D0541657

COUNTRY

Living Legends and Dying Metaphors in America's Biggest Music

NICK TOSCHES

SECKER & WARBURG
LONDON

To Louise

Copyright © 1977 Nick Tosches
Copyright © 1985 Nick Tosches, Inc.

First published in Great Britain 1989 by
Martin Secker & Warburg Limited
Michelin House, 81 Fulham Road,
London SW3 6RB

British Library Cataloguing in Publication Data

Tosches, Nick
Country: living legends and dying metaphors
in America's biggest music
1. American country music to 1985
I. Title
784.5′2′00973

ISBN 0 436 53201 8

Printed and bound in Great Britain by
Butler & Tanner Ltd, Frome, Somerset

Contents

PREFACE
TO THE REVISED EDITION

A decade ago, in the spring of 1975, I signed a contract to write a book called *Living Legends and Dying Metaphors,* which was to be an impressionistic study of country music —rather, of those aspects of country music that most interested me.

As it developed, the months following the signing of that contract marked the beginning of country music's biggest boom, a period that, though inevitable, can be said to start with the crossing over to the pop charts of Willie Nelson's album *Red Headed Stranger,* in July 1975. Redneck chic became the rage. Manhattan's correct saloons swarmed with silly hats as professional Texans and would-be good old boys warmed to their moment in the artificial sun. Willie, Waylon, Dolly, and Loretta, after years of kicking their cans up and down Sixteenth Avenue

South in Nashville, arrived full-blown in the realm of brie, Bloomingdale's, and the Judeo-Christian will to co-op.

I didn't know my editor, Mary Solberg, too well. She told me her brother was the blond guy in "Starsky and Hutch," and she showed me a lacrosse scar on her leg. We rarely spoke, but I knew the new country-music vogue had piqued her enthusiasm for our project. My book was now seen as a timely one, and I was behooved to finish it as soon as possible. She wasn't aware that neither old Willie nor old Waylon, neither Dolly's left nor right breast was to weigh heavily in my scheme of things.

There were so many lost, undone days and nights then in Nashville. My buddy Noel Fox, not quite yet calmed from his gospel-singing years, and I would order an extra beer at lunch and wind up two mornings later at Sheri's, the after-hours joint out by the fairgrounds. The long shadows overtook summer. Outside the windows of my apartment on Elliston Place, I saw gray squirrels and red squirrels conducting the business of their lives with greater sagacity than I.

My mind retains the image of Tompall Glaser in his black-leather rock-star britches, which lately could not be buttoned due to the imperialist expansion of his gut, swaggering across the floor of his Nineteenth Avenue South office at four o'clock in the morning, wielding one of those twelve-inch plastic rulers that school kids tote. "Gotta knock down this here damn wall," he'd declare with a flourish of his ruler, "expand the office by a good two, three feet." He'd nod, self-satisfied with the majesty of his diplopic designs. "And you, Atrocious Tosches," he'd bellow, mispronouncing my name to fit the tiresome rhyme he never tired of turning, waving the little ruler toward me, "you'd better finish that book and put my great ass in it." He'd nod again, Tompall de' Medici, then laugh like the lunatic he was.

Eventually, early in 1977, I did finish it. By then my

original editor at Stein & Day was gone, leg and all, replaced by a fellow named Benton Arnovitz, whom I
never met and who, as far as I knew, had no relatives in
prime time. Old Benton seemed a bit nonplussed by the
manuscript to which he had fallen heir. While the book
was full of half-forgotten country stars, faded honky-tonk
singers, obscure rockabillies, and black musicians of by-
gone generations, while pages and pages of it were given
to the likes of Jimmie Rodgers, Elvis Presley, and Jerry
Lee Lewis, old Willie and old Waylon were referred to
only fleetingly. (Even my friend Tompall Glaser, by far
the most gifted and intriguing of the so-called country-
music outlaws, was mentioned only in passing.) And
while one of the book's longest chapters was devoted to
the subject of sex in country music, the valley of the
shadow of Dolly Parton's cleavage was bypassed com-
pletely. I had wanted to explore the darker areas of country music's history, not its current popularity; to write a
book for those who were interested more in where country
music came from and what it was than in what it had
lately become. My only gesture, really, of putting country
music's recent commerciality in perspective was the re-
printing, under its own chapter heading, of a 1939 *Billboard* article that began, "Real hillbillies rarely have good
night-club acts, says Meyer Horowitz, who ought to
know."

The book was published, as *Country*, in November
1977, three months after Elvis died. Much has happened
in the years since then. Willie Nelson has been absorbed
into the popular mainstream, his Judy Garland pigtails as
familiar now as Frank Sinatra's toupé. But the Stetsons
have grown scarce near where the brie runs, and Boy
George now prances where once Waylon Jennings stonily
stood. Nothing that has happened, however, has called
for any major overhauling of *Country*. It has heartened
me that the very things that may have initially hurt the

book's sales—its lack of timeliness, its reluctance to gaze at length upon the passing stars of the moment—have in the long run proved to be its saving graces. As Ernest Tubb said, beholding his lambent image in the glossy shine of his chartreuse boots: Good taste is timeless.

In this revised edition, many factual errors—dates, names, and so on—have been corrected, and many new facts have been added. Certain sections have been expanded, others trimmed of their excesses. I have tried to follow some historical trails farther, and to bring various biographies up to date. More than a few stories had to be ended, as many of the characters in *Country*, several of whom I interviewed expressly for the book—honky-tonk hero Al Dexter, rockabilly legend Warren Smith, and more—have passed on to the other side. I have also taken this opportunity to recast some prose that now strikes me as extravagant. Whatever I've done here, I hope I've brought the book closer to what I originally wanted it to be: something that could be both read for entertainment and used as history.

I am grateful to the many people whose correspondence has contributed to the amending of *Country*, and to Michael Pietsch of Scribners, who made possible this revised edition. May they, indeed all my friends and readers, never come to know who Hank Thompson really is.

—NICK TOSCHES
New York, 1984

Thela
in the New World

In the spring of 1607 a man named John Laydon, or Lydon, came to America. He was one of a hundred men and four boys who left London in three ships a week before Christmas last. Like the others, he took with him clothes and grain and oil and axes and guns and knives. He also took a fiddle. It had come from Cremona before he was born, and it had belonged to his father. Carved into its dull, dark neck was a strange name: Thela.

All of the 104 perished, by "Swellings, Flixes, Burning Fevers, and by warres, and some departed suddenly, but for the most part they died of meere famine"; all but thirty-eight. With years, new ships came across the ocean and up the river to Jamestown, and in 1630, the year of John Laydon's fiftieth birthday, there were more than twenty-five hundred souls.

First Laydon made soap ash, then pitch. In 1612,

along with the others, he grew tobacco. In 1619 he got a girl from Liverpool, inexpensively. Her name was Lena. She was sixteen and soft, and loud when she drank. He liked her.

His life was as plain as burnished stone. He grew tobacco. He drank whiskey. He broke his leg in '37 and nearly died. He had six sons, and one of them drowned on a bright July morning. In the winter of 1645 he passed away in the night.

He fiddled "as a Man wilde by Fever," wrote his friend Nathaniel Powell. He loved the old tunes, the songs they played back home, and he made some "wondrous newe songs" that Powell mentioned by name in his diary. "Asked their Names, he reply'd the first Song is Devil's Bitche and the other is Drunk Negar, and then laught."

Two of Laydon's sons fiddled, and they had their own sons. It went on: Laydon's blood passed to the Carolinas and to Tennessee. The old fiddle passed too; repaired and dropped and rained upon and repaired and dropped.

Four men sit in a room without windows in Los Angeles. One is the president of the greatest record company in America. His skin is the color of fragile boredom, or mayonnaise. Another is a famous singer and songwriter who records for a subsidiary of the greatest record company in America. His name is not Laydon, or Lydon, but he has the blood, and he has the fiddle with the strange name carved into its neck. The other two men are his friends: his music publisher and his rhythm guitarist, who is also a singer and a songwriter.

The president has summoned the three so that they may hear an acetate of a song the president's young acquaintance has written. "It would be a natural for you," he says to the famous singer. "Just let me know what you think."

The acetate disk is placed on the turntable. In a moment it is obvious, to all but the president, that the song is a weak imitation of a hit the man not named Laydon had written in 1968. But they say nothing.

The tone-arm starts to skip and stutter upon the acetate. The rhythm guitarist takes a coin from his pocket and offers it to the president, to weigh the tone-arm with. The president regards the coin with feral hesitance. He takes it, examines it, and sticks it in his pocket.

"No," another says nicely. "Put it on the record."

The president gently places the coin on the black disk, near the label, where it goes around and around and around.

Orpheus, Gypsies, and Redneck Rock 'n' Roll

At the Henry E. Huntington Library and Art Gallery in San Marino, California, a young pedant, drudging out data for his doctoral thesis on the role of the industrial revolution in British broadside literature, hunches over the only surviving first edition of *The Tea-Table Miscellany*, a collection of balladry and popular verse compiled by Scots poet and wigmaker Allan Ramsay. Poring over the frail, tawny pages of the fourth volume, printed in 1737, the pedant comes upon a ditty called "The Bottle Preferr'd":

> *As great as a monarch,*
> *The moments I pass,*
> *The bottle's my globe,*
> *And my scepter's the glass.*

The table's my throne,
      And the tavern's my court,
The drawer's my subject,
      And drinking's my sport.

At the same moment, at Big Ed's in Orlando, Florida, an unemployed poultry boner orders his seventh shot of Carstairs and slips a quarter into the jukebox. Doyle Holly's 1973 hit "Queen of the Silver Dollar" fills the barroom.

She's the queen of the Silver Dollar,
And she rules this smoky kingdom.
Her scepter is a wine glass,
And a bar stool is her throne.*

The pedant puts pencil to notebook, the drunken poultry boner burps and listens, and the continuum pulses on. Of course, Heraclitus was right. Everything flows; nothing abides.

An eighteenth-century lyric blaring from a jukebox in a topless bar is by no means the most bizarre example of what a crazy bastard sort of thing country music is. Its roots descend deeper into the past than those of any other popular music. In his *Diary* entry for January 2, 1666, Samuel Pepys wrote that a performance of the "little Scotch song of 'Barbary Allen'" by Mrs. Knepp, an actress, brought him "perfect pleasure." Writing in 1765, Oliver Goldsmith said that "an old dairymaid sung me into tears with . . . 'The Cruelty of Barbary Allen.'" Centuries later, this same ancient ballad of mournful love is still being sung and recorded, and discovered anew by fresh ears.

In February of 1976, *Billboard* reported that Wink

---

* "Queen of the Silver Dollar" by Shel Silverstein. Copyright ©
1972 by Evil Eye Music, Inc. Used by permission.

Martindale's 1959 recording of "Deck of Cards" had been added to the playlist of New York radio station WHN after several broadcasts of the record during the Christmas season had got a good response from WHN's audience. With a flourish of historicity, *Billboard* explained that "Deck of Cards" did not originate with Wink Martindale's 1959 hit on Dot Records but that "T. Texas Tyler wrote 'Deck of Cards' about a young soldier being disciplined by his sergeant for having a deck of cards out in chapel. The song explains the deeper meaning the soldier sees in each card." Which is like mistaking an Egyptian potsherd for a piece of Pyrex.

T. Texas Tyler, born David Myrick about 1900 near Mena, Arkansas, had a Number Three country hit with "Deck of Cards" in the spring of 1948 on Four-Star, an independent Hollywood label. (Tyler had been performing "Deck of Cards" since 1939, when he had a radio show at WCHS in Charleston, West Virginia.) There have been assorted versions of Tyler's record by artists such as Rex Cross, Rusty Draper, Phil Harris, Nelson King, Wink Martindale, the Rainbow Four, Tex Ritter (whose cover was first, hitting the charts on July 10, 1948), Larry Robinson, Riley Shepard, the Stewart Family (who changed the recitation into a song), and Tex Williams. There have also been several parodies and derivatives. During the Korean War, Red River Dave, ever the opportunist, recorded a "Red Deck of Cards"; later Red Sovine cut "The Viet Nam Deck of Cards." Ferlin Husky did a "Hillbilly Deck of Cards," and Cowboy Copas did "Cowboy's Deck of Cards."

The truth of "Deck of Cards" is that an almost identical recitation was in use as a church sermon for at least a century before Tyler's birth. The sermon itself was little more than a British folktale variously called "The Perpetual Almanack," "The Gentleman Soldier's Prayer Book," "The Soldier's Bible," and "The Religious Card

Player." Very likely "Deck of Cards" was a medieval
standard. Tyler says he came across the recitation in his
reading during 1938 or 1939. In 1954 he recorded a
version of "Deck of Cards" for Blue Ribbon, a budget
label that presented six ghost versions on each 78-rpm
disk (Tyler, by then, was reduced to covering his own
songs; the other artists on this same disc include an unknown Roy Clark singing "Run 'Em Off" and an unknown
Jimmy Dean singing "Release Me"), and this version was
titled "The Soldier's Prayer Book," probably the title under which Tyler first encountered it.

That such a scrap of kitsch has endured in a way that
the writing of Francis Bacon has not says much about
what's really timeless and what isn't; that the 1959 "Deck
of Cards" was far more popular with pop audiences than
with country audiences says much about who the real
kitschmongers are.

After Four-Star, T. Texas Tyler recorded for Decca,
Capitol, and Starday. In the early sixties he became an
ordained evangelist minister, and he and his wife, Claudia,
traveled America doing God's P.R. On January 23, 1972,
in Springfield, Missouri, Tyler was called in by his Em-
ployer. And Wink Martindale, a former disk jockey from
Jackson, Tennessee, is the host of the television game show
"Tic Tac Dough."

> *Well, I rocked over Italy and I rocked over Spain,*
> *I rocked in Memphis, it was all the same,*
> *Till I rocked into Africa and rolled off the ship*
> *And seen them natives doin' an odd-lookin' skip.*
> *I parted the weeds and looked over the swamp,*
> *And I seen them cats doin' the Ubangi Stomp.*

So begins Warren Smith's 1956 rocker "Ubangi
Stomp." The song was written by Charles Underwood, a
producer, songwriter, and musician who was born in

Iuka, Mississippi, on September 15, 1937. (In 1954 black alto-saxophonist Earl Bostic had recorded an instrumental called "Ubangi Stomp" for King. Underwood's song bore no resemblance to Bostic's beyond the title.) Underwood was deeply involved in the seminal rock-and-roll scene at Sun Records in Memphis, and in 1959 he produced Charlie Rich's hit "Lonely Weekends" on the Phillips International label. In 1961 Charles and his wife moved to Los Angeles, and there in 1962 he engineered two hit records: "Monster Mash" by Bobby Pickett and "The Lonely Bull" by Herb Alpert. In the spring of 1963 Underwood opened the Nashville West studio, which he operated until 1971. He recorded for Warner Brothers in 1966 as the Charlie Underwood Glide Band.

"Ubangi Stomp" typified the tough, churlish strain of country music that evolved in the 1950s. Known as rockabilly, it was the music of men such as Elvis Presley, Carl Perkins, and Jerry Lee Lewis. Aflash with images of sex, violence, and redneck existentialism, rockabilly was the glorious florescence of white rock-and-roll. It seemed such a sexy, pagan horror, such a dangerous new creature, that America feared it, preached against it, and tried to ban it. And yet, deep in its surly soul, rockabilly too carried ancientry. The juxtaposition of "Ubangi Stomp," part of the birth-scream of an era, and its flip-side, "Black Jack David," shard of another millennium, is an improbable but perfect symbol of modern country music's duality.

Warren Smith was born in Louise, a small town in western Mississippi, on February 7, 1932. He moved to Memphis in early 1953, several months after he left the Air Force. He was singing with Clyde Leoppard's Snearly Ranch Boys at the Cotton Club in West Memphis when Sam Phillips, owner of Sun Records and the first to record the rockabilly music of Elvis Presley and others, offered him an opportunity to cut some sides. In February 1956, Smith recorded "Rock 'n' Roll Ruby" for Sun, and it became a regional hit.

Warren Smith.

On March 30, 1956, Warren Smith went into the Sun studio at 706 Union Avenue in Memphis. With a band that consisted of a fiddler, a guitarist, a bassist, and a drummer, Smith cut four sides: "Who Took My Baby," "Movin' On," "I Couldn't Take the Chance," and "Black Jack David." Although none of the recordings from this session was released, at his next session, in August, Smith again cut "Black Jack David," along with "Ubangi Stomp," and the record was issued on September 1, 1956. "Black Jack David" was copyrighted in Smith's name several weeks later, on October 10.

Black Jack David come a-ridin' through the woods,
Singin' so loud and merry.
His voice kept ringin' through the green, green trees;
He spied a fair-haired maiden,
He spied a fair-haired maiden.

Would you forsake your husband dear?
Would you forsake your baby?
Would you forsake your fine, fine home
And go with Black Jack David,
Go with Black Jack David?

No, dear Jack, I cannot go
Away and leave my baby;
I cannot forsake my husband and home
And go with you, Black Jack David,
Go with you, Black Jack David.

Listen, dear lass, my name is Jack,
I've come from afar
Lookin' for a fair-haired lass like you;
Won't you come and be my bride,
Come and be my bride.

Yes, I'll forsake my husband dear,
And I'll forsake my baby,
I'll forsake my fine, fine home
And go with you, Black Jack David,
Go with you, Black Jack David.

Last night she slept on a fine feather bed
Beside her husband and baby,
Tonight she slept on the cold, cold ground
Beside old Black Jack David,
Beside old Black Jack David.

Smith left Sun Records in 1959, having scored one national pop hit, "So Long, I'm Gone." He went on to record for Liberty, on which label he had seven country hits during the years 1960–64, Mercury in Nashville, Skill

in Pasadena, Texas, then Jubal in Nashville. Throughout
the late sixties and seventies, he worked as a safety man
at Heat Control in Longview, Texas, where he lived with
his wife and daughter. His last recordings, made in late
1976, were released in the Lake County album *The
Legendary Warren Smith*. After a successful British tour
with several other rockabilly veterans, Warren Smith died
of a heart attack, on January 30, 1980.

In 1976, twenty years after he recorded it, I asked
Warren Smith the source of the song "Black Jack David."

"I wrote it," he answered.

Cut to Athens, fourth century B.C. In his *Symposium*,
Plato refers to an attempt made by Orpheus, mythical poet
and son of Oegrus the harper and Muse Calliope, to rescue
his wife from the land of the dead. This is the earliest
known mention of Orpheus's wife, Eurydice, and of his
adventure in the lower world. It's also the beginning of
"Black Jack David."

In his fourth *Georgic*, completed in 29 B.C., the Roman
poet Vergil wrote a full account of the myth of Orpheus
and Eurydice. Aristaeus the shepherd, son of sea goddess
Cyrene, had been playing about with Eurydice by the bank
of a river. Pursuing her among the flora, Aristaeus saw
Eurydice fall from the bite of a snake. She died. When

Orpheus discovered this, he sank into pale despair. Eventually he pulled together the nerve to pass through the jaws of Taenarus into the underworld in search of his dead lady. He sang his petition so powerfully that Tartarus quaked. Proserpina, the death-bitch maxima, gave Orpheus permission to take his wife back to the plane of life, the conditional clause being that if he turned to look at Eurydice as he led her to the upper world, she would be returned to the land of death. In a moment of forgetfulness, Orpheus looked back.

Orpheus ambled and cried for seven months, and nothing could crack his sadness. One night during their sacred orgies in honor of Bacchus, the women of the Cicones, angered by Orpheus's refusal of sex, tore his body apart. His meat was scattered about the countryside; his head was lobbed into the river Hebrus. Borne by the river's current, the head opened its bloodied mouth and called the name of Eurydice.

It was Ovid's retelling of the travails of Orpheus in his *Metamorphoses*, written in the first decade A.D., that brought the myth into later European culture, for by the twelfth century Ovid had become the most respected classical poet, and his influence spread throughout the Middle Ages. French, German, and Spanish renderings of *Metamorphoses* were in circulation before the end of the thirteenth century. Dante had Vergil guide him through the underworld, but it was Ovid whom he put in the highest place of honor allowable for a pagan poet. Ovid's version differed little from that of Virgil, except for some added drool-data, as when he informs in perfect hexameter that "Orpheus preferred to center his affections on boys of tender years, and to enjoy the brief spring and early flowering of their youth; he was the first to introduce this custom among the people of Thrace."

One of the most important popularizers of classical literature was the Roman Boethius, whose *De Consolatione Philosophiae*, written shortly before he had his head chopped off in 525, was one of the most widely read works in western Europe until the close of the Renaissance. Boethius too retold the legend of Orpheus and Eurydice, but interpreted it as a parable. "This fable," he wrote, "applies to all of you who seek to raise your minds to sovereign day. For whoever is conquered and turns his eyes to the pit of hell, looking into the inferno, loses all the excellence he has gained."

It was King Alfred's ninth-century translation of Boethius that ushered the Orpheus myth into medieval Britain. That the myth had entered the blood of British culture before the thirteenth century is attested to by such works as Welsh writer Walter Map's *De Nugis Curialium*. Completed about 1190, Map's book includes a passage, captioned *Item de fantasticis aparicionibus*, which tells of the death of a beloved wife, of her husband's grief, and of his success in finding her in the netherworld and bringing her back to the living. Classical myth becomes pop lore.

Here Ireland flows in. Celtic mythology contained a variety of legends in which supernatural men or women lured members of the opposite sex to come and dwell in the underworld. Ultimately, these legends derive from the ancient Celtic myth of the Rival Wooers, in which all the characters were gods and goddesses. *Leabhar na hUidhre*, an Irish manuscript written before 1106, tells one such tale, "Tochmarc Étaíne," or "The Wooing of Étaín." The story is this: Eochaid Airem, King of Ireland, weds beautiful young Étaín. Midir, the fairy ruler of the sidh, or underworld, of Brí Leith, had been Étaín's husband in a previous life, and he now approaches her to come live with him in the underworld. Étaín says that she will leave the king only if he gives her willingly to Midir. The fairy prince challenges the king to a series of chess games for high stakes, and loses them all. Unaware that Midir is cheating him, the king agrees to play one final game for whatever prize the winner wishes. Midir, of course, wins and demands the right to rub up against Étaín. The king stipulates a month's delay. Against the big day, he summons all the armies of Ireland to protect his palace from Midir's entry. But Midir materializes mysteriously. The king keeps his bargain, and when Midir takes Étaín in his arms, the pair rise through the smokehole in the roof. The king and his men ravage all the fairy mounds in Ireland looking for Étaín. At the end of nine years' searching, the king is met with sixty women, all clones of Étaín, sent out by Midir. In time Étaín makes herself known, and the king brings her home in triumph. This tale, which probably made its first appearance in the ninth century, was still very much alive in the late Middle Ages.

Sometime in the twelfth century, an unknown bard of Brittany familiar with the classical myth, Walter Map's pop derivative of it, and the Irish legend of Étaín distilled the three strains into a melic poem called the *Lai d'Orphéy*. Although no manuscript of the lay has been discovered, it is referred to by name in several contemporary works.

Sir Orfeo is a thirteenth-century translation of the *Lai d'Orphéy*, which had probably been written in Old French or Anglo-Norman. The oldest of three *Sir Orfeo* manuscripts dates to the early fourteenth century. In a southwestern dialect of Middle English, the poem describes Lady Heurodis's abduction by a fairy king, Sir Orfeo's sadness and self-imposed exile, his discovery of the fairy palace after ten years, and his recovery of Heurodis. Whoever adapted the lay into English showed a complete ignorance of its classical antecedents. He described Thrace as the ancient name for Winchester and ended his poem with this explanation of how it came into being:

> *Later, Breton harpers heard*
> *How this marvel had occurred,*
> *And made of it a pleasing lay,*
> *And gave to it the name of the king.*

> *So 'Orfeo' it is called today;*
> *Fine is the lay, and sweet to sing.*
>   *Thus did Orfeo quit his care:*
>   *God grant that all of us so fare.*

Over the centuries, *Sir Orfeo* devolved into a common ballad. This ballad seems not to have gained widespread popularity, for only two versions have been recorded. The first was transcribed from a performance by an elderly Scotsman in Unst, Shetland, in 1880 and published in February of that year in *The Leisure Hour*. The old man admitted that his memory had lost much of the original whole of the ballad, which he called "King Orfeo."

> *Der lived a king inta da aste,*
>   *Scowan ürla grün;*
> *Der lived a lady in da wast,*
>   *Whar giorten han grün oarlac.*
>
> *Dis king he has a huntin gaen,*
> *He's left his Lady Isabel alane.*
>
> *'Oh I wis ye'd never gaen away,*
> *For at your hame is döl an wae.*
>
> *'For da king o Ferrie we his daert,*
> *Has pierced your lady to da hert.'*
>
> *And aifter dem da king has gaen,*
> *But whan he cam it was a grey stane.*

The next and last time "King Orfeo" showed up was in April of 1947. Again it was found in Unst. In this later version there is little remaining but a shell.

> *Will ye come in into our ha',*
> *Scowan Earl Grey,*
> *Yes we'll come in into your ha',*
> *For yetter kangra norla.*

And we'll come in into your ha',
And we'll come in among ye a'.
First they played the notes o noy,
Then they played the notes o joy.

Then they played the good old gabber reel,
Scowan Earl Grey,
Which might a made a sick heart heal,
For gettar kangra norla.

Both these ballads reek death. They're skeletal, disjointed, and dull (who cares what "gettar kangra norla" means?). Mere archaeological junk, like so many pieces of rotten hominid skull, these ballads are nothing but connections between the old and the new. "King Orfeo" is an evolutionary discard; it birthed a new brood of balladry, then fell. The abduction, the magick, the search were retained in the offspring of "King Orfeo," but the name of Orpheus was dropped for that of a new, but in his own way mythic, character. From *The Tea-Table Miscellany* of 1737, "Johny Faa, the Gypsie Laddie":

The gypsies came to our good lord's gate,
*   And wow but they sang sweetly;*
They sang sae sweet, and sae very compleat,
*   That down came the fair lady.*

And she came tripping down the stair,
*   And a' her maids before her;*
As soon as they saw her well-far'd face,
*   They cooft the glamer o'er her.*

Gae tak frae me this gay mantile.
*   And bring to me my plaidie,*
For if kith and kin and a' had sworn,
*   I'll follow the gypsie laddie.*

Yestreen I lay in a well-made bed,
*   And my good lord beside me;*

This night I'll ly in a tenant's barn,
Whatever shall betide me.

Come to your bed, says Johny Faa,
Oh come to your bed, my deary;
For I vow and I swear by the hilt of my sword,
That your lord shall nae mair come near ye.

I'll go to bed to my Johny Faa,
I'll go to bed to my deary;
For I vow and swear by what past yestreen,
That my lord shall nae mair come near me.

I'll mak a hap to my Johny Faa,
And I'll mak a hap to my deary,
And he's get a' the coat gaes round,
And my lord shall nae mair come near me.

And when our lord came home at een,
And speir'd for his fair lady,
The tane she cry'd, and the others reply'd,
She's away with the gypsie laddie.

Gae saddle to me the black, black steed,
Gae saddle and make him ready;
Before that I either eat or sleep,
I'll gae seek my fair lady.

And we were fifteen well-made men,
Altho' we were nae bonny;
And we were a' put down for ane,
A fair young wanton lady.

Here, for a change, the sweet young thing doesn't particularly care to be rescued. No mistake about it: For all its similarities to *Sir Orfeo* and "King Orfeo," this ballad was driven by fresh winds.

Gypsies had arrived in Britain before the end of the fifteenth century, and soon began to make pests of themselves. Thievery and assault, along with fortune-telling scams, came to be synonymous with the word *gypsy*. In Scotland, where the gypsies made their British debut, Council Registers are full of charges brought against gypsies named Faa, Faw, or Fall (three spellings of the same name). This division of Faa gypsies seems already to have been established in southeast Scotland by 1470. In the Council Register of Aberdeen under the date of January 22, 1530, two female gypsies were arrested and described as servants of "George Faw, Earl of Egypt." At Falkland on February 15, 1540, James V signed a writ of the Privy Council of Scotland, which granted certain privileges to "John Faw, Lord and Earl of Little Egypt." On June 6, 1541, the writ was withdrawn and John Faw and his brood were ordered to leave Scotland within thirty days under penalty of death. In 1554 Queen Mary gave "Johnne Faw" her royal pardon after he murdered someone. On July 10, 1616, "John Faw," his son James, and several other gypsies were sentenced to death. In 1624 six "Faas" and two other male gypsies were executed. By the nineteenth century, gypsies had forsaken the name Faa for others such as Allan, Barclay, Gordon, Kennedy, Shaw, Tait, and Young.

By the early part of the seventeenth century, one of these Faas, or all of them, had entered into popular legendry. The story has Orphic overtones. John VI, Earl of Cassillis, who was, according to *The Edinburgh Magazine and Literary Miscellany*, "commonly termed 'the grave and solemn Earl,'" wed Lady Jane Hamilton, daughter of Thomas, first Earl of Hadington. (In the year of Lady Jane's birth, 1607, Claudio Monteverdi created the first modern opera, *L'Orfeo*, based on the myth of Orpheus and Eurydice.) When Lord Cassillis was in England on business, the gypsy John Faw and several of his followers traveled to Cassillis and persuaded, some say by magick, the Lady to elope with him to England. She and Faw had not made it across the border when the Earl overtook them, murdering all the gypsies save one. Lady Jane was placed in a dungeon near Maybole, where she remained until her death in 1642.

It will never be known how much of the tale is truth. The *Woodrow MSS* in the National Library of Scotland contain two letters in Lord Cassillis's hand, written after the death of his Lady Jane. In one, addressed to Robert Douglas, minister at Edinburgh, he wrote that "I finde it so harde to digest the want of a dear friend, such as my beloved yoke-fellow was." In the other, addressed to Lord Eglinton, he called his late wife a "dear bed-fellow." It is said Lord Cassillis wed again.

Legend has it that the lone survivor of Faw's band composed the ballad, but it is far more probable that the song was the work of one of the many professional ballad-makers who flourished in Britain from 1550 till the close of the nineteenth century. These men, most of whose names have long been lost, were the first of the breed later to be known as Tin Pan Alley hacks. They churned out songs and sold them for a shilling (rarely more) to printers, who published them in single folio sheets or in chapbooks of eight to sixteen pages, to be sold by peddlers who walked the streets or solicited door-to-door, sometimes singing the latest ballads as they moved along. Much of the work of ballad-makers (except for the period 1550 to 1580, when balladry was indulged in by literary men) was based on news.

Street balladry, the roots of traditional American music, was pop. The purest mountain airs, lustily pursued by sweaty, obsessive folklorists and concerned young things, were once the pop junk of urban Britain. In the preface to his 1888 anthology, *More Lyrics from the Song-Books of the Elizabethan Age,* A. H. Bullen denounced "the poor thin wretched stuff that one hears today." He might as well have been speaking about rock-and-roll. In a way, he was.

Street balladry didn't really die at the end of the nineteenth century. Its center became America, instead of Great Britain; its form of publication became phonograph records, instead of broadsides.

"The Gypsie Laddie" was a hit. Even Robert Burns used it in his 1808 *Reliquies*. When Charles Kirkpatrick Sharpe published a version of the ballad that he got "from the recitation of a peasant in Galloway," in the November 1817 issue of *The Edinburgh Magazine and Literary Miscellany*, he omitted several lines "on account of their indelicacy."

The ballad certainly arrived in America before 1750. It was popular in the New World, too. In almost every state the ballad flourished into the present century. (Versions have also been collected in Nova Scotia.) As it moved, "The Gypsie Laddie" changed. It became "Gyps of Davy," "The Gypsy Lover," "Gypsy Davy," "Black-Eyed Davy," "The Lady's Disgrace," "The Three Gypsy Laddies," and even "The Jewish Lady" in one Virginia version collected in 1932. Sex and violence became nursery rhyme in *The Magic Garden of My Book House,* a 1920 children's book by Olive Beaupré Miller that printed the ballad under the title "The Raggle, Taggle Gypsies."

One of the most popular American titles was "Black Jack David." The phrase "black jack" meant different things in different Scottish and English dialects: cockroach, black leather vest, caterpillar, dark sweetmeat made of treacle and spice; its significance in the ballad title is lost.

In October 1929 a duet with the glittery name of Professor and Mrs. I. G. Greer recorded "Black Jack Davy" for Paramount. Ten years later, in July 1939, Cliff Carlisle recorded "Black Jack David" for Decca. In October 1940 the Carter Family recorded it for Okeh. In 1945 T. Texas Tyler cut it for Four-Star. Carlisle says that he got his version from T. Texas Tyler, even though Tyler didn't

record the song until several years after Carlisle's record;
that Tyler copyrighted "Black Jack David" in August
1939, a month after Carlisle cut it, backs this up. The
Carlisle record went like this:

> *Black Jack David come a-riding through the woods,*
> *Singing so loud and merry.*
> *His voice kept ringin' through the green, green trees,*
> *And he charmed the heart of a maiden,*
> *Charmed the heart of a maiden.*

And so on. Warren Smith was seven years old when
Carlisle's record came out. He was thirteen when T. Texas
Tyler's version was released.

"I wrote it."

You never heard it before that?

"Well, long, long time ago there was one called
'Black Jack David.' I guess I kinda got the idea from it,
but I changed it around altogether. I remember hearin'
this when I was quite young. One of those great big
seventy-eight records. I heard it at some people's house.
And I don't know how I ever came up with the idea that
night for a second side of 'Ubangi Stomp.' I ran outa songs,
and then all of a sudden I just got to hummin' it, and I
set down then and started writin' it then, and we cut it
the same night. I was kinda half-way crazy about it,
y'know, but they kinda half-way banned it there in
Memphis. I guess it was, uh, it was kinda like this man
comin' through there while another man was gone from
home and stole his wife, y'know?"

The
Girl Singer

There is a motel in Cheyenne, at the junction of Inter-states 80 and 25, called Holding's Little America. Cartoon penguins are everywhere: matchbooks, menus, cocktail napkins.

It is the end of July, and the week-long Frontier Days rodeo, held each year since 1896, is winding down. To-morrow afternoon, Sunday, the winning ropers and wres-tlers and riders will be given trophies, and it will be over until next year.

The girl singer and I are in a room, talking and drink-ing, among the penguins. It is four in the morning; the television is cold. The girl singer is dissipated. Earlier to-night she sang at Frontier Park. In the last twenty-eight days she has sung at twenty-seven other places and taped a series of motorcycle-safety commercials in Eugene. Next Thursday night, four towns from now, she will return to her home just north of Nashville. After six days of rest, she'll do it again, this time in the Southeast.

She is blowzy. The musculature of her face is still and sodden, and words come from the corners of her mouth thick and slow. She doesn't seem sad, just wasted. With the care of one who seems to be performing a ritual, she withdraws an envelope from a cosmetics case next to her on the bed. The envelope is opened, and several photographs and a small, thin piece of paper with writing on it are removed. After looking briefly, very briefly, at the piece of paper, she replaces it. She lays the photographs at the foot of the bed, away from her, so that they face me. There are five, black-and-white, each of a different age. The oldest print has a serrated border. A woman sits in a chair, her hair waved in the soft full curls of the 1940s, a small, pointed party hat tilted on her head. At her knee is a small boy, smiling, in a felt cowboy hat, spotted chaps, and miniature Western boots; he awkwardly holds a shiny cap pistol.

The second photograph shows a boy who appears to be in his early teens. He is of medium build, pale complexion. It seems to be winter, but it is difficult to tell. The boy is standing against a wooden wall, wearing a plaid cap and a hunting jacket. There is a rifle, a .22, propped against the wall behind him. He is smiling.

The third photograph shows the boy (by now it is obvious that the pictures are of the same person) in his late teens or early twenties. He is sitting, thinner than before, on a couch, and he has his arm around a pretty girl. He is making a funny face at the camera, a very dumb face really. He and the girl seem very familiar. Perhaps they are married, or brother and sister.

The fourth photograph shows the boy, or young man (he does not appear much older than in the third picture), standing in a softly dark suit with a group of other men, also wearing suits. One of these men is quite old. Everyone is smiling. There seems to be a mural in the background.

In the fifth photograph was a man I immediately recognized, a well-known country singer who was killed in a plane crash in the early 1960s. The young man, slightly older here but still youthful and soft and pale, is at his side in a restaurant, laughing over drinks and coffee and an ashtray full of cigarette butts like fat, white worms.

"Who is he?" asks the girl singer.

"Jim Reeves."

"No. The other one." She moved her hand across all five pictures.

"I don't know."

"Who does it remind you of?"

"No one," I say.

"When would you say this last picture is from?"

"About nineteen sixty-three, maybe sixty-four. He looks the same as he did in all those pictures they published of him when he got killed."

"And the other guy doesn't remind you of anyone?"

I don't answer her this time, for she really is getting annoying.

Now she removes another photograph from the cosmetics case, one that hadn't been in the envelope. It is an early publicity photograph of herself. She looks quite different: Her hair is short and lacquered in the picture, and the airbrushing that was intended to make her face look like burnished ivory made it look instead like a soft, dull cheese. She places this photo with the others.

"They're all me," the girl singer says.

Loud Covenants

Words such as *realism, neoclassicism, minimalism,* and *Dada* are intellectual niceties, terms invented to describe esthetics. Each has a definition easily rote-learned; each has a clear, sensible origin. You can look at the word *Dada* and think, Yes, Tzara invented it, in 1916, to shock the world. It means "hobbyhorse" in French.

But words such as *juke, jazz, honky-tonk,* and *rock-and-roll* are elusive. None of them was invented for the purpose of art; each seems to have its own pneuma, from which the art evolved, like dark, primeval word magick. Ancient black men say they quit playing blues because it's the devil's music. Pale white preachers yell against the sinfulness of rock-and-roll. And it is not impossible that the word *juke,* first encountered among the blacks of Florida and coastal Georgia, late in the last century, has the same source as the Wolof word *dzug,* which means to lead an evil, wicked life.

There is not a clue to the origin of the word *jazz.*
Many of the black musicians who were active in New
Orleans at the turn of the century were asked about the
word, but none knew where it had come from. The November 15, 1890, issue of *The Mascot,* a weekly newspaper of
New Orleans, described the music of a Basin Street jazz
band as "a sad affliction." The band itself was described
simply as "a nigger brass band." The earliest recorded use
of the word is in "Uncle Josh in Society," a 1909 Columbia
recording by Cal Stewart, whose series of rural-dialect
monologues, described in a 1901 Columbia catalogue as
"Uncle Josh Weathersby's Laughing Stories," began in
1898 and remained popular till the late 1920s. The line
is "One lady asked me if I danced the jazz." In the June
17, 1917, issue of *The Times-Picayune,* a writer, in his
finest remedial English, asked, "Why is the jass music,
and, therefore, the jass band?" He damned the music as
"indecent" and a "vice," and concluded that "its possibili-
ties of harm are great." The title of a jazz song, popular
among Storyville performers of the day, responded in-
directly to *The Times-Picayune*: "Kiss My Fuckin' Ass."

The phrase *honky-tonk* was first encountered in the
east Texas–Louisiana–Oklahoma area. In the February 24,
1894, issue of *The Daily Ardmoreite,* published in Ard-
more, Oklahoma, is the report that "the honk-a-tonk last
night was well attended by ball-heads, bachelors and
leading citizens." (Yes, it's right here: "ball-heads.")
New Orleans bars were sometimes referred to as tonks
by blacks of the period. The first use of the phrase in a
song is in "Honky Tonky," a one-step copyrighted by
Charles McCarron and Chris Smith in April 1916. It
was recorded by both the Victor Military Band and
Prince's Band. "Everything Is Hunky Dory Down in
Honky Tonk Town" was featured in the Tin Pan Alley
musical *Everything,* staged at the New York Hippo-
drome in 1918 with a cast that included Houdini. In 1924

Fletcher Henderson and His Club Alabam Orchestra recorded " 'Those Broken Busted' Can't Be Trusted Blues (A Honky-Tonk Blues)" for Vocalion. The next year, Bennie Moten's Kansas City Orchestra cut "Sister Honky-Tonk" for Okeh. Meade Lux Lewis helped birth boogie-woogie in 1927 with his Paramount record "Honky Tonk Train Blues."

In country music, honky-tonk came to be associated with the loud, small-group sound that developed in the redneck bars of east Texas oil-boom towns: amplified guitars and lyrics of sex and whiskey. It's odd that Al Dexter, an east Texan born in 1902, who wrote and re-corded "Pistol Packin' Mama," one of the classic honky-tonk songs (and the first country song to make "Your Hit Parade," which censored "beer" from the song's lyrics), doesn't recall hearing the phrase until 1937. In those days, Dexter wrote songs with a man named James B. Paris.

"One day I went to see Paris, and he said, 'I thought of a title last night that'll set the woods on fire.' I asked him what it was, and he said 'Honky Tonk Blues.' I asked him where he got that idea. I never heard the word, so I said, 'What is a honky-tonk?' So he said, 'These beer joints up and down the road where the girls jump in cars and so on.' I said, 'I never thought about it like that.' He said, 'Use your thinker-upper and let's write a song like that.' "

Dexter and Paris copyrighted their song on February 26, 1937. There had been songs with similar titles ("Hunkie Tunkie Blues" by Hunkie Smith in 1930, "Honky Tonk Blues" by Pat Shelton in 1936), but they weren't country songs. "Honky Tonk Blues" led to Dexter's recording con-tract with Vocalion and a storm of honky-tonk fever in country music. By 1938 even Roy Acuff was singing about "Honky Tonk Mamas." Dexter's late awareness of the phrase is especially weird in light of the fact that he operated an east Texas honky-tonk, the Round-Up Club, in the early thirties.

In 1893, before any of these words appeared in print, anthropologist Richard Wallaschek wrote in his book *Primitive Music* that "the most striking feature of all the savage songs is the frequent occurrence of words with no meaning whatever." A-womp-bop-a-lu-bop, a-womp-bam-boom.

Rock-and-roll. Both verbs came to the English tongue during the Middle Ages, and were soon used as skin-thrill metaphors. "My throbbing heart shall rock thee day and night," wrote Shakespeare in *Venus and Adonis*. An early nineteenth-century sea chanty included the line, "Oh do, me Johnny Bowker, come rock 'n' roll me over." A lyric found in the ceremonial Fire Dance of Florida's obeah worshipers was, "Bimini gal is a rocker and a roller."

In the fall of 1922, blues singer Trixie Smith cut a song called "My Daddy Rocks Me (With One Steady Roll)" for Black Swan Records. It was a hit. The Southern Quartet, a black group that recorded for Columbia, did a version of the song in 1924 under the title "My Man Rocks Me (With One Steady Roll)." By the next year, white kids were on to the song; in February 1925 Harold Ortli and His Ohio State Collegians recorded the song under its original title for Okeh. In 1929 Jimmie Noone and Tampa Red both had versions released by Vocalion.

Trixie Smith's record inspired many lyrical elaborations: "Rock That Thing" by Lil Johnson (Vocalion, 1929), "Rock Me Mama" by Ikey Robinson (Brunswick, 1929), "Rocking and Rolling" by Bob Robinson (Champion, 1930, but unissued), "I'm a Steady Rollin' Man" by Robert Johnson (Vocalion, 1937), "Rock Me Daddy" by Georgia White (Decca, 1937), "Rock It for Me" by Mildred Bailey (Vocalion, 1938), and others.

The metaphor also had a spiritual life, as shown by black gospel recordings such as "Rock, Church, Rock" by Clara Smith (Columbia, 1926) and "Rock My Soul" by Mitchell's Christian Singers (Vocalion, 1939). "She was found with child of the Holy Ghost," says the Bible, and He's still rocking and rolling them in the South. In *White Spirituals in the Southern Uplands,* George Pullen Jackson described an interracial convention of Holy Rollers he attended in Cleveland, Tennessee, in September 1929.

"The spirit moved some to dance, others to speak in the unknown tongue, to shout, to jerk, or to fall in a dead trance. Mourners in ever-increasing numbers fell on their knees, elbows in a folding chair, at the altar, while the exhorters clapped hands to the time of the music, urged the kneeling ones to 'come through,' I imagined, and were quite beside themselves at the appearance of even a faint smile on the face of the praying sinner.

"After half an hour of this, the singing came to an end. Also the instrument strummers, worn out, dropped out one by one, leaving only the piano player and a tambourine whacker, whom I could not see, to carry on the steady and almost terrifying rhythmic noise. Terrifying because it impressed me as being the production of the wild, subconscious human animal, one which we seldom come upon in such frightfully self-regimented herds. But the extreme mesmeric orgies of such primitive groups have been often enough described. And after all, my purpose is simply to make clear how the indigenous song merges into the hypnotic rhythmizing used in this indigenous type of religious practice."

Holy Roller cults are still alive in the South and in some Northern black urban areas. There is still shock in their worship. "And they shall take up serpents, and if they drink any deadly thing, it shall not hurt them," says the Bible, so some sects dance with rattlesnakes round their necks and drink "salvation cocktails," made of strychnine and water.

The eighth line of Psalm 22 is "He trusted in the Lord." But the Hebrew word translated as "trusted" is transliterated *gahlahl,* which didn't mean trust. The 1560

Geneva Bible gave a literal translation of the line: "He roled in the Lord."

The schizophrenia of the rock-and-roll metaphor was the inspiration for "Holy Roll," a funny, dirty 1931 Columbia record by Rufus and Ben Quillian.

By the early thirties, rock-and-roll was more than a fuck-phrase. It described an elusive style of music, a new sensuality of rhythm. In 1931 Duke Ellington recorded "Rockin' in Rhythm" for Victor, and in 1934 Red Nichols cut the same piece for white folks.

In *Transatlantic Merry-Go-Round,* a film released by United Artists in the fall of 1934, the Boswell Sisters (Martha, Connie, and Helvetia, all from New Orleans) sang a song called "Rock and Roll." It was written by Sidney Clare and Richard A. Whiting, a pair of Tin Pan Alley authors born in the 1890s. The Boswell Sisters recorded the song with Jimmy Crier and His Orchestra on October 4 in Los Angeles, and it was issued by Brunswick to coincide with the movie. On October 23, Joe Hayne and His Orchestra covered the song for Melotone. Gladys Presley of Tupelo was pregnant that "Rock and Roll" autumn.

The elusive rhythm spread, became more defined:

"Rockin' Rollers' Jubilee" by Erskine Hawkins (Bluebird, 1938), "Rocking the Blues" by the Port of Harlem Jazzmen, featuring Albert Ammons on piano (Brunswick, 1939), "Keep Rockin'" by Harlan Leonard and His Rockets (Bluebird, 1940), "I Want to Rock" by Cab Calloway (Okeh, 1942), "Rockin' the Boogie" by Hadda Brooks (Modern, 1945), "Good Rockin' Tonight" by Roy Brown (DeLuxe, 1947), "Rockin' the Blues" by Pee Wee Crayton (Modern, 1947), "Shout and Rock" by Billy Williams (Atlantic, 1948), "Rock and Roll" by the Flairs (Modern, 1949), "Rock & Roll" by Wild Bill Moore (Modern, 1949), "Rock the Joint" by Jimmy Preston (Gotham, 1949), "Rockin'" by the Robins (Modern, 1949), "We're Gonna Rock" by Cecil Gant doing business as Gunter Lee Carr (Decca, 1950), "Rock It" by Jimmy McCracklin (Modern, 1950), "Rock 'n' Roll" by John Lee Hooker (Modern, 1950), "Rockin' and Rollin'" by Lil Son Jackson (Imperial, 1950), "Rockin' Blues" by the Johnny Otis Congregation (Savoy, 1950), "Rockin' with Red" by Piano Red (RCA-Victor, 1950), "Rocking After Midnight" by Lowell Fulson (Swing Time, 1950), "All I Do Is Rock" by the Robins (Crown, 1951), "Let's Rock Awhile" by Amos Milburn (Aladdin, 1951), "Rock Little Baby" by Cecil Gant (Decca, 1951), "Rock Me All Night Long" by the Ravens (Mercury, 1952), and "Rock, Rock, Rock" by Willis Jackson (Atlantic, 1952) and Amos Milburn (Aladdin, 1953).

Almost all these records were by blacks, and all of them were popular among blacks. Some were primitive but pure rock-and-roll. Roy Brown's 1947 "Good Rockin' Tonight" was a jump blues, the most popular sort of music among urban blacks of the 1940s (and very popular among whites, as record-sales patterns and TV appearances by such jump blues artists as Louis Jordan indicate). In the summer of 1948, Wynonie Harris cut a version of the same song for King, and the new version was a hit.

Harris's "Good Rockin' Tonight" was a jump blues also, but it was wilder, less mellow than the usual jump blues record. It rocked.

It is impossible to discern the first modern rock record, just as it is impossible to discern where blue becomes indigo in the spectrum. It is right to say, however, that by 1950 black music was rocking strong. Imperial issued Fats Domino's first record, "The Fat Man," in 1949, and it sold well. In 1951 occurred several pure and unmistakable rock-and-roll hits: "Sixty Minute Man" by the Dominoes on Federal, "It Ain't the Meat" by the Swallows on King, "Rocket '88' " and its sequel, "My Real Gone Rocket" by Jackie Brenston and His Delta Cats on Chess.

The Dominoes' "Sixty Minute Man" was not only the biggest rhythm-and-blues hit of 1951, but also the first rock-and-roll record to make the pop charts, which is especially surprising in light of its theme. Billy Ward, ringleader of the Dominoes, was born in Los Angeles on September 19, 1921, and began composing classical pieces when he was a teenager. He was a Golden Gloves champion, soldier, journalist, and voice coach at Carnegie Hall before forming the Dominoes in the late forties. In 1950 he enlisted seventeen-year-old Clyde McPhatter as lead tenor singer, and by the end of 1951 the Dominoes were the most famous black group in America. In 1955 they cut a salty epilogue to their biggest hit: "Can't Do Sixty No More."

After "Sixty Minute Man," other black rock-and-roll records appeared on the pop charts: "Crying in the Chapel" by the Orioles (Jubilee, 1953), "Gee" by the Crows (Rama, 1954), "Sh-Boom" by the Chords (Cat, 1954), "Hearts of Stone" by the Charms (DeLuxe, 1954), and "Ling, Ting, Tong" by the Five Keys (Capitol, 1954) and the Charms (DeLuxe, 1955). But none of these, except for "Sixty Minute Man," was a hard-ass rock-and-roll record, and the collective sound was closer to that of the Ink Spots than to that of Wynonie Harris and the others.

One of the first pure rock records. Sam Phillips produced it in Memphis in March 1951. Singer Jackie Brenston's name was used on the label, but the band was really Ike Turner's, an eighteen-year-old piano player and disc jockey from Clarksdale, Mississippi.

There were many hard-rocking country records in the years before Elvis Presley's debut. Although it was never as popular among whites as it was among blacks, the metaphor had been used by early country singers. Uncle Dave Macon was the first to use it, when he cut "Rock About My Saro Jane" for Vocalion in 1927. He later said he got the song in 1887, from black singers in Nashville. Jimmie Davis recorded "Rockin' Blues" for Victor in 1932, but it was not released. Cliff Carlisle cut "My Rockin' Mama" for Bluebird in 1936. Buddy Jones recorded "Rockin' Rollin' Mama" for Decca in 1939.

As black music began rocking in the forties, a parallel development occurred in country music. It was called hillbilly boogie, and it was pioneered by men such as the Delmore Brothers, Moon Mullican, and Arthur Smith (whose 1945 Super Disc recording of "Guitar Boogie" led eventually to his MGM "Mountain Be Bop" of 1949). The first country boogie record was "Boogie Woogie," recorded in 1939 for Bluebird by an obscure Georgia-based performer named Johnny Barfield, who accompanied himself on guitar. In some of their King releases, such as "Freight Train Boogie" (1946) and "Whatcha Gonna Gimmie" (1952), the Delmore Brothers went beyond boogie into an effervescent sort of country rock. Pianist Freddie Slack

JOHNNY BARFIELD

B-8272	Boogie-Woogie Everybody's Tryin' to Be My Baby
B-8318	Why Don't You Give Me My Memories?
	Don't Cry, My Darlin'
B-8415	It Ain't No Good
	My Poodle Doodle Dog
B-8506	The New "Boogie Woogie"
	That Little Shirt My Mother Made for Me

and sexy Texas singer Ella Mae Morse cut "House of Blue Lights" for Capitol in 1946, and it was such a fine, tough rocker that Chuck Berry recorded it twelve years later. Red Foley's "Tennessee Saturday Night" on Decca was one of the best-selling country records of 1948, and it rocked. "Rootie Tootie," Hank Williams's third MGM release, cut in 1947, was a jivey rocker, whirling with nonsense lyrics, funky call-and-response, and hot licks. Carl Perkins recalls that the rhythm of Hank's 1953 "Kaw-Liga" inspired Sun thinking. (And there is persistent rumor that Hank Williams left behind a tape of R&B performances, but that it's been suppressed in the interests of his image.) A handful of Tennessee Ernie Ford's early records, on Capitol, such as "Smokey Mountain Boogie" (1949), "Shotgun Boogie" (1950), and "I Don't Know" (1953), are among the best and strongest examples of country music's gropings toward rock-and-roll. The Maddox Brothers and Rose, a West Coast Okie group, recorded stuff that not only rocked, but also contained many of the vocal fireworks—yelps, screams, howls—that became watermarks of rockabilly. They cut "New Mule Skinner Blues" (a version of Jimmie Rodgers's "Blue Yodel No. 8") for Four-Star in the late forties; it was copied by the Fendermen in

Released in May 1953.

1960, and became a Number Five rock hit. Their "Hang-over Blues" (Decca, 1952) is pure gutter-rock. In 1956, the year Elvis broke, the Maddox Brothers and Rose recorded "The Death of Rock & Roll" for Columbia. In early 1954, a few months before Elvis cut his first sides, Joe Almond and His Hillbilly Rockers recorded "Gonna Roll and Rock" for Trumpet Records of Jackson, Mississippi.

The first white rock-and-roll star was Bill Haley. He was born William John Clifton Haley in the Detroit suburb of Highland Park, on July 6, 1925. When he was seven, his family moved to Booth Corner, a small town in southeastern Pennsylvania. During his high school years, Haley began playing country music. As a disk jockey at WSNJ in Bridgeport, New Jersey, in 1945, Haley took the name Yodeling Bill Haley. One of his idols was Bob Wills, and when Haley cut his first records, in 1949, for Cowboy, a small Philadelphia label run by James E. Myers (who later helped write "Rock Around the Clock"), he called his group Bill Haley & the Four Aces of Western Swing. The Cowboy records included versions of recent country hits: George Morgan's "Candy Kisses," Red Foley's "Tennessee Border," and Hank Williams's "Too Many Parties, Too Many Pals."

After Cowboy, Haley cut several records for Center, Keystone, and Atlantic. Late in 1951 he cut his first rock records, for Holiday, a Philadelphia label run by Dave Miller. His Holiday debut was a version of Jackie Brenston's "Rocket '88'," which had been a Number One R&B hit earlier in the year. Haley continued to look at the R&B charts for inspiration. In 1952 he cut a pair of duets with someone named Loretta ("Bill and Loretta with the Saddlemen," the labels read): "Pretty Baby," a Griffin Brothers R&B hit of the year before, and "I'm Crying," which Memphis Slim had cut earlier in 1952.

Haley still showed his ties to country music. His last record for Holiday was "Jukebox Cannonball," a thin parody of "Wabash Cannonball," and when he began recording for Essex (also a Dave Miller label), his first release was "Icy Heart" in 1952, plainly inspired by Hank Williams's "Cold, Cold Heart" of 1951.

The flip-side of "Icy Heart," however, was "Rock the Joint," a wholly violent and fiery rocker—not merely a cover of an R&B hit (Jimmy Preston's 1949 original was on Gotham, a Philadelphia independent), but a lumination.

In the spring of 1953 came Haley's first hit, "Crazy,

Man, Crazy." It rose to the Top Twenty, at a time when "Song from Moulin Rouge" by Percy Faith was Number One. "Crazy, Man, Crazy" was the first white rock hit, but already, somewhere between "Rock the Joint" and the spring of 1953, Haley had let the fire die. In "Rock the Joint" he reveled; in "Crazy, Man, Crazy" he merely performed.

Decca signed Haley in 1954, largely on the basis of "Crazy, Man, Crazy." In April of that year, Haley recorded "(We're Gonna) Rock Around the Clock," which went unnoticed. His second Decca release, a cover of Joe Turner's "Shake, Rattle and Roll," hit the Top Ten. His next record, "Dim, Dim the Lights," crossed over to the R&B charts.

"Rock Around the Clock" was written by a pair of Tin Pan Alley veterans, lyricist Max Freedman and composer Jimmy DeKnight. Freedman, born in 1895, had written "Sioux City Sue," "Song of India," and "Blue Danube Waltz." DeKnight was really James Myers of Myers Music. When Evan Hunter's 1954 novel, *Blackboard Jungle*, was made into a movie, James Myers was chosen as technical advisor (perhaps because he was known to have several acquaintances under the age of sixty-five— Max Freedman, for instance). Myers suggested that "Rock Around the Clock" be used as the film's theme song.

Blackboard Jungle was released in March 1955. Bosley Crowther of *The New York Times* questioned whether the film was "a desirable stimulant to spread before the young." *Blackboard Jungle* was banned in Memphis. Clare Booth Luce, ambassador to France, demanded the film be withdrawn as an entry at the Venice Film Festival, and so it was. What fine publicity.

In May "Rock Around the Clock" hit the charts, and it rose to Number One. In June it crossed over to the R&B charts, where it hit Number Four.

"Rock Around the Clock" became the best-selling

rock record in history, with sales of almost seventeen million to date. But what I find more fascinating, more important about the record, and about Bill Haley, is this: "Rock Around the Clock" was recorded three months before Elvis made his first record, and it was a hit nine months before Elvis appeared on the pop charts. Viewing Haley's earlier records, such as "Rock the Joint," as the first white rock-and-roll, and "Rock Around the Clock" as not only the first Number One rock hit, but also the first clear example of rock gone wholly astray, of fake Tin Pan Alley rock, one can plainly see that in the brief span from 1952 to 1955 rock-and-roll had already risen and fallen. When Elvis broke in early 1956, it had all gone down already. All that remained was for it to be done again, grander and louder; end cycle. The year the Beatles broke, 1963, Elvis was reduced to "Bossa Nova Baby," and Bill Haley, even further into the dim, was doing stuff like "Midnight in Washington" for Newtown Records, rarely to be heard from again until his death, on February 9, 1981. And in 1976 my buddy Richard Meltzer saw two fourteen-year-old girls looking through the bins in a Los Angeles record store. One came upon a Beatles album and called to her friend, "Hey, look! Paul McCartney was in a band before Wings."

In 1952, the year of "Rock the Joint," twenty-nine-year-old disc jockey Alan Freed was hosting his "Moondog Rock and Roll Party," a nightly show broadcast from WJW in Cleveland. Freed's programming of black music for white kids was actually the idea of Leo Mintz, an acquaintance of Freed's who operated the biggest record store in Cleveland. In March 1952 Freed promoted his first concert, which he called a Moondog Ball, at the Cleveland Arena. The Arena had a capacity of ten thousand, and there were about nine thousand tickets sold in advance. On the night of the show, between twenty and thirty thousand kids showed up. They smashed the doors open, overwhelmed the police, and screamed. "Everybody had such a grand time breaking into the Arena," said Freed, "that they didn't ask for their money back."

On September 8, 1954, Freed broadcast his first program at WINS in New York City. In New York Freed called the show simply "Rock and Roll Party" after he was enjoined from including the word *Moondog* by a large blind person named Moondog, who was a familiar figure in the midtown area. In 1953 Moondog had cut some jazz percussion sides for Decca. (He continues to be seen alurk in Manhattan streets, with his staff, horned Viking helmet, flowing robe, and long white whiskers. In the late sixties he cut an album for Columbia.)

Freed became the king of rock-and-roll, and the shows he produced at the Brooklyn Paramount are legendary. At his 1956 Labor Day week shows, he grossed $221,000, an unheard-of take for a rock promoter in those days.

A scandal bloomed near television quiz shows in 1959. On November 4 of that year, twelve-year-old Patty Duke, who was then working on Broadway in *The Miracle Worker*, revealed before Congressman Owen Harris's Subcommittee on Legislative Oversight that she had been given the answers in advance of her appearance on "The $64,000 Challenge" in 1958. Duke had won $32,000 as an expert on singing groups. The person who gave her the answers was Shirley Bernstein, associate producer of the program and sister of culture-creep Leonard Bernstein. *The New York Post*'s headline covered the entire front page: "THEY EVEN FIXED THE KID." There was a photo of small, smiling Patty.

The TV payola scandal spread to radio. Disk jockeys were accused of taking money in return for airplay. Buy some spins; buy some hits. On occasion the currency was not cash, but small parcels of white stuff, or the ministrations of vagina and jowl.

New York District Attorney Frank S. Hogan, who was among the first of the inquisitors of TV payola in the summer of 1958, obtained commercial-bribery indictments against eight fast-talking humans. One was convicted, and two pleaded guilty and paid fines; charges against the other five were dropped. Alan Freed was one of the two who pleaded guilty. In 1960 he was indicted on the charge of accepting $30,650 from six record companies in exchange for, ahem, promotional services. Freed was indignant: "This is the backbone of American business." He changed his plea to guilty in the end and in return was handed a six-month suspended sentence and a $300 fine. Later he was indicted on charges of evading payment of taxes on $37,920 in payola. The king withdrew to an exile in Palm Springs, where he died of uremia in 1965.

Monday, July 5, 1954. The most popular albums in America are Jackie Gleason's *Tawny*, Frank Sinatra's *Songs for Young Lovers,* and the soundtrack of *The Glenn Miller Story*. The top song on the Hit Parade is "Three Coins in the Fountain." The biggest-selling R&B artists are the Midnighters, and the biggest-selling country artist is Webb Pierce. There has been a white rock-and-roll star: Bill Haley.

On this summer day something is happening in Memphis that will overwhelm the whole of American music. Within the Sun Record Company at 706 Union Avenue, Sam Phillips is cutting a first session on a local punk named Elvis Presley.

Samuel Cornelius Phillips had got into the record business by way of radio. Born near Florence, Alabama, on January 5, 1923, Phillips began working as a radio announcer after dropping out of high school in 1941. At night he studied engineering, podiatry, and embalming. In 1942 he was a disc jockey at WLAY in Muscle Shoals, and the next year at WHSL in Decatur. In 1945 he worked at WLAC in Nashville, and from 1946 to 1949, he worked at WREC in Memphis, where he also promoted shows at the Hotel Peabody.

With the money he had saved as a disc jockey and promoter, Phillips opened a recording studio in October 1949 at 706 Union Avenue, where he made recordings of Southern blacks and leased them to independent labels: Chess, Modern, Meteor, Trumpet, and others. He also recorded weddings and the drolleries of Rotarians, transcribed them onto one-sided LPs, and charged nine dollars a throw.

One of the early records that Phillips cut and leased was Jackie Brenston's "Rocket '88'," recorded in March 1951. Some of the record's success as a rocker must be attributed to Phillips. He added extra amplification to Willie Kizart's guitar work, and in doing so, added much brash dimension to the overall sound of the record.

Other bluesmen whom Sam Phillips recorded were Bobby Bland, Little Milton, James Cotton, Sleepy John Estes, Earl Hooker, Walter Horton, Howlin' Wolf, B. B. King, and Joe Hill Louis.

In 1952 Sam decided to start his own record label. He took his brother Judd on as partner and paid a commercial artist on Beale Street to design a logo for the label, which Sam called Sun.

The early months of Sun Records are a faded picture. The first known Sun record, "Blues in My Condition" coupled with "Selling My Whiskey," by Jackie Boy and Little Walter, is Sun 174. Phillips cut these sides by Jack Kelly and Walter Horton in the Union Avenue studio on February 25, 1952, and assigned the coupling the catalogue number 174. (Independent labels rarely inaugurated with logical designations. Instead of giving their first releases catalogue numbers such as 1 or 100 or 1000, they chose numbers with personal meanings—lucky numbers. Later on, independent labels took to giving their first releases high numbers, to fool distributors into thinking

A 1951 check signed to Chester Burnett (Howlin' Wolf) by Sam C. Phillips. Wolf was produced by Phillips from late 1950 to the summer of 1952.

the label had been in business for a long time, and thus received better treatment or credit.) It is not known, however, when this first Sun record was issued, if indeed it was. Sun 178, "She May Be Yours (But She Comes to See Me Sometimes)" by Joe Hill Louis was reviewed in the March 28, 1953, issue of *Billboard*.

In any case, Sun started as a blues label. Walter Horton, Joe Hill Louis, Rufus Thomas, Memphis Ma Rainey, the Prisonaires, and Junior Parker were among the first Sun artists.

Sun's first country record was "Silver Bells" by the Ripley Cotton Choppers, a quartet from Ripley, Tennessee. It was released in October 1953, with HILLBILLY stamped in red upon its yellow label. With subsequent releases, it became obvious that Phillips was trying to wrest a new sound from his country sessions.

"Boogie Blues" by Earl Peterson, a country singer from Lansing, Michigan, who had known Phillips since his disc-jockey days, was issued in March 1954. This wry, uptempo song featured a yodeling vocal. It also bore the

HILLBILLY stamp. Peterson was basically an old-line country singer, but "Boogie Blues" possessed a lively, youthful edge. The next year, Peterson recorded the song for Columbia.

Hardrock Gunter's "Gonna Dance All Night" was released in May of 1954. Sidney Louie Gunter, born in Birmingham, Alabama, on September 18, 1918, had been a disc jockey since 1939 and a recording artist since the late forties. He was best known for his 1949 "Birmingham Bounce" on the Bama label. Red Foley and Leon McAuliffe both covered "Birmingham Bounce" in 1950; Foley's version, on Decca, was a Number One country hit. In 1951 R&B singer Amos Milburn covered the song for Aladdin. After releasing three records on Bama, Gunter recorded for Bullet in late 1950, then for Decca in early 1951. In the fall of that year he became First Lieutenant Sid Gunter and was stationed in Fort Jackson, South Carolina. Back in the studio in the summer of 1953, he cut two singles for MGM. In 1954, the year of his Sun release, Gunter joined the WWVA "Jamboree" and recorded for King. Although he remained with the Jamboree and continued to record for small labels (Emperor, Cross Country, Cullman) throughout the fifties, Hardrock Gunter had all but faded by 1962, the year his atrocious "Hillbilly Twist" was released by Starday. Gunter eventually retired to Colorado, where, in 1972, calling himself simply Rock Gunter, he issued an album of guitar performances of Hank Williams's songs, distributed through Thurston Moore Enterprises.

Interestingly, "Gonna Dance All Night" predated the existence of Sun. Recorded in Birmingham in 1950 and released by Bama in July of that year, Gunter leased the recording, along with several others, to Sun almost four years later. Just a few weeks after Sam Phillips first heard Gunter singing "We're gonna rock 'n' roll," Elvis was in the Sun studio, fulfilling Gunter's roundabout prophecy.

A Sun record released in June 1954, a month after
"Gonna Dance All Night," came closer to the panting It:
"My Kind of Carryin' On" by Doug Poindexter and the
Starlite Wranglers. It fluttered, shook like a creature
flirting with madness. Sam must have slept well that night.

"My Kind of Carryin' On" was Poindexter's only Sun
single. In 1955 he retired from the music business after
the breakup of his band. His lead guitarist, Scotty Moore,
and his bass player, Bill Black, had joined with a new
singer. Today Poindexter sells insurance in Memphis.

Monday, July 5, 1954. Rock-and-roll exists. Sam
Phillips, Elvis Presley, Scotty Moore, and Bill Black are
in Sun's poky, thirty-by-twenty-foot studio messing with
"Blue Moon of Kentucky," a song Bill Monroe and His
Blue Grass Boys had cut for Columbia in 1945. Phillips
has that weird bastard sound in the dampness of his brain,
and he looks at Presley and hopes.

Finally the sound is in the air—materialized, magic—
captured on magnetic tape. It's a curious, physical sound.
Rockabilly they would come to call it in a year's time.

Sam Phillips grins. "Hell, that's different," he says.
"That's a pop song now, Levi. That's *good.*"

Elvis Aron Presley was nineteen then (he was born
in Tupelo, Mississippi, on January 8, 1935). Six years
earlier, in 1948, his family had moved to Memphis, and in
the spring of 1953 Elvis was graduated from Humes High
School. His picture in *The Herald,* the Humes High yearbook, shows a boy with sideburns, Corinthian pompadour,
and a hint of acne. He had participated, the yearbook says,
in R.O.T.C., Biology Club, English Club, History Club,
and Speech Club. The summer after graduation, Presley
went to work for the Precision Tool Company. He left that
job after a brief time and began working at the Crown
Electric Company, which paid him $42 a week to drive a
truck.

On a Saturday afternoon in 1953 (Haley's "Crazy,

Man, Crazy" was in the air), Elvis made his first visit to
the Sun studio. As a sideline operation, Phillips still main-
tained his Memphis Recording Service, administered by
Marion Keisker, former Miss Radio of Memphis. It was to
the Memphis Recording Service, not Sun Records, that
Elvis came that afternoon. He paid Keisker the four-dollar
charge, entered the studio with his acoustic guitar, and
recorded two songs directly onto a double-sided ten-inch
acetate disk. On one side Elvis cut "My Happiness," which
had been a pop hit for Ella Fitzgerald, and for several
other acts, in the summer of 1948, when Elvis was thirteen.
On the other side he did "That's When Your Heartaches
Begin," a mawkish ballad written by Zeb Turner and recorded by Bob Lamb on Dot in 1951.

Struck by Presley's voice, Marion Keisker recorded
the end of "My Happiness" and the whole of "That's When
Your Heartaches Begin" on a length of discarded tape.
Seventeen years later, Marion Keisker MacInnes told Elvis
biographer Jerry Hopkins, "The reason I taped Elvis was
this: Over and over I remember Sam saying, 'If I could
only find a white man who had the Negro feel, I could
make a billion dollars.' This is what I heard in Elvis, this
. . . what I guess they now call 'soul,' this Negro sound.
So I taped it. I wanted Sam to know."

Keisker made a note of Presley's address, 464 Alabama
Street, and the next time she saw Phillips she played the
tape of Elvis's performance. Sam seemed mildly interested, but did not pursue the matter.

On January 4, 1954, Elvis returned to the Memphis
Recording Service. Marion Keisker was not in, but Phillips
was. They spoke, Sam calmly and plainly and easily, Elvis
nervously. He paid Sam four dollars and cut another
acetate: "I'll Never Stand in Your Way," a 1941 country
song written by Clint Horner, and "Casual Love Affair."

In the early summer of 1954, about eight months
after Elvis had first visited the Sun studio, Sam Phillips

received a demonstration record of a song called "Without You," cut in Nashville by an unknown black singer. Sam was so impressed by the demo that he wanted to release it on Sun. He called Nashville in search of the singer and to obtain permission to issue the record. He was told that no one knew who the kid was, that he had been hanging around the studio when the song arrived and they let him demo it. Phillips decided to find someone else to record the song.

"What about the kid with the sideburns?" said Marion Keisker. Pause for commercial.

Elvis was called that same Saturday afternoon, and he rushed to the studio. Phillips played the demo for him. Elvis sang it, and it was ridiculous. He tried again, then again, but it was still ridiculous. Phillips gave up on "Without You" and suggested that Elvis try "Rag Mop," a song written by Johnnie Lee Wills (Bob Wills's brother) and Deacon Anderson. Wills had had a Top Ten country hit with it in 1950, on the Bullet label. The same year, the Ames Brothers had had a Number One pop hit with it, and Lionel Hampton had had a Top Ten R&B hit with it. It seemed an easy song (the lyrics are impressively dumb), but again Elvis was awkward and plain.

Sam, disturbed, asked Elvis just what in hell it was that he could sing. Oh, anything, Elvis replied. So do it, Sam said. And then, we are led to believe by the grooms of history, it poured forth, a crazy rush of disparate sounds: gospel (earlier in 1954, Elvis had almost joined the Blackwood Brothers, a gospel quartet that performed regularly on the WMPS "High Noon Roundup"), hard-core country, R&B, pop. For hours it went on, not a cool Apollonian eclecticism, but fevered glossolalia.

Sam called Winfield Scott Moore, better known as Scotty, the twenty-two-year-old guitarist who had recorded with Doug Poindexter several weeks before. On

Sunday, Independence Day, Elvis and Scotty met at Scotty's home, where they fooled with several recent country songs, such as Eddy Arnold's "I Really Don't Want To Know" and Hank Snow's "I Don't Hurt Anymore," both recent hits on RCA-Victor, and a few of singer Billy Eckstine's MGM sides. After a few hours, bass player Bill Black, Scotty's neighbor, who had also played at Doug Poindexter's session, dropped in. He was not impressed, but the next evening, July 5, Black found himself in the Sun studio with Phillips, Presley, and Moore. It was Sam's idea for Scotty and Bill not to bring the rest of the Starlite Wranglers with them—no fiddle, no steel guitar. Sam had a different kind of country session in mind.

The first recording of "Blue Moon of Kentucky" was never released legally. (In 1975 Bopcat Records, a Dutch label, bootlegged the tape and included it in the album *Good Rocking Tonight.*) The version that was issued was recorded either the same night or the next night. Although this piece of history is clouded, it seems likely that the released version of "Blue Moon of Kentucky" was cut the same night as the version that caused Sam Phillips to utter, "Hell, that's different. That's a pop song now, Levi. That's *good.*" (Those words can be heard on *Good Rocking Tonight.*) They were in the groove then, touching tongues with the philosophers' stone Sam was seeking, and it's difficult to imagine their calling it a night at that moment of celebration.

"Blue Moon of Kentucky," as released on Elvis's first record, Sun 209, is surer, tougher than the earlier take. Presley is dizzy with the confirmation of his prowess. "Blue Moon of Kentucky" is daring to the point of mania. It is Elvis walking on steel blades, through orange-white flames, invincible with the knowledge he sees in Sam's eyes, hears in his own voice, and feels in his own flushed skin; the knowledge that right now, this moment, he,

Elvis Aron Presley, is the greatest singer in Memphis and the universe. Nothing, not sex, not the eyes of bank tellers, would ever again disarm with its mystery.

I think Elvis Presley will never be solved. It is strange enough that at the time of his first recordings, Elvis declared his idol to be Dean Martin, but to hear him at an August 22, 1957, press conference proclaim Pat Boone to be "undoubtedly the finest voice out now," and call Patti Page and Kay Starr his favorite female singers—this is modestly terrifying, a wild illogic.

Elvis never revealed himself. He was found dead on his bathroom floor early on the morning of August 16, 1977, at the age of forty-two. Traces of thirteen different drugs were found in his system—grim corroboration of the sensational allegations that had been published less than a month before in a hastily written paperback called *Elvis: What Happened?* by three former Presley lackeys.

"It don't mean a damned thing," Colonel Parker was rumored to have remarked on Elvis's death. "It's just like when he was away in the army." As sales rose on the third day, the excitement grew more and more ecstatic. Mourners lost their lives, crushed in the frenzied funerary convergence on Memphis. The cemetery tomb, to which Elvis had been delivered in a Cadillac hearse the color of the Resurrection raiment, was defiled by unholy thieves in search of grisly spoils; and the body was reinterred within the hallowed, guarded walls of Graceland, laid beside the body of his mother, Gladys, beneath a stone cross.

Like the fourth-century impresario who hauled Saint Stephen's coffin through Christendom, a holy huckster toured the South in Elvis's limousine, allowing people to sit in it for a fee and to have their pictures taken in it for an additional charge. (When I encountered him that fall at the Tennessee State Fair Grounds in Nashville, he was also doing a brisk business hawking photocopies of Elvis's autopsy report and death certificate.)

Morbid tribute records flooded forth in waves of formaldehyde and glucose. One of them was Billy Joe Burnette's "Welcome Home, Elvis." Sung as if by the twin brother, Jesse Garon, who died at birth, the song warmly welcomed Elvis to the Great Beyond, where mama was "waitin' for ya, Elvis. Yeah, she's right over there, And soon our daddy will take our hand, and we'll be a happy family once again." In time there was a record called "The Shroud of Memphis," which celebrated a miraculous retention of Elvis's image in the manner of the Turin winding-sheet. It is distressing that of all the books about Elvis published since his death, the most successful has been the most ghoulish, *Elvis* by Albert Goldman.

The wonder of Elvis will never die; no carrion bird can kill it. There was more mystery, more power, in Elvis, singer of "Danny Boy," than in Bob Dylan, utterer of hermetic ironies. It is the sheer, superhuman tastelessness of Elvis that shakes the mind. In 1965, as Western civilization lay on its tummy peeking over the brink at the rapids of psilocybin and "(I Can't Get No) Satisfaction," Elvis, for all the world to see, was hopping about singing "Do the Clam." And the same week "Do the Clam" was released, Dean Martin came out with "Send Me the Pillow You Dream On," a Hank Locklin country hit from 1958. A few years later people began speaking of the revolutionary pop-country fusion wrought by the Byrds and Bob Dylan. Could Bob Dylan do the Clam? I bet Dino could.

One thing is certain. In an age bereft of magic, Elvis was one of the last great mysteries, the secret of which lay unrevealed even to himself. That he failed, fatally, to understand that mystery, gives anyone else little hope of doing so. After all, the truest mysteries are those without explanations.

After "Blue Moon of Kentucky," Elvis and the boys

ELVIS PRESLEY

The first feature article on Elvis appeared in the September 1955 issue of Country Song Roundup. *"There's no doubt about it," concluded the anonymous writer, "this youngster is a real 'Folk Music Fireball.'"*

cut "That's All Right," a song originally recorded by Mississippi-born bluesman Arthur Crudup, also known as Big Boy Crudup, for Victor in 1946. As Elvis performed it, it was no more a blues song, and no less a country song, than "Blue Moon of Kentucky." Where Bill Haley's versions of R&B songs were playfully mimetic, Elvis's were creative. He had no restraining concept of commercialism. Not yet, at least.

Elvis's first record, "Blue Moon of Kentucky" c/w "That's All Right," was released on July 19, 1954. Sam Phillips took a copy of the record to Dewey Phillips, the disc jockey who hosted the "Red Hot and Blue" show at WHBQ, and he broadcast "That's All Right." Listeners called in their enthusiastic reactions. At WHHM disk jockey Sleepy Eye John began spinning "Blue Moon of Kentucky." The record took off, and as the weeks passed, "That's All Right" became the Number One country record in Memphis.

That is when rockabilly became fact, and Elvis its avatar. On September 25, Elvis's second record was issued, a coupling of "Good Rockin' Tonight" (the 1947 Roy Brown song) and "I Don't Care If the Sun Don't Shine," written by Mack David, author of "Bibbidi Bobbidi Boo" and "La Vie en Rose." Elvis made his debut on the Opry,

Roy Brown's original "Good Rocking Tonight," released in September 1947.

Wynonie Harris's hit version, released in February 1948.

as a guest in Hank Snow's segment. He sang both sides of his first single. After the show, Jim Denny, the boss of the Opry Artists Bureau, told Elvis he should go back to driving a truck. Elvis cried all the way home to Memphis.

On October 16, Presley played the "Louisiana Hayride," where he went over so well that he was brought back the following week to become a regular performer. The December 11 *Billboard* called him "the youngster with the hillbilly blues beat."

The third Elvis record, released on January 8, 1955, was "Milkcow Blues Boogie," originally cut by Kokomo Arnold on Decca in 1935 and subsequently done by several country artists: Cliff Bruner (Decca, 1937), Johnnie Lee Wills (Decca, 1941), Moon Mullican (King, 1946), and the Maddox Brothers and Rose (Four-Star, 1948). The flip was "You're a Heartbreaker," a strong country weeper, written by Charles Alvin Sallee, that was closer to a honky-tonk performance than any of Elvis's other Sun sides.

In "Milkcow Blues Boogie," it is obvious that Elvis is no longer innocent of commercial affectations. After a well-rehearsed false start, Elvis, in a voice that foreshadowed every black-and-white beatnik movie of the late fifties,

---

Bill Monroe

★★★★ *Roanoke*
★★★★ *Cheyenne*

This is a must for them what likes good instrumental records, with the pickin' on both sides excellent. (**Decca 29406**)

Morgan Sisters

★★★★ *You Play Fiddlesticks*
★★★ *Evergreen*

Fiddlesticks is a fast tune well-sung by the girls who might have a big one this time. (**King 3913**)

Elvis Presley

★★★★★ *Milkcow Blues Boogie*
★★★★ *You're A Heartbreaker*

Two excellent sides by one of the bright newcomers in the country fields. (**Sun U-140**)

Marvin Rainwater

★★★★ *I Gotta Go Get My Baby*
★★★ *Daddy's Glad You Came Home*

Marvin does a top job on *Baby* with the Ridge Riders doing some fancy pickin' on both sides of this release. (**Coral 61342**)

Fred Rose

★★★★ *A New Flame*
★★ *Old Man Of The Sea*

Fred renews an old romance, and gets off a real good record. *Old Man* is just along for the ride. (**MGM K-11909**)

Record reviews from the April 1955 issue of Country & Western Jamboree.

says, "Hold it, fellas. That don't move. Let's get real, real gone." It was the "Rock Around the Clock" syndrome, Elvis's first plunge into schmaltz.

"I'm Left, You're Right, She's Gone," written by Bill Taylor and Sun steel-guitarist Stan Kesler, and "Baby Let's Play House," recorded by Arthur Gunter on Excello earlier in the year, comprised the fourth single, issued on April 1, 1955. (Bill Taylor later revealed that his song was

based on a Campbell's Soup advertisement, and that he wrote it while taking a bath.) For the first time, one of Presley's records hit the national country charts—"Baby Let's Play House" rose to the Number Ten position. As "Baby Let's Play House" was high on the charts, Elvis's last Sun disc was issued: "Mystery Train," an R&B song Junior Parker had cut for Sun in 1953, and "I Forgot To Remember to Forget," written by Charlie Feathers and Stan Kesler. In "Mystery Train" Scotty Moore showed the influence of Merle Travis. His guitar break toward the end of the record is an echo of the licks used by Travis in his 1946 "Sixteen Tons." The record became a double-barreled hit, rising to the Number One position on the country charts. Elvis Presley, rock-and-roll madman, had the best-selling country record in the nation: The year 1955 belonged to Elvis Presley and *Blackboard Jungle*.

Late in 1955, Elvis signed with RCA-Victor. On January 5, 1956, in Nashville, Elvis cut his first sides for his new label. Now, in addition to Scotty and Bill and drummer D. J. Fontana (who had joined the group early in 1955), Nashville cats were involved: guitarist Chet Atkins, pianist Floyd Cramer, vocal group the Jordanaires. Elvis's first RCA-Victor recording, "Heartbreak Hotel,"

was released in February 1956. It became the Number
One song on both the country and the pop charts.

"Heartbreak Hotel" was a superlative rockabilly song,
full of austerity, sex, and stone-hard rhythm. The story of
"Heartbreak Hotel" is this: Mae Boren Axton, songwriter
and Hank Snow's P.R. lady, was shown a newspaper clipping by her friend Tommy Durden, another songwriter.
The clipping reported a suicide by a young man who had
left a one-line note: "I walk a lonely street." Axton and
Durden wrote the song around the line and made a tape
of it within a half hour. The song was offered to the Wilburn Brothers, who declined it.

For the next two years, Elvis continued to cut strong
rockabilly for RCA-Victor: "Hound Dog," originally done
by Willie Mae Thornton on Peacock in 1952 and covered
by Tommy Duncan (formerly lead singer with Bob Wills)
on Intro in 1953; "Don't Be Cruel," written for Elvis by
Otis Blackwell (the demos Blackwell made, at Charlie
Brave's Allegro studio in the basement of 1650 Broadway
in New York City, were masterworks; all the vocal fillips
and rhythmic heat of "Don't Be Cruel," "Great Balls of
Fire," "Fever," and other hits were copied directly from
Blackwell's demos); "Jailhouse Rock"; "Hard Headed
Woman." Elvis sometimes reached beyond the usual
sources; "Love Me Tender" was taken from the traditional
ballad "Aura Lee."

With each new session, Elvis grew further from rockabilly. By the time he was drafted into the army in 1958,
the golden days of rockabilly had passed.

As all things that contain more creativity than
formula, more emotion than intellect, rockabilly cannot
be precisely defined. As the word implies, rockabilly is
hillbilly rock-and-roll. It was not a usurpation of black
music by whites because its soul, its pneuma, was white,
full of the redneck ethos. When Elvis cut Big Boy Crudup's
"That's All Right," he was no more usurping black culture

TV News and Views

By ROBERT JOHNSON
Press-Scimitar Staff Writer

I never had a better time than yesterday a f t e r n o o n when I dropped in at Sam Phillips' Sun Record bedlam on Union at Marshall. It was what you might call a barrel-house of fun. Carl Perkins was in a recording session . . . and he has one that's going to hit as hard as "Blue Suede Shoes." We're trying to arrange an advance audition for you Memphis fans before the song is released in January. Johnny Cash dropped in. Jerry Lee Lewis was there, too, and then Elvis stopped by.

Elvis headed for the piano and started to Fats Domino it on "Blueberry Hill." The joint was really rocking before they got thru.

Elvis is high on Jerry Lee Lewis. "That boy can go," he said. "I think he has a great future ahead of him. He has a different style, and the way he plays piano just gets inside me."

Elvis debunked the newest rumor: "No, I haven't bought 200 acres at Collierville," he said. "How do those stories get started?"

He talked earnestly about the Toledo incident. "I talked to that fellow for at least 15 minutes, trying to be nice to him and keep him from starting anything, but finally it just got out of hand."

I never saw the boy more likeable than he was just fooling around with these other fellows who have the same interests he does.

If Sam Phillips had been on his toes, he'd have turned the recorder on when that very unrehearsed but talented bunch got to cutting up on "Blueberry Hill" and a lot of other songs. That quartet could sell a million.

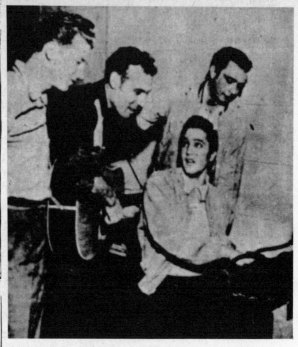

MILLION DOLLAR QUARTET—The only thing predictable about Elvis is that he's unpredictable. Yesterday Carl (Blue Suede Shoes) Perkins was cutting some new records at Sam Phillips' Sun Record studio on Union at Marshall. Elvis dropped in. So did Johnny Cash. Jerry Lee Lewis was already there. Elvis headed for the piano, and an old-fashioned barrel-house session with barbershop harmony resulted. In the picture are Sun's new discovery, Jerry Lee Lewis, at the left, Carl Perkins, Johnny Cash and the virtuoso at the little 88 is Elvis.

Our only regret! — that each and everyone of you wonderful d. j.'s who are responsible for these boys being among the best known and liked in show business could not be here too!

We thought however that you might like to read first-hand about our little shindig --- it was a dilly!

Sincerely grateful,

Sam Phillips

Sun press release, December 1956.

Fame's center aisle, 1956: Colonel Parker explains the Faustian Clause to Elvis; behind him, Irish McCalla, Sheena Herself, gazes west, towards all darkness.

than Wynonie Harris was usurping white culture when he cut country singer Hank Penny's "Bloodshot Eyes" three years before. Presley's version of "That's All Right" is better than the original, just as Harris's version of "Bloodshot Eyes" is better than its original.

There was an affinity between rockabilly and black music of the 1940s and '50s, as there had been an affinity between Western swing and black music of the 1920s and '30s. But it was not, really, more than an affinity. Of the sixteen known titles Elvis recorded as a Sun artist, five were derived from R&B records: "That's All Right," "Good Rockin' Tonight," "Milkcow Blues Boogie," "Baby Let's

Play House," and "Mystery Train." (Two of these, in turn, were derived to a certain extent from country records: Arthur Gunter's "Baby Let's Play House" from Eddy Arnold's 1951 hit "I Want To Play House with You," and Junior Parker's "Mystery Train" from the Carter Family's 1930 "Worried Man Blues.") During his Sun years, as during the decades since, Elvis derived the bulk of his music from country and pop sources.

What blackness there was in rockabilly in no way constituted an innovation in country music. The black enculturation in the music of old-timers such as Jimmie Rodgers and Bob Wills was far greater, far deeper. Nor was there much of a technical nature in rockabilly that country music had not known before. The slap-bass technique, one of the watermarks of classic rockabilly, can be heard in country records of the pre-War era—for example, hear bassist Ramon DeArmon in the Light Crust Dough-boys' 1938 Vocalion record "Pussy, Pussy, Pussy." The echo effect heard in many Sun rockabilly recordings had been used, less subtly, by Wilf Carter in his Victor records of the 1930s and by Eddy Arnold in his 1945 "Cattle Call." (The unique echo sound of the Sun studio was achieved through the use of a tape-loop delay and a 7½-ips, instead of the more advanced 15-ips, two-track recorder. The added echo effect heard in Scotty Moore's guitar relied on a custom-built amplifier, made in Cairo, Illinois, by a man named Ray Butts. Moore got the second amp that Butts built; the first went to Chet Atkins, the third to Carl Perkins, and the fourth to Roy Orbison. When he ceased working with Elvis in September 1957, Moore put the amp in a closet. Several closets later he withdrew it at Carl Perkins's request and plugged it in for one of Carl's Mercury sessions early in 1975.)

What made rockabilly such a drastically new music was its spirit, a thing that bordered on mania. Elvis's "Good Rockin' Tonight" was not merely a party song,

The low cost of rockabilly.

but an invitation to a holocaust. Junior Parker's "Mystery Train" was an eerie shuffle; Elvis's "Mystery Train" was a demonic incantation. Country music in recent years had not known such vehement emotion, nor had black music. Rockabilly was the face of Dionysos, full of febrile sexuality and senselessness; it flushed the skin of new housewives and made pink teenage boys reinvent themselves as flaming creatures.

PEEPLES MUSIC PUBLISHING CO.

917 LAIRD ST.   PASADENA, TEXAS

February 11, 1956

Sun Record Co., Inc.,

706 Union,

Memphis, Tenn.

                    Hi Lo Pub. Co.
                    Sun Record No. 234- By Carl Perkins
            Re.-"BLUE SUEDE SHOES"
Gentlemen:

This letter is to inform you that the song entitled,

"BLUE SUEDE SHOES" was officially published by Peeples

Music Pub. Co., 917 Laird St., Pasadena, Texas and cleared

through BMI on the date of August 22, 1955.

At the present time I hold the copyright to said song, and

the one of the same title, theme and tune which you just

recently released is so similar in every detail, that I

could not possibly release the one I have in my catalogue.

The writers feel that the song belongs to them and I am sure

that if you knew the reasons why they make their claims, that

you would be interested.

We would prefer to make an amicable settlement regarding the

publishing rights to this song; but we do feel that the song

belongs to us.

Please let me hear from you immediately regarding this matter.

                              Yours truly,

                              Curt Peeples.

                              Peeples Music Pub. Co.

A 1956 letter contesting the rights to "Blue Suede Shoes."

February 15, 1956

Mr. Curt Peeples
Peeples Music Publishing Company
917 Laird Street
Pasadena, Texas

Dear Mr. Peeples:

We have your letter dated February 11th, and postmarked February 14th.

While we can appreciate your concern if you have a song of the same
title in your catalogue, we can assure you that it would be an amazing
artistic coincidence if there should be the duplication you speak of
between your copyrighted composition and the "BLUE SUEDE SHOES" that
Sun Record Company, Inc., has recorded.

The song recorded and released on Sun record #234 is a joint work of
two of our artists, Johnny Cash and Carl Perkins and was virtually
composed, over a period of several months, in our studios.

As you know, titles alone cannot be copyrighted, and many songs of
identical title can be composed, copyrighted, recorded and published
without any infringement of one another's rights.

We have no desire to intrude on anyone's rights and interests, and if
you wish to furnish us with a lead sheet of the composition that you
have copyrighted, we shall be glad to have an impartial professional
lead sheet man run a comparison of the melodies. Again we say, however,
that should any appreciable similarity be shown, it would be a surprising
coincidence, as we know under what circumstances the Sun recorded song
"BLUE SUEDE SHOES" was composed and written.

With kindest regards, we are,

Appreciatively,

SUN RECORD COMPANY, Inc.

Sam C. Phillips,
President

SCP:mk

Sam Phillips's reply.

He reached in his pocket and he flashed a quart.

Although Elvis was the avatar, the unforgettable boy-daddy of rockabilly, there were others. In Memphis, and across the South, burning ever north, they drove country music berserk.

Carl Lee Perkins was born on a welfare-supported tenant farm near Tiptonville, Tennessee, on April 9, 1932, the second of three brothers. His early years were spent on a plantation in Lake County, Tennessee, where his family were the sole white sharecroppers. In 1945 the Perkins family relocated in Bemis, where Carl began working as a laborer in a battery plant, then at a bakery in nearby Jackson.

In 1945 Carl won a talent show in Bemis. He taught his brothers, Jay B. and Clayton, to play guitars, and together the three performed locally as the Perkins Brothers Band.

Late in 1953, after he and his Mississippi-born wife, Valda Crider, moved to Parkview Courts, a government-subsidized housing project in Jackson, Carl sent demo tapes to various record companies in Nashville and New York. In December 1954, after a few unsuccessful attempts, Perkins had an audience with Sam Phillips at Sun. Several weeks later, in February of 1955, Sam issued Carl's first record on the Flip label (a Sun affiliate): "Movie Magg," which Carl had authored in 1945, and "Turn Around," a straight country piece.

With "Movie Magg" it became immediately apparent that Perkins was a consummate rock guitarist, given to rapid-fire, high-note runs on his Les Paul Gibson. The Flip record got an impressive disc-jockey response in Memphis, as had Elvis's records during the previous seven months, and Sam signed Carl on as a regular Sun artist.

During the next years, until Carl left Sun in 1958, he had only seven singles released, or less than two a year. This small number of releases is odd in light of the fact that four of these records were country hits and three of these four crossed to the pop charts. One of them, "Blue Suede Shoes," was a Top Ten hit on the country, pop, and R&B charts in 1956. Most likely Carl's records were over-pressed in anticipation of another hit the magnitude of "Blue Suede Shoes."

Like Elvis, Carl Perkins sometimes used black material, as in his 1957 "Matchbox," a hard-edged version of Blind Lemon Jefferson's 1927 "Matchbox Blues" (which had been recorded by several country acts before Perkins: Larry Hensely in 1934, Joe Shelton in 1935, Roy Shaffer in 1939, Roy Newman and His Boys also in 1939, and the Shelton Brothers in 1947). Unlike Elvis, however, Perkins was a consummate songwriter who was at his best in stuff such as the 1956 "Dixie Fried," a torrent of whiskey and violence, and the 1957 "Put Your Cat Clothes On" (unreleased until 1971), an anthem of redneck rock.

From Sun, Perkins went to Columbia, where he tried to recapture the success of "Blue Suede Shoes" with a series of wardrobe-rock contrivances: "Pink Pedal Pushers" and "Levi Jacket" in 1958, "Pointed Toe Shoes" in 1959. In 1963 he went to Decca. After Decca he signed with Dollie, an independent Nashville label, and in 1968 he returned to Columbia, where he stayed till 1973, when he joined Mercury, with whom he released only one album and a handful of singles.

* * *

I believe in an ultimate and absolute rhythm.
   —Ezra Pound
      Sonnets and Ballate of Guido Cavalcanti

He who controls rhythm/controls.
   —Charles Olson
      "Against Wisdom as Such"

It was three o'clock in the morning, and the master bedroom of Graceland was still. Elvis Presley lay in his orange silk pajamas, dreaming. It was the same old dream.

He strode through Tupelo along Highway 78 in the late afternoon, toward the home of Mary. He had not seen her since that sexy, ruinous morning in 1955, and he was happy as he turned the corner onto Fourth. There was the house, where she waited in magic underwear. Suddenly he knew he was walking without shoes and socks. Pleasance became dread, and he flushed with panic. He would go across town, where in this dream his mother lived, and there get shoes and socks. If he hurried, there was time. He took a shortcut through a backyard he recognized, but he was soon lost, running barefoot and scared through strange, derisive streets, until he came to a meadow like none he had ever seen, and afternoon became night and the meadow became endless and he screamed.

The white telephone at Elvis's bedside was ringing. He reached and pressed a small silver button on the box of walnut and black glass that sat near the phone. Its dark face lighted, 3:07. Beneath the time, in smaller lines, was the date, November 23, 1976. He lifted the receiver. It was Robert Loyd, a Graceland security guard, calling from the guard post downstairs. There was trouble.

At the gate Jerry Lee Lewis leaned against his 1976 Lincoln Continental. He held a .38-caliber derringer, and he was drunk. He had come to liberate Elvis, to speak with Elvis, to murder Elvis, to sing with Elvis. He demanded Elvis come to the gate. Then he demanded he be brought in to Elvis. He waved the gun and yelled curses. His eyes tightened with wrath, and he shouted for Elvis. Loyd was scared, and he asked Elvis's advice. Ignore him, Elvis said.

Jerry Lee raved on, and Loyd called the cops. Memphis patrolman B. J. Kirkpatrick arrived to find Lewis sitting in his car, holding the derringer at his knee. The trigger was cocked. He was arrested and charged with public drunkenness and carrying a pistol, then released on $250 bond pending a hearing the next morning. Jerry Lee did not appear in court for the hearing, and a warrant was issued for his arrest. Later in the day the warrant was dismissed by Judge Albert H. Boyd at the request of Lewis's lawyer. The night after the disturbance Jerry Lee entered Doctors Hospital for treatment of peptic ulcers and influenza.

Less than twenty-four hours before his arrest at Graceland, Lewis was arrested at a street corner near his home in Collierville, east of Memphis. After driving his thirteen-year-old daughter, Phoebe, to school, he overturned his $46,000 Rolls-Royce. He was charged with reckless driving, driving while intoxicated, and driving without a license. Collierville police chief, H. A. Goforth, Jr., said Lewis was given a Breathalyzer test but it proved negative. The police were baffled by this thaumaturgy and could do nothing but free him on $250 bail pending a hearing.

After this arrest Jerry Lee told a reporter he resented that the press treated Elvis as royalty and him, Jerry Lee, as white trash. "You all hate my guts or something," he said. "I'm no angel, but I'm a pretty nice guy." Hours later he waited, gun cocked, outside the big house on Elvis Presley Boulevard.

That Monday night, not long after Jerry Lee had magicked the Collierville Breathalyzer, his father, Elmo Lewis, was arrested near Robinsonville, Mississippi, and charged with speeding and driving while intoxicated. He refused to take an alcohol-content test and was placed in Tunica County Jail. On Tuesday morning he was released on $300 bond pending a hearing later in the day. The elder Lewis fled across the state line to Tennessee.

On the afternoon of September 29, his forty-first birthday, Jerry Lee shot Norman "Butch" Owens, his bass player, in the upper chest with a .357 magnum. Owens survived, and Jerry Lee told police he thought the gun was empty. A hearing was set for nine o'clock, October 14, but Jerry did not appear.

The week after he shot his bass player, Jerry Lee was arrested at his home and charged with disorderly conduct. Neighbors had complained that Lewis was shouting obscenities at them.

There had always been legal fires. Until 1975 Jerry Lee kept an office in Memphis: Jerry Lee Lewis Enterprises, Inc., Suite 805, 3003 Airways Boulevard. But one night he blasted twenty-five holes through his office door with a .45 automatic, and he was asked to leave.

Back in the early sixties, before San Francisco first uttered the word *psychedelic*, Jerry Lee and his band, the Memphis Beats, were arrested at a motel in Grand Prairie, Texas, and charged with possession of seven hundred amphetamine capsules; two hundred were for the band, five hundred for Jerry Lee. In March 1975, after San Francisco last uttered the word *psychedelic*, federal narcotics agents boarded Lewis's Convair 640 at the Denver airport and took what a government spokesman called "a substantial amount of drugs." Lewis claimed it was a setup. The dope was confiscated, but no arrest was made.

Believe it: Jerry Lee Lewis is a creature of mythic essence, a Set, a Baptist Dionysos aflame with glorious cowardice and self-killing guilt. He was—in a way, still is—the heart of redneck rock 'n' roll, and one of the greatest country singers who ever lived. Talk about rock-and-roll depravados: Jerry Lee makes them all look like Wayne Newton. Talk about honky-tonk heroes: Next to Jerry Lee, they're a bunch of frat-party pukers. "I was born feet first, been rockin' ever since," he'll tell you if he's in a good mood. His vassals and kin will tell you more: Jerry Lee can out-drink, out-dope, out-fight, out-cuss, out-shoot, and out-fuck any man alive. He is the last American wild man, *homo agrestis americanus ultimus*. "Just don't get too close to him and you won't get hurt," said Waylon Jennings. In all ways he is a lord of excess. "I've seen him eat four steaks and then eat again in a couple of hours," said his sister Linda Gail.

In 1975 Donnie Fritts (also known as the Elegant Alabama Leaning Man), a Nashville songwriter and actor in several Sam Peckinpah movies, wrote a song for Jerry Lee called "A Damn Good Country Song." Jerry Lee cut it, and Mercury released it as a single.

> *Well, I took enough pills for the whole damn town;*
> *Jerry Lee Lewis drank enough whiskey to lift any*
>   *ship off of the ground.*
> *I'll be the first to admit it;*
> *I sure wish that these people would quit it,*
> *Cuz it's tough enough to straighten up when*
>   *they won't leave you alone.*
> *My life would make a damn good country song.**

He was born on September 29, 1935, in Ferriday, Louisiana, the second son of Elmo and Mary Ethel Lewis. The older son, Elmo, Jr., was killed in a car wreck at the age of nine. After Jerry Lee came two daughters, Frankie Jean and Linda Gail. Frankie Jean says her daddy, a carpenter, helped build Angola Prison Farm; she says Jerry Lee started playing piano in 1944, and that "Silent Night" was the first song he could play straight through. In the fall of 1949, Ferriday's Ford dealer presented a show in his parking lot to hail the new line of cars. Jerry joined the band and sang and played piano for twenty minutes. He raped the down-home crowd with his version of "Drinkin' Wine Spo-Dee-O-Dee," which had been an R&B hit twice that year, first by Stick McGhee and then by Wynonie Harris. The crowd dropped a glorious $13 in Jerry's kitty, and he decided to go professional.

The next year Jerry worked at the Blue Cat Night Club in Natchez. On Saturdays he had a twenty-minute radio program at WNAT in the same city. His sister Linda

---

* "A Damn Good Country Song" by Donnie Fritts. Copyright © 1975 by Combine Music Corporation. Used by permission.

Gail recalls that he hitched to New Orleans to make a record, but none was made. He brought home his report card: twenty-nine F's.

After quitting high school, he attended Southwestern Bible Institute, a school of the Assembly of God in Waxahachie, Texas. (In 1963 the institute changed its name to Southwestern Assemblies of God College. According to its bulletin, the college "embraces standards of living and conduct that are the same as those generally accepted by the Pentecostal churches in America. These are characterized by clean conduct and conversation, modest apparel in dress, high standards of moral life, and a deep consecration and devotion in spiritual life.") Jerry Lee was expelled for ravaging "My God Is Real" during a performance in chapel.

Back in Ferriday, he became a door-to-door seller of vacuum cleaners. He quit in 1952, when he got a regular job at the Wagon Wheel in Natchez, drumming in a trio led by Paul Whitehead, a blind pianist. Sometimes Whitehead switched to trumpet or accordion, and Jerry was then allowed to play piano.

Jerry Lee first married when he was sixteen. The marriage to Dorothy Barton, a preacher's daughter, lasted barely a year. In 1953 he married Jane Mitcham of Natchez, and on November 2 of that year his first son, Jerry Lee, Jr., was born. (On November 13, 1973, Jerry Lee, Jr., was killed in a car wreck near Cockrum, Mississippi. He had spent part of the year in a nuthouse, which he attributed to the evil effects of marijuana upon his brain. A few weeks before his death, he was saved at an Assembly of God revival.)

Soon after his son was born, Lewis went to Shreveport to audition for the "Louisiana Hayride," a show broadcast by KWKH and patterned after the Grand Ole Opry. The Hayride's newest star was Elvis Presley, who had made his debut there in October. Lewis recorded an

audition disc for Slim Whitman, who was boss of a Hayride package tour. Whitman listened to the record. "I
Don't Hurt Anymore," a then-current country hit by
Hank Snow, was on one side; "If I Ever Needed You" was
on the other. He handed the disk to Lewis and said,
"Don't call me; I'll call you." Jerry Lee remembers Whitman as "that old nub-fingered sonofabitch."

Jerry Lee came to Sun Records in Memphis early in
1956. Sam Phillips, who owned Sun, had recently sold
Elvis to RCA-Victor for $35,000 (which he still truculently
denies ever regretting), and he was in the market for a
new punk prodigy.

Lewis's first record was a coupling of "Crazy Arms,"
the Ray Price hit that was still on the charts when Jerry
Lee cut it in the fall of 1956, and "End of the Road," an
original song. He did not pursue writing in subsequent
years (of the several hundred titles he has cut in the past
twenty-five years, only a handful bear his signature. Since
1966 he has recorded only one new original composition,
an unreleased song called "Alvin," cut in Nashville in
1970). However, in "End of the Road" Jerry Lee proved
himself a masterful evoker of lurid mood and dark thirst,
and it is poetically just to look at the song as a statement
of purpose, an existential anthem of the career to follow:

> *Well, the way is dark,*
> *Night is long,*
> *I don't care if I ever get home:*
> *I'm waitin' at the end of the road!*

Radio station WHBQ premiered Jerry Lee's first
record. In July 1954 the station had premiered Elvis's
first record.

Jerry Lee had the two biggest hits of Sun's history:
"Whole Lot of Shakin' Going On" and "Great Balls of
Fire." The former was written by Dave Williams and Roy

The original version of "Whole Lot of Shakin' Going On," made in New York, March 1955.

Hall (using the pseudonym Sunny David) and first recorded by Big Maybelle in March 1955. Later that year, Roy Hall cut the song for Decca, and by the end of 1955 two more versions followed, by Decca big-band singer Dolores Fredericks and by the Dot pop group the Commodores. Jerry Lee learned the song from Johnny Littlejohn, a drummer who sometimes played at the Wagon Wheel in Natchez with Paul Whitehead's group.

"Whole Lot of Shakin' Going On" was cut by Lewis early in 1957 and released on April 15, his second record. On August 31 it hit the Number One slots on both the country and R&B charts (only one other person in the history of popular music had Number One hits in both of these markets: Elvis), and in September it hit Number Two on the pop charts. In October the record appeared on the British charts, where it soon reached Number Eight. In the end, the record sold six million copies worldwide. Jerry Lee sang it on "American Bandstand"; Dick Clark recalls that Lewis was the only guest he encountered who refused to lip-sync. (In many ways Jerry Lee is a purist, or more precise, a primitivist. "I don't like no overdubbin'," he has said. "When you're makin' love to a woman, ya can't go back in and overdub.")

Recorded in the fall of 1957 and released on November 3, "Great Balls of Fire" peaked in January 1958, when it was Number One country, Number Two pop, Number Five R&B, and Number One in Britain. The song was written for Lewis by Otis Blackwell (who had written "Don't Be Cruel" and "All Shook Up" for Elvis, and whom Jerry Lee described as "a little colored fellow in a derby hat"), and it was intended that Jerry Lee would perform the song in the Warner Brothers film *Jamboree,* his movie debut. Directed by Roy Lockwood and featuring Lewis, Fats Domino, Count Basie, Carl Perkins, Slim Whitman, Frankie Avalon, and others, *Jamboree* was released in December 1957. Lobby cards described the film as "a fast-spinning love story behind the scenes of today's brand new kind of Tin Pan Alley!"

"Great Balls of Fire" was a fine and sleazy record, the yell of a tribe sloughing its senses. The day the record was released, the Commies fired their second silly Sputnik, a half-ton ball circling nine hundred miles up, a dog panting fearfully within, stranger than any Egyptian glyph. Eisenhower lay numb and still from a stroke; Nixon, large wet cow liver of a human, ruled. Charlie Starkweather, five-foot-two "red-headed peckerwood" (the words of his confession), thrashed and skidded through Nebraska and Wyoming murdering and murdering and

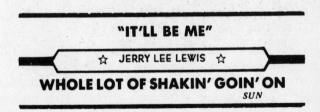

"IT'LL BE ME"

☆   JERRY LEE LEWIS   ☆

WHOLE LOT OF SHAKIN' GOIN' ON

SUN

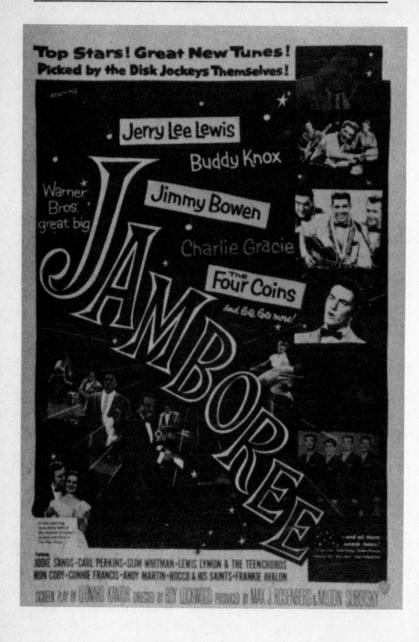

murdering. How many times did Starkweather gnash and grin with sexy delight as "Great Balls of Fire" crackled from his car radio?

By 1958 Jerry Lee Lewis was on top. Of all the rock-and-roll creatures, he projected the most hellish persona. He was feared more than the rest, and hated more too. Preachers railed against him, mothers smelled his awful presence in the laundry of their daughters, and young boys coveted his wicked, wicked ways.

My friend Michael Bane grew up in Memphis in the fifties, and he has tenebrious memories of the Killer's role in local society.

"There was this dive, I mean a real dive, called Hernando's Hideaway. It was located just south of town, toward the Mississippi line—a great two-story house, all black. When we drove by, my parents would snort and say, 'That's where people like Jerry Lee Lewis play.' My mother was real adamant about how, essentially, he was the garbage of the earth. She couldn't stand him; she couldn't stand thinking about him.

"He kind of balanced things out in Memphis. He made Elvis acceptable. Elvis tried to be good. Folks could look at him and say, 'This is a good boy.' But Jerry Lee was always a shitkicker. There were always horror stories. There was always an aura of extreme violence to Jerry Lee."

Jerry Lee Lewis is the greatest song stylist in country music. (He himself will tell you there have been only three real stylists in the whole of music: Al Jolson, Jimmie Rodgers, and Jerry Lee Lewis.) A recording by Jerry Lee is as unmistakable as a passage by Faulkner. Bursting phrases recur throughout Jerry Lee's music. "Think about it!" he yells before a strafe-force barrage of ascending triplets. (Scholars, please note: The first "Think about it!" is found in "Foolish Kind of Man," in the 1971 album *Touching Home*.) Pindar would have loved it: *"Think*

about it!" How similar to Faulkner, who while writing his
third novel fell upon the word *indomitable* and for the rest
of his days did not write a book without a handful of
grand, truculent *indomitables.* And Jerry Lee is permitted
his vast liberties, as Faulkner was permitted his. Jerry Lee
is the only country singer who can get away with yelling
at his audience, referring to his musicians as mother-
fuckers, just as Faulkner got away with statements such
as his description of a mule in *Flags in the Dust:* "Misun-
derstood even by that creature (the nigger who drives
him) whose impulses and mental processes most closely
resemble his."

The piano, the wife/gun of Jerry Lee's music, came
late to country music. In 1775 John Behrent of Philadelphia made the first American piano, and in 1823 Jonas
Chickering of Boston began the first steady manufacture
of New World pianos. (He constructed them with cast-iron
frames, to withstand the rigors of shipment in America.)
In 1860 there were about twenty-two thousand pianos in
the States. The upright piano, the kind Jerry Lee played
in his Ferriday home, was invented about 1800 and was
first known as the *pianino* or *piano droit.* One of the first
makers of uprights was an American, J. I. Hawkins of
Philadelphia. Its smaller size and weight took it places
where pianos had never been: bars, whorehouses, tent
shows, and small homes. In it, Southern music found a
new tool. One of the first Opry performers, Theron Hale
(born about 1883 in Pikeville, Tennessee), used a piano
in his band as early as 1926. Al Hopkins's Hill Billies, Dr.
Bates's Possum Hunters, Ed Poplin, and other Opry acts of
the late twenties also used pianos.

Two country pianists wrought influences on Jerry
Lee: Moon Mullican and Del Wood. Mullican (his true
first name was Aubrey) was born March 27, 1909, in
Corrigan, Texas; he died New Year's Day, 1967, in Beaumont, Texas. He was the first country piano player to

record in a boogie-woogie style. Though the phrase didn't occur on record till 1928, when Clarence "Pinetop" Smith, a blues singer who was murdered at the age of twenty-three, cut "Pinetop's Boogie Woogie," the style originated in the early twenties. Its father was Jimmy Yancey (1894–1951), who used the eight-to-the-bar pattern and improvised contrapuntally in both bass and treble. Yancey was not recorded until 1939, but he was the mentor of Meade Lux Lewis (1905–1964), whose 1927 "Honky Tonk Train Blues" was the first true boogie-woogie record. The style spread through the thirties, with Albert Ammons (1907–1949) and Pete Johnson (1904–1967) its most famed masters. By 1940 boogie-woogie was popular among white audiences, and Tommy Dorsey, the Andrews Sisters, Bob Crosby, Woody Herman, and others were having pop hits with songs like "Beat Me Daddy, Eight to a Bar" and "Boogie Woogie Bugle Boy." The first boogie-woogie country record was Johnny Barfield's "Boogie Woogie" in 1939. The Delmore Brothers coined a phrase when they cut "Hillbilly Boogie" in 1945.

Moon Mullican recorded with Cliff Bruner's band in the late thirties. Bruner: "When I left Milton Brown, I hired Moon as my piano man. Moon developed his own, he used to call it 'three-finger' style. And he didn't play very good when I hired him, but he developed into a fine piano man, terrific showman. Later on, he and I had a band together for a few years. Called it Cliff Bruner, Moon Mullican, and The Showboys."

In 1945 Mullican signed with King Records. There were hits: "New Pretty Blonde (New Jole Blon)" (1947), "I'll Sail My Ship Alone" (1950), "Mona Lisa" (1950), "Cherokee Boogie" (1951). Then for ten years Moon was in the shadows; in 1961 he had one last hit, "Ragged But Right" on Starday. While performing at the Kansas City Auditorium in 1962, Moon had a heart attack (he weighed 275 pounds at the time). He continued to record, for

Kapp and independent labels such as Hall and Spar. On
the last day of 1966, Moon made a New Year's resolution
to lay off pork chops. He died before the first day of 1967
ended.

Del Wood (shortened from Adelaide Hazelwood)
was born February 22, 1920, in Nashville. She was an old-
fashioned piano player with a hard, clear barrelhouse style.
Her first and only hit was "Down Yonder," a 1951 instrumental on the Tennessee label. The tune was an old one,
written by New Orleans pianist L. Wolfe Gilbert in 1920
and performed by the Brown Brothers in the musical *Tip
Top* that same year. Wood's version hit the pop charts
first (it rose to Number Six), then crossed to the country
charts, where it entered at Number Nine but disappeared
after one week. She made her Opry debut on February
23, 1952, and has performed regularly in the show since
then. After leaving the Tennessee label in early 1953, Wood
recorded for Republic, then RCA-Victor. In her Chart
album, *Are You from Dixie?*, recorded in the late sixties,
she performed a thing called "Psychedelic Mockingbird,"
an original composition.

Jerry Lee loved Del's record of "Down Yonder," and
when he first came to Nashville in the fifties, she was one
of the few people who treated him with kindness. When
he made his belated Opry debut, on January 20, 1973, he
interrupted his performance (the Nashville corpus held its
breath in grim anxiety) and invited Del Wood onstage.
She sat at the piano with him, and together they partied
out "Down Yonder," then they embraced. In 1969 Bob
Dylan had offered a song to Jerry Lee ("To Be Alone with
You"), and Charles Conrad had brought a cassette of
Jerry Lee's music to the moon aboard Apollo XII. Quoti-
dian stuff: Jerry Lee misplaced Dylan's demo, looked to
the full moon for a moment. But a chance to play piano
with Del Wood—that was something! (The next October,
John Lennon came backstage to Jerry Lee's dressing room

at the Roxy in Los Angeles; he knelt gracefully and kissed
Jerry Lee's foot. Jerry Lee looked down to see if his shoe
shine had been smarmed.) Jerry Lee also liked the work
of Merrill Moore, the popular jazz pianist from Iowa who
recorded "House of Blue Lights" (1953), "Down the
Road Apiece" (1955), and other jazz-rockers for Capitol.

A striking antecedent of Jerry Lee's style is heard in
the music of Cecil Gant, a black singer and pianist who
was born in Nashville in 1915, and who died there, of
pneumonia and alcohol, in 1951. He recorded from 1944
to 1951 for Gilt-Edge, Bronze, Four-Star, Sound, Bullet,
Dot, Down Beat, Swing Time, Imperial, and Decca. His
first release, "I Wonder," issued by Gilt-Edge of Los
Angeles in 1944, was a hit, and Gant remained a well-
known and successful artist till his death.

Much of Cecil Gant's music was boogie-woogie, but
it was wilder, tougher, than the classic boogie styles. His
"Nashville Jumps," recorded for Bullet in 1947, is one of
the perfect party records.

Seen ya goin' up Cedar Street hill,
I know you got your whiskey from Jack Daniel's still!
Nashville really jumps, really jumps all night long;

I'd rather be in Nashville than to be way back down home.
Yeah, jump, Nashville!

Before the last stanza, Gant yells, "Gimme another drink
and I'll be all right!"

Some of Gant's records were what can only be called
rock-and-roll. The most striking of these is "We're Gonna
Rock," recorded in July 1950 in New York City for Decca.
The piano introduction of "We're Gonna Rock" is indis-
tinguishable from Jerry Lee's Sun style.

It is not unlikely that Sam Phillips signed Lewis because he brought to mind black pianist Ike Turner, who
had played in the classic Jackie Brenston rock sessions
Phillips had produced in 1951. Elvis, the white boy who
sang like a black man, was lost, over the lea, sold
to RCA-Victor for $35,000. Here was a white boy who
played piano like a crazy nigger; maybe history would
repeat itself. It didn't.

Jerry Lee fell in the spring of 1958. Arriving for a
tour of England in May, he was made victim of a seedy
media-gale which tsk-wailed and screamed that his wife
(he had married a third time), Myra Gail, was also his
thirteen-year-old cousin. With his usual speed, Jerry responded to the British press: "Myra and I are legally married. It was my second marriage that wasn't legal. I was
a bigamist when I was sixteen. I was fourteen when I was
first married. That lasted a year; then I met Jane. One day
she said she was goin' to have my baby. I was real worried.
Her father threatened me, and her brothers were hunting
with hide whips. So I married her just a week before my
divorce from Dorothy. It was a shotgun wedding." Britain
was not pleased. It was announced in the London *Times*
of May 28 that the tour, which was to have lasted until
June 29 and included appearances at twenty-seven Rank
theatres, had been canceled. Through all this, J. W. Brown,
Myra's thirty-one-year-old daddy, played bass in Jerry
Lee's band.

Hometown hero, May 1958.

Jerry Lee and Myra Gail were belatedly divorced in the fall of 1970. (They had two children: Steve Allen, named for the man who was responsible for Lewis's TV debut, was born in 1959; Phoebe Allen was born in 1963. Steve Allen Lewis drowned in the family pool in 1962.) In court Myra testified that their marriage was "a nightmare." Jerry Lee was placed under court injunction "not to threaten, molest, or intimidate" his twenty-six-year-old cousin.

In October 1971 he wed Jaren Pate. They had one child, Lori Leigh, born in April 1972. In 1974 Jaren filed for legal separation, and their marriage after that developed as much in as out of courtrooms—until the afternoon of June 8, 1982, when Jaren was found dead in the little swimming pool of a Collierville, Tennessee,

Jerry Lee and Myra Gale, after the fall, Memphis, June 1958.

neighbor. A year later, almost to the day, on June 7, 1983, Lewis married Shawn Michelle Stevens, a twenty-five-year-old cocktail waitress from Garden City, Michigan. Seventy-eight days later, on the morning of August 24, she was a corpse, bruised and bloodied in the bridal bed of the Nesbit, Mississippi, mansion that Lewis had bought in the spring of 1973. On the night after Shawn's death, her sister Denise phoned Lewis from Michigan.

"I said, 'What happened?'" Denise later told *The Detroit Free Press*; "and Jerry said, 'Your sister's dead, and she was a bad girl.'"

According to an autopsy report delivered the next month to DeSoto County, Mississippi, authorities by one Dr. Jerry Francisco, Shawn Lewis died of an overdose of methadone. Exactly eight months later, on April 24, 1984, Lewis took the hand of his sixth bride, a pretty twenty-two-year-old girl named Kerrie McCarver. "JERRY LEE LEWIS' BRIDE REFUSES TO LIVE IN HOUSE OF DEATH" was the headline of the May 8 issue of Rupert Murdoch's *Star*. Inside, Jerry Lee's sister Frankie Jean was quoted as saying that Linda Gail Lewis, the youngest Lewis sibling, "told me that she saw demons at the house." Frankie Jean told the *Star*, "There's something wrong there. I'm going to take a Catholic priest there—I believe God can do anything."

Back in the spring of 1958, before the sixth bride was born, there was no *Star* to keep us abreast of the tenebrous developments of the Lewis demonology. *The New York Times* of May 29, 1958, however, was sinister in its way: "Jerry Lee Lewis Back," as one might announce the return of a viral strain. In the same issue of the *Times* was an advertisement for the film *High School Confidential*, which opened the next day at the Loew's State in Times Square: "Exploding Tomorrow with Even More Shock!" Scenes were depicted: wielded switchblade, belly-to-belly kiss, punch-out.

High School Confidential was Lewis's second movie. Starring were Russ Tamblyn, John Drew Barrymore, Mamie Van Doren, and Charles Chaplin, Jr. Jack Arnold, the director, had previously made *With These Hands* (1950), *Girls in the Night* (1953), *It Came from Outer Space* (1953), *The Creature from the Black Lagoon* (1955), *Return of the Creature* (1955), and *The Incredible Shrinking Man* (1957).

Lewis had cut the title song of *High School Confidential* on April 21, 1958, before his ruined English tour. Released on May 20, the record never broke the pop Top Twenty. The effects of the scandal were severe. In the June 9 issue of *Billboard*, a full-page advertisement appeared. "An Open Letter to the Industry from Jerry Lee

Lewis" began, "Dear Friends: I have in recent weeks been
the apparent center of a fantastic amount of publicity and
of which none has been good. . . ."

But nothing was healed. "High School Confidential"
was Jerry Lee's last appearance in the Top Ten of the
country charts until 1968, and his last appearance, period,
in the Top Twenty of both the pop and R&B charts. Six
months earlier radio sations had held loud elections:
Who's the King of rock 'n' roll? Elvis or Jerry Lee? (In
many areas, such as that of WHB in Kansas City, Lewis
had won two to one.) Now his price dropped to $500 a
night, and disc jockeys wouldn't play his records.

Jerry Lee Lewis kept pumping. That word Faulkner
loved: *indomitable*. In 1968 he rose anew with a series of
country hits that started with "Another Place, Another
Time," the best honky-tonk song of the sixties, for Smash.
Of the Sun rockabilly triumvirate—Elvis, Carl Perkins,
and Jerry Lee—he is the only one still making 101-proof
rockabilly on a grand scale.

The mythology of Jerry Lee Lewis has a thousand
devoted Hesiods. Since the beginning, Jerry demanded
to close every show he appeared in. In 1958 Alan Freed
insisted that Lewis precede Chuck Berry in a show. They
still talk of that show, how Jerry Lee had the crowd
screaming and rushing the stage, how he took a Coke
bottle of petrol from his jacket pocket and doused his
piano with one hand as the other hand banged out "Whole
Lot of Shakin' Going On," how he set the piano aflame,
his hands still riding the keys like a madman as the kids
went finely and wholly berserk with the frenzy of it, and
how Jerry Lee stalked backstage stinking of lighter fluid
and wrath, turned to Chuck Berry, and said, real calm, as
the sound of the kids going crazy and stamping and
yelling for more shook the walls, "Follow *that*, nigger."

A record-company executive recalls another meeting
between Jerry Lee and Chuck Berry. The executive was

producing a concert in which both singers were to appear. Jerry Lee started a fight with Berry backstage; much drinking and aggravation followed. When the executive called for the curtains to be opened, there at center stage stood Jerry Lee, Chuck Berry, and Elmo Lewis. Chuck Berry was holding a knife to Jerry Lee's throat, and Pappy Lewis had the open end of a shotgun pressed to the base of Berry's skull. The audience uttered no sound.

There is said to have been a time when Jerry Lee's drummer, Morris "Tarp" Tarrant, was eager to have Jerry smoke marijuana, perhaps in the hope that it would soften the lines of his personality. On a night when there was much potent Jamaican dope circulating, Jerry Lee consented to try it. Tarp rolled a very fat joint, a thing of true

Backstage.

Jerry Lee Lewis proportion, and Jerry sat with it, consuming its smoke in deep, strong sucks. All awaited the verdict, the birth of Jerry Lee, flower child, cherub of peace and soft colors. He rose. "Not bad," he said, then quickly swallowed five small pills, grabbed a fifth of Old Crow, and departed into the night.

Somewhere in the direst gut of Alabama, Jerry Lee was playing a honky-tonk. It was a gas-money date. Pick up some cash and split. Toward the beginning of the second set, a drunken, thick, red man encroached Jerry Lee. He was angry. "My wife's crazy about you," he said, motioning to a female dissolved in darkness and smoke and the blurred vision both men shared. "She bought every record you ever made. But I think you're a piece a shit, and you know what I just did? I went home and busted ever one of them records. Whatchoo think about that, boy?" Jerry Lee moved his face close to the drunk's, captured his pupils with his own, and in a voice neither loud nor soft, said, "Good, now she's gotta go out and buy 'em all over again."

There was a wife, one of them, whom Jerry Lee left sleeping in a Nashville motel room. He returned to the room moments before dawn. He carried a lighted cigar and a submachine gun. The wife was awakened in a novel way, as the wall above her head was shattered with metal.

Merle Haggard tells of his night with Jerry Lee in 1974. "We were in that little room at the bottom of the King of the Road in Nashville, and he had already busted some guy in the mouth that night, a guy who was a life-long fan of his. The guy was just in awe of Jerry Lee. I knew the guy, and he was a piano player. This guy was sitting there watching Jerry Lee play and all of a sudden —BAK!—Jerry took his whiskey bottle and busted it in his face, cut the guy's face all up to pieces. I found Jerry Lee that next morning, about six o'clock. I had just heard about what he'd done and, well, I figured he was in one of those rare moods. He said, 'Well, let's go out and pick.' So we did."

A former employee of Mercury Records in New York tells of the night he was supposed to deliver Jerry Lee to the ABC TV studio to tape the "Dick Cavett Show." Jerry Lee was very, very drunk. "Are you sure you want to do the show?" the employee kept asking him. And Jerry Lee kept nodding and falling back asleep. The limousine pulled up in front of the studio, twenty minutes before taping, and the employee shook Jerry Lee and his manager, Judd Phillips, awake. "Is this the bus depot?" they asked peering out at some private geometry of gin.

Writers have not had much success interviewing Jerry Lee. One night in Brooklyn in 1973, an editor of *Country Music* asked Jerry Lee a question. The interviewee responded by leaping across the table, breaking off the butt of his pint bottle of Heaven Hill, and sticking the interviewer in the neck with it.

I attended a Jerry Lee Lewis recording session in Memphis. Pappy Lewis was there. On his way to the studio, Pappy had been chased down the highway by the Memphis police as he rushed along in Jerry Lee's white, custom-built Lincoln (1-FZ541) at a speed of 110 miles per hour. Pappy's reaction to his situation was ingenious. He increased his speed until he put enough distance between himself and the police so that he was invisible to them. Then he skidded the car to the side of the road, jumped in the back seat, and waited. The police arrived in a moment. "Glad you showed up, boys," Pappy said. "That crazy man drivin' this car was like to get us killed. When he saw your light flashin', he stopped the car and ran off into them trees there." The cops stared dully at the vacant driver's seat. "My son's Jerry Lee Lewis. He's makin' a record on Poplar Avenue, and I gotta be there. This is his car. I'm in no condition to drive myself. How's

Jerry Lee and his father, Elmo, seven miles over Babylon, 1972.
Photo courtesy of Malcolm Temple.

about one you boys takin' me? Jerry be purty mad I don't git his car back to him." He was driven to the studio.

Earlier in the day, at Jerry Lee's office, the scene was something like this: Jerry was on the telephone, shouting. "He's gonna sue *me?* You tell that sonofabitch husband of yours that if he tries to sue me I'm gonna come over there and give him the biggest ass-whuppin' he ever got in his life." There were perhaps twelve other people in the room. Everyone was drunk, and a few were falling asleep as Jerry shouted into the phone. It was ten o'clock in the morning. For some reason, Jerry Lee was drinking bourbon and orange juice, a combination the color of wan excrement. "He's on a health kick," somebody suggested. Pappy Lewis decided to try some orange juice in his bourbon, so he asked someone to give him the Tropicana container from Jerry's desk. Jerry Lee banged the hand with the receiver as it was about to touch the orange juice. From the wielded receiver, a woman's voice was faint and shrill: "What the fuck was that?" Jerry was indignant. "What the hell you doin' my orange juice?" A voice attached to the hand, a drunken voice, answered, "It's for your father." Jerry Lee returned the receiver to his ear. "Shoot. Tell him to go buy his own fuckin' orange juice. You still there, darlin'?"

At the recording session was a one-armed man named Paul. He introduced himself. "Mr. Lewis, you probably don't remember me—"

"Right," Jerry said.

Soon the one-armed man was very drunk, and he beat his wife, who seemed to be a short Indian. She left him, for good it seemed. The one-armed man said, "Fuck her." He approached a girl who sat quietly in a corner. "Hey, baby, what's shakin'?" He dangled his armless, folded sleeve in her face. The girl was repulsed. Judd Phillips, who had been sleeping, said to the one-armed man, "Watch it or I'll snitch the other one off." Jerry Lee laughed, low and dark. The girl ran from the studio.

Pappy Lewis seemed to be speaking in Hittite. Only Jerry could comprehend him, or perhaps he was merely faking. "You know you ain't supposed to drink." Pappy responded in Hittite and spilled an eight-ounce Dixie cup of whiskey into his lap, a deed he loudly regretted, in Hittite. With Pappy was the son of his girlfriend. The future son-in-law was about thirty, drunk but not in the Hittite fashion. It surfaced that Pappy could not remember his fiancée's name, but he was sure the fiancée was mad with him. "Get a dime; call your mama," he said, in English, or something like it.

An obviously psychopathic youth with eyes the size of gull eggs ran about telling anyone he could catch, "I'm a writer for *TV Guide*. I write about country artisez. Did you ever hear of the Grateful Dead? They played at my wedding. My wife's a model. She poses for artisez. She poses naked: tits, hiney, everything. She makes more money than you and me both. I hired a private eye to follow her around all day, and he keeps a little book of all the people she fucks behind my back. He's very expensive."

A woman with bleached hair was referred to by all as "the curse of the family," a distinction of awesome implication.

A man dressed in black and carrying a bottle of Peter Pan Port introduced himself to the curse of the family. "Don't get fresh," she said, frequently. He was the drummer with Bobby and the Spotlites, the house band at Hernando's Hideaway. There was a pack of cigarettes sticking from each of his pockets. Every pack was open, and he smoked from them variously. Memphis session organist James Brown was in the studio. The drummer from Hernando's Hideaway saw him and screamed, "Oh, my God, don't tell me Jerry Lee's got spooks in his band!" The curse of the family applied lipstick.

Judd fell asleep on the floor. Jerry Lee gently kicked him awake and said, "Take out your teeth and I'll marry ya." Judd returned to sleep.

Through all this, Huey Meaux was trying to produce a record. Carl Perkins was in the studio, playing guitar on several cuts. Every few minutes a large, barefoot, suet-thighed lady turned to Huey Meaux and yelled, "Make Carl Perkins play the 'Blue Suede Shoes'! Please!" Carl, a reformed alky, seemed ill at ease.

Billy Lee Riley, the man who cut "Flying Saucers Rock 'n' Roll" for Sun in 1957, materialized, looking like five thousand concentrated volts. He spread his hands before him as if holding a birthday cake. "Man, I got me a pill this big, and when I take a bite the damn thing grows right back." Then he smiled, baring a large space between his teeth, and departed quickly.

It was the only recording session I ever saw that was fun.

In a Fort Lauderdale club in the spring of 1973, my friend Al Bianculli taped several hours of Jerry Lee speaking. Judd and Pappy were there, but mostly unconscious.

"Jerry, what were you doing between nineteen fifty-two and nineteen fifty-six?"

"I don't remember. I was a ramblin' man, a gamblin' man. . . . My ancestors come from Alabama. Come by covered wagon. Settled in Ruston, Louisiana. . . . Still own the town, the Lewises. . . . They did, they settled there, in Ruston. . . . They own that town. Ruston, Louisiana. Nice town. They sent me a telegram when I done the Steve Allen show, complimenting me, you know. . . . 'We'd love to meet you sometime.' Said who they were. And, hell, they're worth millions, as far as money goes. They wouldn't tolerate Daddy or [unintelligible] or [unintelligble]. . . . My great-grandfather owned a plantation. He owned Monroe, Louisiana. *Owned* it, lock, stock, and barrel. That's Louisiana history. Old Man Lewis. He had a hundred and fifty slaves. Then they freed all the slaves. He wasn't a slavedriver or anything. They made 'em leave. . . . He owned it. . . . I can show you the house where he was raised up himself, the house that he owned. . . . That big funeral home right there on Ouichita Cliff, right in Monroe, Louisiana. That was his home. . . . Monroe was once all a plantation. If you think I'm tellin' you a lie, you just check your history book. It's taught in history books. . . . J. P. Hardy's Little Club, the one I worked in . . . [unintelligible] . . . called it the Little Club. . . . I worked out there way over on—what's that street? That big old place out there. I was eighteen years old. I played out there, and this guy was crippled. He's crippled. Had hands like this. Played his guitar like this. And he can *play*. He was workin' out there, and had this guy on steel guitar, one of the greatest steel guitar-players

you ever heard in your life. . . . And that's the first time I
met Otis Brown. He walked in, and at that time he was
a hell of a man; he had them sleeves rolled up. And, boy,
you could tell that he was a tough shot. So he wiped out
about six. Had a few beers. And then he wanted to come
up and play fiddle. And I thought he could play! And he
was Aunt Jane's son. I never met [unintelligible], didn't
know him, period. But Otis Brown I knew, I'd heard of
him. I thought he could play. He got up there and—he,
you know, he was my first cousin—so the steel guitar-
player says, 'That sonofabitch can't play nothin'.' Made
me mad, y'know? And he was right, he couldn't [laughs].
. . . Well, son I've lived a hell of a life. You wouldn't believe the experiences. . . . How many things are there left
for me to do? How many roads am I to travel? Or am I
livin' in my final hour? . . . [fades]. . . .

"Jim Reeves. He's a good old boy, but you haveta get
to know him. [Reeves died in a plane crash in 1964.] A
strange person. We had some pretty good times together.
Yeah, he drank. At that time I didn't drink that much. He
did. He did drink pretty good, I know that, he drank
pretty good. He told me, 'I'll tell ya, if RCA ever brings
me out to do another record hop without the right kind
of band, they can kiss my ass.' That's the first time I'd
ever met him. I said, 'What's your problem?' He said, 'I
just don't like that band.' And the guy that's playin' drums
is just beatin' on it: boom-a-boom-boom-a. You wouldn't
believe it. Jim Reeves went out there with his guitar and
he said, 'Boys'—and he was real nice; I knew right then,
there's a pro—he says, 'I don't think I need ya to back me
up. Just lay out and let me play the guitar.' Just him and
the guitar, and it was beautiful. He hung it in. He tore 'em
up, man. He proved his point. And I come, 'Great Balls of
Fire,' and that damn band. Cat out there with a mustache
had a bass drum hung round his neck and he's beatin' on
it. . . . Me and Jim got together after that and we made

every club in town. . . . He was a fine person. . . . Strange cat, just couldn't get close to him. . . . He did 'Four Walls.' Just him and a guitar. He liked me, though. He enjoyed gettin' with me, and he'd drink. . . . Jim Reeves, Merle Haggard, they're two funny cats. Great talents, but funny cats. . . . Hell, I don't care about it myself. I'll fight my way through those damn hotels and I'll be nice and I'll be a piano-player and I'll sing and I'll just be what I am. I ain't gonna be no strange cat. I ain't gonna back off in no corner and hide. . . . You're gettin' a hell of an interview, ain't ya? . . . [fades]. . . .

"Dr. Jekyll and Mr. Hyde. That's what that bitch al-

Jerry Lee Lewis and his cousin Mickey Gilley, 1976.

ways called me. . . . The Killer! . . . [Pappy wakens, yells: 'Killer Diller!']. . . . Armadilla! . . . Know what armadillas are?"

"Amarillo, Texas?"

"Hell, Louisiana's got more of 'em than Texas. Grave robbers, them things."

"Is that how you got the name 'Killer'?"

"WHAT!"

"You said 'Killer Diller,' and then you said 'Amarillo!' "

"Arro-dillo! You know what arro-*dillos* are?"

"I never seen one in person, but I seen pictures of 'em."

"Then you know what I'm talkin' about, doncha? That ain't where I got the name 'Killer.' I ain't a grave robber. You callin' me a grave robber? What the fuck are you talkin' about! Damn . . ."

Patsy Lynn Kochin, esteemed deposed president of the Jerry Lee Lewis Fan Club, told in her *Newsletter* of a night she spent with Jerry Lee in a Boston Ramada Inn. It is one of my favorite passages.

"Jerry would play the piano with one hand and sing while he found what he was looking for in the Bible using the other hand. He then read Acts Ch. 2. . . . Jerry also spoke on the last days which he says we are living in— the end almost here. . . . Then he told us why the South lost the war. . . . Jerry then explained the difference in a ninety-nine-year sentence and a hundred-year sentence. . . ."

The truth is that Jerry Lee has always known the end is almost here, must be almost here, and that the almost-here end is the heart of it all; without it, there is no rock-and-roll, no jukebox epiphany, just pale, soft people looking from the window. Without the obsession or the fever or the fear of the almost-here end, all is reasonable and mere.

Foreign students of dissolution receive a lesson from the master.

Somehow that is why Jerry Lee Lewis leaned with a loaded gun beneath the window of Elvis Presley in the hour of the wolf. Elvis had turned his back on the Church of the Almost-Here End, sold his soul to MOR, but Jerry Lee kept pumping—Holiness! Tongues!—and with each new clawsome, wild wife, with every new midnight violence, every extravagance of face, he slid further from grace. The King and the Killer: This was their desert. To Elvis it was a droll annoyance, but to Jerry Lee the midnight deed was glory, no mere D&D scene, but 1 Sam. 17:49, .38-style. In the cold, brilliant handcuffs, the creature known in certain parts of Mississippi as Colonel Hermes Trismegistus, in parts of Tennessee as God's

Garbage Man, squinted into the dark and thought a thought: Did they have Breathalizers in the Old Testament days?

On May 3, 1977, Memphis City Court Judge Albert Boyd declared Jerry Lee Lewis not guilty of the charges for which he was arrested at 3764 Elvis Presley Boulevard the previous November. Rock on, Judge.

May the voice never end that for so long has said these words of virtue: "Just gimme my money and show me where the piano is." If it does, so does the Church.

Jerry Lee's 1958 scandal marked the beginning of the end for Sun. In 1957 Jerry Lee, Johnny Cash, and Bill Justis had given Sam Phillips great crossover hits. By the fall of 1958 Lewis and Justis had ceased to have hits, and Cash had signed with Columbia. Judd Phillips went up against payola allegations, and he and Sam broke their relationship.

"I think Sam's problem," said Judd in 1972, "was that he never really believed in them—he was afraid. He never really had faith. He never really believed that Elvis Presley, Jerry Lee Lewis, Johnny Cash would be the giants they are today. He thought it was just a passing situation. And as a consequence we let all these artists slip away from us."

In the summer of 1958 Judd formed his own company, Judd Records, in Sheffield, Alabama. (In 1960 he sold out to NRC in Atlanta.) Early in 1959 producer Jack Clement, who had been at Sun since 1955 and had been responsible for much of Sun's most imaginative production work (such as Jerry Lee's 1957 doo-wop recording of Hank Williams's "You Win Again"), was fired by Sam after a disagreement.

Early in 1961 Sam opened a studio at Seventeenth Avenue in Nashville. He began using many of the city's pop-country musicians in his sessions: Floyd Cramer, Hank Garland, Buddy Harmon, Bob Moore, Pig Robbins,

Billy Sherrill, and others. But Phillips failed to make Sun a part of the ever-more-lucrative Nashville sound.

Sun lingered. In 1966 Sam shut Phillips International, the subsidiary he had formed in the fall of 1957. From 1964 to 1968, Sun released only twenty singles, most of them junk. In 1968 Sun Records came to its end. On July 1, 1969, Nashville entrepreneur Shelby Singleton, Jr., acquired from Sam 80 percent interest in the Sun catalogue and became the major stockholder in a new Sun International Corporation. Since 1969 Singleton has released a flow of budget-line Sun reissues.

Presley, Perkins, and Lewis were the most famous, most successful rockabilly artists. Others, less enduring, less famed, made music often as good, sometimes better.

Vincent Gene Craddock, better known as Gene Vincent, was born in Norfolk, Virginia, on February 11, 1935. He served in the navy during the Korean War. Later crippled in a motorcycle accident, he attributed his limp and leg brace to a fanciful combat injury. (Un-Americanism did not become a salable commodity in rock 'n' roll for another decade yet.) Thin, wan, crippled, Vincent was an unlikely pop star, but a pop star he nonetheless became.

After performing at station WCMS, Vincent and his band, the Blue Caps, were brought to Capitol by Sheriff Tex Davis, who worked at WCMS. In the spring of 1956 his first disc was released: "Be-Bop-A-Lula" (inspired by a *Little Lulu* comic) c/w "Woman Love." On the country charts "Be-Bop-A-Lula" hit Number Five, and on the pop charts Number Nine. It was basically a light, cute lyric, but Vincent delivered it with psychopathy, rendering it a perverse, gothic performance, and one of the perfect rockabilly records. "Woman Love" was an obvious emulation of Elvis, but it possessed the powerful sense of the macabre that came to be Vincent's trademark. It is an overtly sexual record, full of glottal twitches and orgasmic pantings.

"Be-Bop-A-Lula" was Vincent's only country hit, and his only Top Ten pop hit. Capitol issued nineteen singles by Vincent before he left the label in 1961. During the next ten years he recorded for Challenge, Forever, Dandelion, and Kama Sutra, all without commercial success. On October 12, 1971, Gene Vincent died in Saugus, California, from internal hemorrhaging. He was thirty-six and drunk.

Of the major rockabilly artists, Buddy Holly alone never had a hit record on the country charts. Born Charles Hardin Holley in Lubbock, Texas, on September 7, 1936, Buddy's musical heritage was hard-core country, but by the mid-fifties he had developed an interest in black music. After several years of clubs and radio in the Lubbock area, Holly was signed to Decca early in 1956, and on January 26, in Nashville, Owen Bradley produced Holly's first session. In April a single was released: "Blue Days, Black Nights" and "Love Me." Four more discs followed, including the classic "That'll Be the Day," but little happened. In March 1957, Buddy Holly and the Crickets were signed to Brunswick/Coral, and late that year "Peggy Sue" became Holly's first hit, eventually rising to Number Three on the pop charts. Within the next two years Holly had five more pop hits, but none entered the Top Ten.

On February 3, 1959, near Fargo, North Dakota, an airplane carrying Holly, Richie Valens, and the Big Bopper (J. P. Richardson) crashed, killing all aboard. Waylon Jennings, who was in Holly's band at the time, gave his seat to the Big Bopper at the last minute.

Although Buddy Holly was a rockabilly artist, he was very different from the rockabilly mainstream. His was a softer music, and his records sounded less neurotic, effervescent instead of turbulent. All was tasteful, nothing clashed. Holly was the gentleman of rockabilly, the first soft rocker. In Holly's records, rockabilly deflects from country music toward a more refined, Apollonian form, perhaps best exemplified by the music of the Everly Brothers, who thrived from 1957 to 1961. With their harmonious sound and rosy-romantic material, the Everly Brothers were the pivotal rockabilly act, rooted deeper in pop than in country. This was the last, inevitable current. With Buddy Holly the mania had ebbed. Now it was nothing but a genetic echo.

In 1957 pop singer Guy Mitchell recorded "Rock-a-Billy" for Columbia, and it hit the Top Twenty. By October there was a 20th Century–Fox film *Rockabilly Baby,* staring Les Brown and Irene Ryan. It was over.

The country-music corpus reacted in its way to rockabilly. Johnny Cash, who was not really a rockabilly artist, was the butt of bigotry in Nashville simply because he recorded for Sun (1955–1958). In 1976 Cash said, "Y'know, myself, back in fifty-six, I had a hard time breaking into the country-music community in Nashville. I came up to the Grand Ole Opry to talk to Jim Denny, who was the manager of the Opry. 'I Walk the Line' was Number One. I had an appointment—but I sat in his outer office about two hours before he ever saw me. Finally he let me come in, and the very first question was, 'What makes you think you belong on the Grand Ole Opry?'"

In 1974 Faron Young spoke of rockabilly: "I said, yeah, Jerry, I remember when you were cutting 'Whole Lot of Shakin''—you didn't give a damn whether country music existed or not. You better get down on your knees every night and thank the Lord for Webb Pierce and Faron Young and Hank Snow—that they kept working and kept this business alive so you'd have something to come back to. If it had been left up to you back then, you wouldn't have given a damn if it had gone plumb under."

Many old-line country artists tried to cash in on rockabilly. Good taste is timeless, but money is better. The month after Elvis's first record was released, RCA-Victor issued "Hep Cat Baby" by Eddy Arnold (the song was written by Tin Pan Alley veteran Cy Coben); it hit Number Nine on the country charts. Bill Monroe went and cut a new version of "Blue Moon of Kentucky" later in the year, and Marty Robbins, who had joined the Opry in 1953, covered "That's All Right" for Columbia (it rose to Number Nine). In 1955 Billy Jack Wills (Bob Wills's youngest brother) cut "There's Good Rockin' Tonight" for MGM.

In 1956 came "Country Boy Rock 'n' Roll" by Don Reno & Red Smiley (King), "Hula Rock" by Hank Snow (RCA-Victor), "So Let's Rock" by Bob Wills (Decca), and "Teen-Age Boogie" by Webb Pierce (Decca). In 1957 came "Rock & Roll Fever" by Cecil Campbell (MGM), "Rockin' and Rollin'" by Carson Robison (MGM; Robison always rolled with the current—at the height of the McCarthy hearings, he had recorded "I'm No Communist"), and "Shake Baby Shake" by Wayne Raney (Decca). In 1958 came Tex Williams's belated exhortation to "Let's Go Rockabilly" (Decca).

A few country artists were stimulated in a good way by rockabilly. Arthur Smith's 1958 "Guitar Bustin'" (MGM) is a killer, and Little Jimmy Dickens's 1958 "I Got a Hole in My Pocket" (Columbia) created a roaring hard-rock sound that foreshadowed things to come.

There were also closet rockabilly singers. George Jones cut "Rock It" and "Heartbreak Hotel" for Starday under the name of Thumper Jones. (His "Heartbreak Hotel" was also issued by Tops under the name of Hank Smith and the Nashville Playboys.) Cowboy Copas used his real name, Lloyd Copas, when he cut "Circle Rock" for Decca. Johnny Dee, who recorded rock songs such as "Sittin' in the Balcony" and "Teenage Queen" for Colonial, a Chapel Hill, North Carolina, label, was really John D. Loudermilk. Some of Buck Owens's 1957 rockabilly records, cut for Pep and Chesterfield, listed the singer's name as Corky Jones. Johnny Paycheck had not yet

changed his name from Donny Young when he recorded
"Shaking the Blues" and other rockers for Decca in 1960.
(Paycheck's real name is David Lytle. He got his current
name from Johnny Paycheck, a small-time heavyweight
who was KO'd by Joe Louis in two rounds in 1940.)

When I asked George Jones about his Thumper
Jones recordings, he said, "I don't guess I'm gonna ever
live that down. I was actually getting started in the business about nineteen fifty-four or so when all this rock-and-
roll really started movin' in, and of course, you know,
you didn't have stations back then that played all that
much country to start with. So especially with rock-and-
roll getting as strong as it was at that time, it seemed like
country music was really a losin' battle except for the
three or four major artists that had it made at the time,
like Lefty Frizzell, Ernest Tubb, Roy Acuff, some of those
people. So we decided to try one, sorta rockabilly-like. I
was sorta ashamed to even do it at the time 'cause I was
so country, so I just used a different name, went under
the name of Thumper Jones."

George did like Elvis, however. "Oh, yes, quite a
bit. I liked quite a bit of the things that came out then,
because really you didn't have much else to like. You
didn't have the radio stations playin' enough of the country music for you to really have a chance to listen to
nothin' but country, so it was a lot of it forced upon us
really."

The Thumper Jones single "Rock It," released in
April 1956, was made after the emergence of Elvis and
after Jones had achieved two country hits of his own. (The
first of these, "Why, Baby, Why," was released in July
1955, as Elvis was making his first appearance on the
country charts.) What truly intrigues is the very early
Starday single by George, not Thumper, Jones, released
in April 1954—"Play It Cool, Man, Play It Cool."

Even Northern R&B labels tried to stick their hands

up rockabilly's skirt. In 1956 Fortune Records of Detroit released "You Ain't No Good for Me" by Elvis-imitator Jimmy Lee. United Records of Chicago released a rockabilly "Honey Hush" by John Hampton in 1957. The next year Apollo in New York issued "You Shake Me Up" by Andy Anderson, and Federal in Cincinnati released "Mercy, Mercy, Mercy" by Joe Penny. Rockabilly records by black artists, such as G. L. Crockett's 1957 "Look Out Mabel" on Chief, a Chicago blues label, were rare.

Rockabilly left a deep mark on both country music and rock. When the Beatles reached America in 1964, they came with a version of Carl Perkins's "Matchbox." In country music, traces of rockabilly run thick. Hear Mickey Gilley (Jerry Lee's cousin), or Gary Stewart, or a hundred other men.

Rock was feared and hated by so many. Some reacted in an almost medieval manner. In August 1955, Rev. Robert Gray of Trinity Baptist Church in Jacksonville, Florida, yelled to his congregation that Elvis Presley had "achieved a new low in spiritual degeneracy."

In 1956 Billy Rose spoke before the Anti-Trust Subcommittee of the House Judiciary Committee. (In 1953, the year of Bill Haley's "Crazy, Man, Crazy," the Songwriters of America had filed an antitrust action against BMI, accusing that company of conspiracy "to dominate and control the market for the use and exploitation of musical compositions.") Said Billy Rose, "Not only are most of the BMI songs junk, but in many cases they are obscene junk. . . . It is the current climate on radio and TV which makes Elvis Presley and his animal posturings possible." Mr. Rose's compositions include "Barney Google," "You Tell Her, I Stutter," and "I Got a Code in My Doze."

At a press conference in Washington, D.C., in 1957, actress Helen Hayes claimed that her son (later known as James MacArthur, sidekick of Jack Lord in "Hawaii

Five-O") had been well on the path to juvenile delin-
quency, brought on by rock-and-roll records. She cured
him by playing a Beethoven record.

Same year, same place: Vance Packard, author of
The Hidden Persuaders, said, "Our airways have been
flooded in recent years with whining guitarists, musical
riots put to switchblade beat, obscure lyrics about hug-
ging, squeezing, and rocking all night long."

In October 1976, Darryl Faulk, youth pastor of the
Capitol Assembly of God Church in Carson City, Nevada,
rose to cry that "most Christians are not aware that secular
music is poison." From somewhere the pastor recruited
twenty young people to make a public pyre of rock-and-
roll albums. The fire department, however, stopped this
exhibition, saying that when consumed by fire, polyvinyl
gives off toxic fumes. The pastor and his army com-
promised: They burned the album jackets and stomped
hell out of the records. This was said to have had a more
droll, less evangelical effect than intended.

Emmett Miller, 1

Emmett Miller is one of the most intriguing and profoundly important men in the history of country music.

He was the first recording artist to sing in the wry, bluesy yodeling style that was later associated with Jimmie Rodgers. He was also the first country singer to record with horns and drums. The mongrel jazz-country music of Bob Wills is rooted strongly in the work of Emmett Miller. In his September 23, 1935, recording of "I Ain't Got Nobody," issued on the Vocalion label, Wills plainly imitated Miller's earlier recording of the song. Wills even patterned much of his persona and many of his mannerisms on Miller's, most notably the jivey exclamations and detached comments that interpolate most of his recordings.

It is not known exactly when Emmett Miller was born or when he died. Nor is it known where he came from or where he went. We don't even know what he looked like, really.

Emmett Miller was a white man from the South, born late in the nineteenth century. On October 25, 1924, he made his first record, "Anytime," for Okeh in New York City. On November 7, 1924, Miller had his second Okeh session in New York City, and the result was "The Pickaninnies' Paradise." I've never heard either of these records, nor do I know of anyone who has.

Miller's third Okeh session was on September 1, 1925, in Asheville, North Carolina. Two records resulted: "Big Bad Bill (Is Sweet William Now)" c/w "Lovesick Blues," and "You're Just the Girl for Me" c/w "I Never Had the Blues."

More than two years passed. On January 15 and 21, 1928, Miller cut five nonmusical sides: "Thousand Frogs on a Log," "Brother Bill," "On the Rock Pile" (never issued), "Sam and His Family," and "Hungry Sam." These are black-dialect routines with jazzy backdrops; they feature Miller in his Sam persona, assisted by one Roy Cowan. More than any of his other work, these rare performances give credence to the theory that Miller worked as a blackface entertainer. (And it is intriguing to hear in "Brother Bill" snatches of imagery that much later were associated with Bo Diddley's "Who Do You Love?")

On June 12, 1928, Miller cut four sides at the Okeh studio in New York: "God's River Blues," "I Ain't Got Nobody," a new version of "Lovesick Blues," and "Lion Tamers." The musicians at this session were Tommy Dorsey (trombone), Jimmy Dorsey (clarinet and alto sax), Eddie Lang (guitar), Leo McConville (trumpet), Stan King (drums), and Arthur Schutt (piano). A man named Dan Fitch assisted Miller in the brief dialogues that prefaced many of the cuts. These records were issued under the name of Emmett Miller and His Georgia Crackers, as were his later Okeh releases.

Miller had six more Okeh sessions in New York. With

slight variations, the same Georgia Crackers were used.

August 9, 1928 (Manny Klein may have replaced Leo McConville on trumpet): "Anytime" and "St. Louis Blues."

September 14, 1928: "Take Your Tomorrow" and "Dusky Stevedore."

January 8, 1929 (the voice of Charles Chiles was added on the last song): "I Ain't Gonna Give Nobody None of My Jelly-Roll," "She's Funny That Way," and "You Lose."

January 19, 1929 (Joe Tarto was added on bass): "Right or Wrong," "That's the Good Old Sunny South," and "You're the Cream in My Coffee."

September 5, 1929 (Leo McConville may have replaced Manny Klein on trumpet, and the voice of Phil Pavey, who had cut two records for Okeh in February, was added on the last song): "Lovin' Sam," "Big Bad Bill Is Sweet William Now," and "The Ghost of the St. Louis Blues."

September 12, 1929 (Gene Krupa replaced Stan King on drums): "Sweet Mama (Papa's Getting Mad)," "The Pickaninnies' Paradise," and "The Blues Singer from Alabam'."

Several of these recordings were issued in England on the Parlophone label, and in France and Germany on the Odeon label.

In Atlanta on September 24 and 25, 1929, Miller joined Fiddlin' John Carson, Frank Hutchison, Narmour and Smith, Moonshine Kate, Bud Blue, the Black Brothers, and Martin Malloy to record "The Medicine Show," a three-disc revue of music and comedy.

On October 17, 1930, Miller's last Okeh recordings were made. These were dialect routines with Pick Maloney: "Sam and Bill at the Graveyard," "The Licker Taster," and "Sam's New Job" (Parts I–II). "Sam's New Job" was Miller's final Okeh release, issued on October 25, 1931.

On September 1, 1936, Miller emerged in New York to cut four sides for Bluebird. The personnel are unknown, except that Gene Cobb sang on the first three cuts. These were Miller's final recordings: "I Ain't Got Nobody," "The Gypsy," "Anytime," and "Right or Wrong."

Then Emmett Miller vanished.

Most of those who knew Miller are dead. In 1976 I called Joe Tarto, who had played bass at Miller's last three New York Okeh sessions. Tarto now lives in New Jersey.

"The only Miller that I knew was Eddie Miller," said Joe Tarto.

"But you played at three of Emmett Miller's sessions, didn't you?"

"Glenn Miller?"

"No. *Emmett* Miller. You played on his records."

"To be honest with you, I don't recall. There was so many of them, I lost track. I really did."

Joe Tarto suggested I call Chauncey Morehouse, a popular jazz drummer of the 1920s and '30s who Tarto said had a good memory. Morehouse also lives in New Jersey. While he was able to give me some interesting information on the lesser-known musicians on Miller's records (Chauncey recalled that Stan King was well-known for his unswaybale beat, that Arthur Schutt was an awesomely heavy drinker, and that Manny Klein, a house-man in the NBC band with Chauncey, once played with Toscanini), he had no memory of Emmett Miller.

"The only Emmett I ever knew was back in Chambersburg, Pennsylvania. Emmett Waugaman. His father ran a drugstore."

"And Emmett Kelly, the clown," added Mrs. Morehouse, who was listening on another line.

"When we were at NBC," said Chauncey, "the dates came so fast that we'd go out and do a date and come home and I'd be layin' in bed at night and I'd think, 'Who in the hell was the leader of that session?' We were always working. It's hard to remember. A lot of guys thought Chauncey was a fag name."

Finally I was led to Seger Ellis, a jazz pianist, who recalls meeting Emmett Miller at the Okeh studio in the Amalgamated Bank Building at Union Square in Manhattan. Ellis, who was born in 1904, has lived in Houston for many years.

"I was under contract to Okeh at the time he recorded. [Ellis recorded for Okeh from November 30, 1926, to November 23, 1930. In the late 1940s, Ellis cut some country-pop sides for Victor under the name of Harry Houston, a name suggested by Steve Sholes. He says he enjoyed listening to country music when he was younger.] He used to do a lot of yodeling, right? He was probably in his late twenties or maybe early thirties then. I think he was about a medium-sized man, a little on the plump side, if I remember correctly. I think he was balding. He'd lost most of his hair, or a lot of it. And he was definitely from the South, either Texas or Arkansas, I believe. I'm not sure. I only met him the one time. He had a big seller. I can't remember the name of it. He was no kid at the time; he'd been battling around for a long

time. He happened to make this one record for Okeh and
it sold real big and they got him back for another one, and
the next session he didn't have anything that moved at
all. And that was sort of the end of him. I think he played
some guitar, but not on record.

"He was a fun-loving guy, it seems. He was also sort
of a loner, as far as I know. I don't know anybody who
knew him real well. They didn't even know him real well
around Okeh, I don't believe."

Ellis, who had used the Dorseys in many of his sessions, assured me that Emmett Miller's music "wasn't the
kind of stuff they wanted to play. It was just a record date
to them. It would've been Justin Ring's idea. He was
musical director down at Okeh, and he practically A&R'd
everybody's dates. He's dead now."

I asked Seger if Miller was considered a jazz singer
or a country singer. "Oh, definitely country."

The mystery of Emmett Miller, I think, will never be
penetrated. Perhaps someday a trunk of Miller lore will be
discovered in the basement of a long-shuttered Hatties-
burg whorehouse. Perhaps someday, some further day,
Miller will be revealed to have been a truant Tau Ceti
cartographer. Perhaps he operates a candy store in
Bayonne.

The surviving Emmett Miller discs are among the
rarest of records. Several years ago, a West Coast bootleg
label called the Old Masters inaugurated a series of jazz
reissue albums with *Emmet Miller Acc. by His Georgia
Crackers,* a set of fourteen Okeh sides. There were no liner
notes or illustrations, and Emmett's name was misspelled.
But the music was there, pressed in beautiful clear green
plastic. Now that album, released in an edition of one
thousand, is itself a rarity.

The unavailability of Emmett Miller's recordings is
lamentable, for his music is as striking and bizarre in
these days as it was in the 1920s. There was never another

voice like Miller's. Seger Ellis called it "freakish"; it was congested, nasal, full of after-hours liquor and crazy times. He often swirled his lyrics off into high, weird yodels—a manic but wholly pleasant effect. He was the greatest song stylist of his generation, and until Jerry Lee Lewis came along no one jumped songs with such sheer country class.

Yodeling Cowboys and Such

The word *yodel* is from the German *jodeln,* which means, literally, to utter the sound *jo.*

In the early nineteenth century, performances of yodelers were common on the British stage. Sir Walter Scott in his *Journal* entry of June 4, 1830, wrote that, "Anne wants me to go to hear the Tyrolese Minstrels, but . . . I cannot but think their yodeling . . . is a variation upon the tones of a jackass."

Yodeling became a part of American minstrelsy. The first yodeling minstrel was Tom Christian, who made his debut in Chicago in 1847. Daniel Decatur Emmett (1815–1904), the composer and minstrel who wrote "Dixie" in 1859 for Bryant's Minstrels, was the author of several songs that showcased what he had learned from visiting European showmen.

The first yodeler to make records was probably one

L. W. Lipp, who cut cylinders for the New Jersey Phonograph Company in 1892. Eddie Giguere, "the well-known yodeler of the Police Patrol Company," made some for Columbia in 1894. Most renowned of the early yodelers was George P. Watson, who cut several cylinders for the Edison company. His earliest were "Leben auf den Alpen" and "Emmett's German Yodle," both released in 1897. Watson recorded three more of Dan Emmett's compositions: "Emmett's Lullaby," released in 1899, and "Medley of Emmett's Yodles" and "Emmett's Yodle Song," both released in 1901.

Yodel records were most popular during the first two decades of the twentieth century. A Columbia catalogue of 1917 includes a section with many selections by George Watson. A 1920 Victor catalogue lists seventeen Yodel Songs, and again many of them are by George Watson (recording contracts were not what they are today).

The first country record to include yodeling was "Rock All Our Babies to Sleep," cut by the blind Georgia singer Riley Puckett (1894–1946) for Columbia in April 1924. The following September, Puckett recorded his second yodel disc, "Sleep, Baby, Sleep." George Watson had recorded English and German versions of this song for Edison in 1897. (The song itself was an 1869 hit by S. A. Emery.) At his first recording session on August 4, 1927, in Bristol, Tennessee, Jimmie Rodgers also cut "Sleep, Baby, Sleep," the first yodel record by the man who became famous as America's Blue Yodeler.

Herb Quinn, a black musician who lived near Rodgers in Mississippi in the early twenties, says that Rodgers's blue yodeling was much copied by both white and black musicians of the era. In Quinn's phrase, "everyone who could pick a guitar" started yodeling like Rodgers.

A few blues singers yodeled on record, such as Stovepipe Johnson in "Devilish Blues" (Vocalion, 1928) and Tampa Red in "Worried Devil Blues" (Bluebird,

1934). Bessie Smith had cut "Yodeling Blues" for Columbia in 1923, but she didn't bother to yodel. Perhaps Bessie yodeled when she performed the song in concert; if she did, it's likely that Jimmie Rodgers heard her.

Rodgers was the most famous of country music's blue yodelers, and several important singers copied his style directly. The best-known Rodgers imitators were Jimmie Davis and Gene Autry, who both started recording in 1929.

I think the mysterious Emmett Miller blue-yodeled earlier and better than Jimmie Rodgers. One of the best-known yodeling performances in country music, Hank Williams's "Lovesick Blues," would not have been without Miller.

"Lovesick Blues" was copyrighted on April 3, 1922, by Jack Mills, Inc., in New York City. The words were written by Irving Mills (born on January 16, 1894, in Russia; Mills later wrote many more standards, such as "It Don't Mean a Thing If It Ain't Got That Swing," "Mood Indigo," and "Caravan"); the music was written by vaudeville piano player Cliff Friend (born on October 1, 1893, in Cincinnati). Later Cliff Friend held that he sold all his rights to "Lovesick Blues" for $500.

Elsie Clark cut "Lovesick Blues" for Okeh late in 1922. Emmett Miller recorded his first version of the song, with yodeling, on September 1, 1925, in Asheville, North Carolina, and it was released by Okeh during the next month. In 1927 blues singer Bertha Chippie Hill also recorded the song for Okeh. On June 12, 1928, Miller cut another version of "Lovesick Blues" in New York City, this time with several well-known jazz musicians behind him (Tommy Dorsey, Jimmy Dorsey, Eddie Lang, and others). Again Miller yodeled. The record was released by Okeh in July 1928, c/w "Big Bad Bill Is Sweet William Now." The disc bore the name of Emmett Miller and His Georgia Crackers.

In December 1939, Rex Griffin, the Alabama-born honky-tonk singer who had written the classic suicide song, "The Last Letter," in 1937, released "Lovesick Blues" on Decca. Griffin's version is a paragon of simplicity: The only accompaniment is his own acoustic guitar. Vocally, Griffin copied Miller in every accessible way, including the wholly strange yodeling that was Miller's watermark. As similar to Miller's version as it is, Rex Griffin's "Lovesick Blues" is a hillbilly song, pure and simple.

Hank Williams copied "Lovesick Blues" directly from Rex Griffin's record. He began singing it at the Louisiana Hayride late in 1948 and recorded it for MGM soon after. When he performed it during his debut at the Grand Ole Opry on June 11, 1949, he became myth, the archetypal country singer. Released on February 25, 1949, Hank's "Lovesick Blues" stayed on the charts for forty-two weeks, the most successful country record of the year. To many people the song, like Hank, is archetypally country. There are those who would not hear that it was written by a Jew from Russia, that it was midwived by a redneck jazz singer who would have been thrown off the Opry.

Many different styles of yodeling could be heard in country records of the 1920s and early '30s: the archaic, nineteenth-century yodel, which can be heard in records such as "Rockin' Yodel" by the Leake County Revelers (Columbia, 1928) and "We Have Moonshine in the West Virginia Hills" by Harvey and Earl Shirky (Columbia, 1930); the minstrel-show yodel, a sort of fake blue yodel (Swiss yodel, black lyrics) that probably predated the yodeling of both Rodgers and Miller, heard in records such as Frank Welling's "Yodelin' Daddy Blues" (Supertone, 1929); and pop-country yodeling, as in Jimmy Long's "Yodel Your Troubles Away" (Champion, 1929).

For me, the ultimate country yodel record is the two-part "Yodel Blues" that Van and Pete recorded for

Okeh in 1928. This is a great, dark, otherworldly piece of music that brings together the glimmering beads of a hundred ancient songs. There is a spare and brilliant steel guitar, hot and cold and monomaniacal, and a voice so seething with desolate power that it nearly chills the skin. The yodels here are not decorative, not, as Jimmie Rodgers called them, the "curlicues I can make with my throat," but feral and haunting, no closer to Switzerland than the nearest dark alley.

> *Well, I thought I heard*
> *A rumble down in the ground,*
> *Awooo, I said down in the ground;*
> *It was only the devil*
> *Chainin' his sweet mama down.*
> *There's a change in the ocean,*
> *In the deep blue sea:*
> *That sweet mama don't come back,*
> *You'll see a change in me.*

The novelty yodel reached an extreme in the early recordings of Wilf Carter, or Montana Slim (born on December 18, 1904, in Guysboro, Nova Scotia). Carter's Victor recordings featured what he called a three-in-one yodel, an effect that relied on the use of echo techniques in the studio.

After Jimmie Rodgers, many of the most successful country artists yodeled: Jimmie Davis, Gene Autry, Cliff Carlisle, and others. In the late 1930s, yodeling could even be heard in Western-swing records, such as "Blue Yodel #1" by Bob Wills and His Texas Playboys (1937) and "Dirty Hangover Blues" by W. Lee O'Daniel and His Hillbilly Boys (1939). "Will There Be Any Yodelers in Heaven?" asked the Girls of the Golden West (Bluebird, 1934).

By the 1940s yodeling had become rare in country

records. It seemed to represent an earlier, more boorish era, and singers and producers shook it loose. There were isolated, wonderful exceptions, such as Hank Williams's 1949 version of "Lovesick Blues."

Today very few country singers would dare yodel even if they could. Nevertheless, most Jerry Lee Lewis albums include at least one great, whiskey-drenched yodel. (Jerry Lee has been yodeling since the Sun days; he recorded "Lovesick Blues" in 1958 and Jimmie Rodgers's "Waiting for a Train" in 1962.) And Tompall Glaser yodeled on several recordings he made in 1975 and 1976, such as "T for Texas." Like Jerry Lee, Tompall is one of the very few singers who can interpret the classics of Rodgers and others in a knowing, exciting way.

In Hollywood in the 1930s was born the yodeling cowboy, one of the mightiest pop hallucinations of all time. Yodeling was not unknown among cowboys. By all accounts, it was no less common than fiddling among oceanographers or tromboning among rare-book dealers.

Cowboys, real cowboys, did make records. One of the best cowboy singers was Jules Verne Allen (1883–1945), a cattle driver from Waxahachie, Texas, who worked in the last of the great drives from the Rio Grande to Montana. On April 21, 1928, in El Paso, Allen made his first sides for Victor. He cut six sessions, twenty-four songs in all, for Victor; the last was on April 27, 1929. Four of Allen's records were of noncowboy songs: "Po' Mourner," "Two Fragments," "You Mean Somebody But You Don't Mean Me," and "A Prisoner for Life" (the first two are of minstrelsy; the second pair are pop). All the remaining twenty records are representative of cowboy music. "Zebra Dun" does not sound so unlike some of Hollywood's cowboy records (it is true that the early L.A. cowboy style was a mixture of the less esoteric cowboy songs and the singing styles of men such as Gene Autry), but some of Allen's other songs reveal a black influence that Hollywood ignored. (His "Jack o' Diamonds," for example, contains lyrics from "Make Me a Pallet on Your Floor.") Allen also cut a version of the classic "Chisolm Trail." The truth of "Chisolm Trail" is that it is a wondrously dirty song. It was recorded by folklorists in its original state (the Robert W. Gordon Collection of American Folk Song at the University of Oregon includes a dirty "Chisolm Trail," collected by Gordon in the late 1920s) but was rarely published. In his *Adventures of a Ballad Hunter* (1947), John A. Lomax wrote that some of the verses of "Chisolm Trail" would "burn up" the horn of the recording machine.

I fucked her standin' and I fucked her lyin',
If she had wings I'd a-fucked her flyin'.
The last time I seen her, and I ain't seen her since,
She was scratchin' her cunt on a barb-wire fence.

Included among the other authentic cowboy singers of the 1920s and early '30s were Dick Devall, J. D. Farley, Newton Gaines, Paul Hamblin, Billie Maxwell, Haywire Mac McClintock, Carl T. Sprague, and Jack Webb. I think the greatest cowboy record is "Texas Ranger," recorded by Jack and Bernard Cartwright for Victor on August 11, 1929, in Dallas. "Texas Ranger" is a very old song, and it was sung by cowboys as early as the 1830s, when it was often called "The Texas Ranger Boy." The only instrument in the recording by the Cartwright brothers is a sere, droning fiddle, and the lyrics are rawly sweet. There is a plot, full of death and romance and endlessness.

Cowboys were active in the West from the 1820s on. In the late 1880s their numbers began to lessen. Also during the 1880s the mythic cowboy appeared, the forebear of the L.A. yodeler. The first cowboy novel had been published in 1864, *The Hermit of the Colorado Hills* by William Bushnell. Here the cowboys were called herders and given an innocent nobility, not unlike that given to redskins during the Romantic movement of the seventeenth and eighteenth centuries. Cowboy fiction hit its stride in the work of Joseph E. Badger, Jr., who first turned to the West for his inspiration in 1879. Badger's titles included such winners as *Solemn Saul, the Sad Man from San Saba* and *Daddy Dead-Eye, the Despot of Dew Drop* (yes, there were Dew Drop Inns a hundred years ago).

In *The Cowboy Clan; or, The Tigress of Texas,* an 1891 book by William Levi Taylor, a woman is made to sing the first Hollywood cowboy song.

> *Lie down now cattle, don't heed any rattle,*
> *But quietly rest until morn.*
> *For if you skeedaddle, we'll jump in the saddle*
> *And head you off, sure as you are born.*

During the 1880s, cowboys began parodying their own reputations. There are photographs, staged by bored cowboys, of fake lynchings and fake gunfights. Some cowboys became notoriously clothes-conscious; it was not too rare to encounter a sagebrush dandy who had paid two months' wages for a pair of the fancy cowboy boots of soft leather and decorative stitching that appeared in the 1880s.

There are many truisms of the Old West. One was a widespread hatred of cows, a hatred that often birthed sadism. It was not considered odd to rub sand into a cow's eyes to rouse it, or to twist its tail until the cartilage snapped. Jack Clement wrote a song that includes the line, "Some cowboys hate cows, and I'm one of those."

Cowboys disliked blacks also, and Mexicans, who were referred to as greasers. The racism of cowboys was so strong that even a Time-Life book on cowboys (*The Cowboys,* 1973) informs, without qualification, that "the white majority of cowhands were unabashed racists." It is also true, however, that roughly 30 percent of cowboys were either black or Mexican. Several black cowboys, such as Jim Taylor, Jessie Stahl, Nat Love a/k/a Deadwood Dick, Isom Dart, and Cherokee Bill, became quite well known. (Born Cranford Goldsby, Cherokee Bill has been called the black Billy the Kid. Hanged at the age of twenty, Cherokee Bill was asked if he had any last words. Bill commented, "I came here to die, not make a speech." His mom claimed the remains.) In 1946 Astor Pictures released a Western musical with a black cast, *Beware*, which featured jump blues artist Louis Jordan, Valerie Black, and Milton Woods, the "colored Basil Rathbone." Louis Jordan, who was born on July 8, 1908, in Brinkley, Arkansas, and who died on February 4, 1975, in Los Angeles, made several films in addition to *Beware*, such as *Reet, Petite and Gone* (1947) and *Look Out, Sister* (1948). Jordan recorded for Decca from December 1938 until January 1954. After Decca, his glory ever ebbing, he recorded for Aladdin (1954), X and Vik (1955), Mercury (1956–57), Lou-Wa (1960), Warwick (1961), Melodisc (1962), Tangerine (1962–64), Pzazz (1968), Black & Blue (1973), and Blues Spectrum (1974).

Cowboys were known to belch frequently, and to produce other uncomely sounds; but to yodel? *Nein*.

Emmett Miller, 2

Emmett Miller sits on a bed. He wears light trousers, light vest, white shirt, and dark bow tie. He is leaning forward slightly, toward the camera. His left hand rests on his knee. There are a diamond ring and a long, lighted cigar. Close to his right stands a woman, young and thin and pale. Her hair is bobbed. She smiles, but there is a drunken, puffy reluctance in her face. Emmett Miller's arm surrounds the girl's thighs, lifting her skirt almost to her hips. Where his hand holds the inside of her leg, there is another diamond. The girl's thin, silvery garters show above her knees, and her legs are pretty and dully incandescent in her fine silk stockings. Near the girl is a small, low table, on which are three glasses, variously full, and a bottle of Crawford's Five Star. The wallpaper is of a thousand trellised roses.

Emmett Miller has no face. There is a hole in the

photograph where it was burned away by a cigarette, a hole of precise and perfect wrath. A piece of chin, a sliver of ear pressed to a girl's hip, one temple and its dark receding hairline—this is all. By the line of the chin and the tightness at the ear and temple, it seems Emmett Miller is smiling.

On the back of the photograph, in crisp, faded blue: "Me and Emmett—Union Square Hotel, New York City— 8/10/28—Sitting on Top of the World!"

I found the photograph, brittle and tawny with its age and its travel, sticking from between pages of *Countries of the World, Vol. II*, in a junk store in Southport, North Carolina, a small ocean place near the bottom of the state. I asked the owner of the store where he had got the book, but he didn't recall. I bought the photo for a nickel.

That was in 1972. A year later it was blown out a ninth-floor window in Manhattan, off the kitchen table of someone I disliked. I watched after it, trying to follow it as it fell, but I didn't see it touch the ground.

Stained Panties and
Coarse Metaphors

In December 1975, Ron Thompson, program director of WWVA, the eminent fifty-thousand-watt country station in Wheeling, West Virginia, dispatched an open letter to the music industry:

"Due to the profanity and distasteful lyrics we have been receiving on records by name artists, WWVA has initiated the following policy. WWVA AM/FM will not air suggestive or profane lyrics. We will delete questionable words and phrases before we play a record. Should the title fail to pass our code of ethics, or if an edit is impossible, the record will not be aired.

"Frankly, we are tired of receiving letters from parents, asking us to explain 'one night stands,' etc. to their children. 'Hell' and 'damn' have become old hat and the sensationalism being used to sell records today has gone too far. It is not our policy to be moral crusaders, but we will not jeopardize our standing in the community. We feel that country music and modern country music stations are the last oasis in the industry. We will not ignore our responsibility to you."

Doc Williams (born Andrew John Smik, Jr., in Cleveland, Ohio, on June 26, 1914), a singer who has performed in WWVA's "Jamboree U.S.A." since May of 1937, said in an interview with Michael Gast of *The Wheeling News–Register*, "I admit that the risqué titles and lyrics problem comprises less than five percent of the country output today, but I fear that the trend will spread, destroying the purpose and very character of a music form that draws on the best and noblest of the American experience."

Program director Thompson and performer Williams were speaking of records such as Tanya Tucker's "Would You Lay with Me (in a Field of Stone)," Conway Twitty's "You've Never Been This Far Before," and Loretta Lynn's "The Pill," hits of 1974 and 1975 that were about fucking. Bob Knight, who succeeded Thompson as WWVA's program director, said the station's antismut campaign met with favorable response, that 350 letters of support and only one letter of opposition had been received.

Like others loud with indignation for the pollution of country music, the folks at WWVA were gravely ignorant of the heritage they claimed to hold so dear. Country music is less sexy, less vulgar than it ever has been. When *Billboard*, on March 25, 1939, published its first list of top-selling Hillbilly Records, it did so with a note that "double-meaning records are purposely omitted from this column." Of the four disks included in that list, two were by Jimmie Davis, one of the most popular, and most intriguing, country singers of the pre-War era.

Born to sharecroppers in Quitman, a small place in northern Louisiana's Jackson Parish, on September 11, 1902, James Houston Davis graduated from the Beech

Springs Consolidated School in a class of three. He attended a New Orleans business school after working briefly at a sawmill. He received a B.A. at Louisiana College in Pineville, then went on to Louisiana State University in Baton Rouge. At L.S.U. he became a member of the Tiger Four, a college vocal group that entertained at theaters in Baton Rouge. After receiving his M.A., Davis joined the faculty of Dodd College in Shreveport, where he taught history and social science. Later he became criminal clerk at the Shreveport City Court.

Victor catalogue, 1930.

ORTHOPHONIC
RECORDING

10-INCH
LIST PRICE 75c

OLD FAMILIAR TUNES AND NOVELTIES

Singing

V-40302 {
My Louisiana Girl
My Dixie Sweetheart
Yodeling with Guitars
        Jimmie Davis

V-40299 {
On Top of the Hill
Never Leave Your Gal Too Long
with Orchestra
Bud Billings-Carson Robison

V-40300 {
Somewhere in Arkansas
The Rambling Woman
with Guitars and Banjo
    Ashley's Melody Makers

V-40303 {
Jake Walk Blues
Reckless Night Blues
with Guitar, Banjo and Kazoo
    Allen Brothers

Jimmie Davis

V-40307 {
The Story of Freeda Boldt
Sunny Tennessee
with String Band
        Floyd County Ramblers

22523 {
High-Powered Mama
In the Jail-House Now—No. 2
Yodeling with Guitar
        Jimmie Rodgers

Jimmie Rodgers

The Music You Want · When You Want it · On Victor Records

While holding down his civil-service job, Davis also performed regularly at station KWKH in Shreveport. He sang a country music that drew heavily from the blues of the deep South, more heavily even than that of his idol Jimmie Rodgers.

A Victor talent scout was impressed by Davis's performances at KWKH, and on September 19, 1929, a week after his twenty-seventh birthday, Jimmie was brought to Memphis, where he cut four songs for Victor. From 1929 to 1933, Davis recorded sixty-eight sides for the company.

A contemporary of Jimmie Rodgers, Davis was a notable disciple of the elder Victor singer. (Another important follower of Rodgers, Gene Autry, also made his first recordings in 1929.) Like Rodgers, Davis was an urbane, eclectic performer who was influenced by black music as well as by the rural white tradition. Part of Jimmie Davis's repertoire was songs such as "The Baby's Lullaby" and "You're the Picture of Your Mother," frail and wispy stuff of an earlier day. The best and most striking part of his repertoire, however, was a series of songs that dealt with sex plainly or in crypto-lubricities, but never without an extremely raunchy sense of humor.

Much of Jimmie Rodgers's music was sexy ("Blue Yodel No. 9," "Let Me Be Your Side Krack," "What's It"), and in songs such as "Pistol Packin' Papa" he showed himself to be a master of the wet metaphor:

> *And if you don't wanna smell my smoke,*
> *Don't monkey with my gun.* *

Davis went further than Rodgers. In "Tom Cat and Pussy Blues," recorded in November of 1932, he sang of the heated interactions of "cock and pussy." In "Organ-

---

* "Pistol Packin' Papa" by Jimmie Rodgers and Waldo O'Neal. Copyright © 1931 by Peer International Corporation. Copyright renewed. Used by permission.

Grinder Blues," recorded in the same session, Davis sang drolly of impotence and the controversial animal-gland treatment popularized by such charlatans as Kansan John R. Brinkley (who after losing his license to practice medicine in June of 1935, concentrated on operating XERA, his powerful border station in Del Rio, Texas, which broadcast programs by country acts such as the Carter Family). Davis looked to a new tumescence.

> *Gonna get me some monkey glands,*
> *Be like I used to was;*
> *Gonna run these mamas down,*
> *Like a Dominicker rooster does.* *

(In *Sanctuary*, published thirteen months before, William Faulkner, who worked on the other side of the river, had his character Miss Myrtle remark, "Maybe he went off and got fixed up with one of these glands, these monkey glands." But the earliest literary reference to monkey glands was penned far from the Mississippi: George Bernard Shaw spoke of "weekly doses of monkey gland" as a fortification against old age in the 1924 introduction to his play *Saint Joan*.)

In "High Behind Blues," recorded in February 1932, he professes melic lust for dark meat.

> *When I get to Mexico,*
> *Gonna get me a big, big brown;*
> *No matter how big she is,*
> *I'm the man can hold her down.* †

At times Davis borrowed directly from earlier blues records, as in "Sewing Machine Blues."

> *Gonna telephone to heaven*
> *To send me an angel down;*
> *If you haven't got an angel, St. Peter,*
> *Send me a high-steppin' brown.*

He finishes the song with a cheerful leer.

> *It ain't your fancy walk, gal,*
> *It ain't your vampin' ways;*
> *It's the way you do*
> *Just before the break of day.* *

In "Red Nightgown Blues," cut in **February** of 1932, Davis fancies himself the object of nymphomaniac attack.

> *We bought the license,*
> *Went to see Parson Brown;*
> *Corrine couldn't wait*
> *And she throwed me down.* †

Feminine aggression and much panting ensue. At one point, Davis has Corrine refer to him dearly as "my meat." But perhaps Davis's most unforgettable Victor allusion is in his 1930 recording of "She's a Hum Dum Dinger from Dingersville," where he likens the pelvic torque of his beloved to "a mowin' machine."

In the fall of 1934 Jimmie Davis signed with newly

---

* "Sewing Machine Blues" by Jimmie Davis. Copyright © 1932 by Peer International Corporation. Copyright renewed. Used by permission.
† "Red Nightgown Blues" by Jimmie Davis. Copyright © 1932 by Peer International Corporation. Copyright renewed. Used by permission.

formed Decca Records. In his earliest Decca recordings, Davis sounds as he did in his Victor work; records such as "Shirt Tail Blues," his second release by Decca (October 1934), represent the peak of Davis's Jimmie Rodgers phase. But soon the yodels vanished from Davis's records, and with them, the raw, vivid instrumentation.

Becoming more of a mainstream artist, Davis made records with Buddy Jones, the Musical Brownies, and Lani McIntire and His Hawaiians. Even Jimmie's voice changed; it got warmer, lighter, and less churlish. At first he did not wholly forsake raunchy material, but what remained of it was greatly toned down. For example, "Mama's Getting Hot and Papa's Getting Cold," released in November 1935, is merely cute. By 1938 the dirty songs had ceased; Jimmie Davis was a crooner.

Davis's first major hit with Decca was "Nobody's Darlin' But Mine," a dark song of death and fidelity vows, released in April 1935. Davis himself recorded three sequels to "Nobody's Darlin' But Mine": "Answer to Nobody's Darlin' But Mine," "That's Why I'm Nobody's Darlin'," and "By the Grave of Nobody's Darlin'." An even bigger hit was "It Makes No Difference Now," written by Floyd Tillman, then a member of the Houston-based Blue Ridge Playboys. First released by Cliff Bruner's Texas Wanderers on Decca in September 1938, then by Jimmie Davis in November, Tillman's masterpiece of sultry fatalism crossed over to become a national pop hit when Bing Crosby cut it, also for Decca, in 1941. Tillman, however, had sold ownership of the song for a few hundred dollars (he retrieved it when the copyright was renewed in 1966, and today he shares the copyright with Davis).

In 1939 Jimmie Davis and Charles Mitchell, who played steel guitar with Davis, wrote the most popular and most valuable song in the history of country music: "You Are My Sunshine." The song was first cut by the Rice Brothers Gang for Decca and released in November

The PINE RIDGE BOYS

B-8263	You Are My Sunshine / Farther Along
B-8331	When Mother Prayed for Me / The Clouds Will Soon Roll By
B-8360	The Convict and the Rose / Where the Old Red River Flows
B-8556	Old Shep / Mississippi River Blues

1939. There followed a version by Bob Atcher and Bonnie Blue Eyes on Okeh, and another by the Pine Ridge Boys on Bluebird, then the two best-known country versions: Jimmie Davis's on Decca (released in March 1940) and Gene Autry's on Okeh (released in June 1941). In 1941 Lawrence Welk recorded the song for Decca, and later in the year Bing Crosby cut it for the same label. Since then, no one has been able to maintain a thorough recording history of the song, although Roy Horton of Peer International Corporation, the publisher of the song, contends there is no doubt that "You Are My Sunshine" is the most valuable copyright in country music, the two dubious challengers being Ted Daffan's 1943 "Born to Lose" (also a Peer song) and Pee Wee King and Redd Stewart's 1948 "Tennessee Waltz" (published by Acuff–Rose).

And here's an amusing tale. Lloyd Copas, better known as Cowboy Copas, was one of the most popular country performers in the late 1940s. He recorded for King Records, the Cincinnati independent label operated by Sidney Nathan. Each month, Copas traveled from Cincinnati to Nashville for the purpose of buying songs from writers. When he returned with the songs, Nathan repaid him half of the cost. Copas took authors' rights of the songs, and Nathan took the publishing rights for his Lois Music. One month Copas returned to Cincinnati with a new batch of songs. He told Nathan that he had refused one good song because the writers wanted too much money for it, twenty-five dollars.

"It's called 'Tennessee Waltz,'" Copas explained, "and all it is, is a copy of Eddy Arnold's 'Missouri Waltz.' And I don't want people goin' around sayin' I'm followin' Eddy Arnold."

Nathan expressed agreement, but added that maybe, for superstitious reasons, Copas should pick the song up next time he was in Nashville. He gave Copas an extra ten-dollar bill.

Next month Copas returned from Nashville, again without the song. "They sold it, huh?" Nathan asked.

"Well, no, Mr. Nathan," said Copas. "The bastards put the price up to fifty dollars, and I wasn't going to pay that much."

Sid Nathan smiled and patted Copas's back. "You done right," he said. "There ain't no song in the world worth fifty dollars."

In 1938 Jimmie Davis became Shreveport's Commissioner of Public Safety. In 1942 he was made State Public Service Commissioner, a job Huey Long had held. Davis sang his way into both positions.

In 1944 Jimmie Davis was offered the nomination for governor on the Louisiana Democratic ticket. He campaigned for office with "You Are My Sunshine" as his rallying theme. The opposition ran advertisements in newspapers, listing some of his older, profaner songs. (His 1936 "Bed Bug Blues" was called "depraved vulgarity.") Davis won. (This was not the first time country music became an important factor in politics. In 1886 brothers Robert and Alf Taylor ran against each other for governor of Tennessee. Their public debates culminated in one-on-one fiddling contests.)

CHARLES MITCHELL and his Orchestra

B-8716	Jersey Side Jive —FT
	The Sun Has Gone Down on Our Love —FT —VR
B-8736	Rainbow Island —FT —VR
	You Don't Love Me Any More —FT—VR
B-8757	I Still Believe in You—FT—VR
	Broken Hearted—FT—VR

Davis's term of office was not an especially eventful one; Louisiana politics had calmed considerably in the years since Huey Long's death. In 1947 Davis was featured in *Louisiana,* a Monogram film directed by Phil Karlson. Davis's previous B-movies were *Strictly in the Groove,* the 1942 film in which he sang "You Are My Sunshine," and *Frontier Fury,* a 1943 Western. His last film was *Square Dance Katy* in 1950.

Charles Mitchell, the steel-playing coauthor of "You Are My Sunshine," was given a government job. Fred Rose was appointed an honorary State Colonel in 1945. Jimmie's term ended in 1948.

In 1960 Davis was again elected to the governorship of Louisiana. Like his opponent, Chep Morrison, Davis ran on a segregationist platform. As in 1944, the dirty songs were dragged from the closet. He finished his term in 1964. After a fling at running for a third term in 1971, Jimmie Davis left politics.

In the 1950s Davis practically abandoned worldly music for sacred. He left Decca/MCA in December 1973, and signed with Canaan Records, a gospel-music company in Waco, Texas. For Canaan he cut a religious version of "You Are My Sunshine" called "Christ Is My

Sunshine." In 1976 Paula Records in Shreveport released his "Walkin' My Blues Away," a strong, bluesy song he had first released on Decca in February 1943. For the most part, however, the Jimmie Davis of the 1970s was a gospel singer.

In the spring of 1976, John Maginnis, editor and publisher of the Baton Rouge tabloid *Gris-Gris,* interviewed Davis at his office in Baton Rouge. Maginnis asked Davis about the sort of music he enjoyed. Country and gospel, Davis answered, "but I don't like country if it's vulgar."

Jimmie Davis was certainly not the first to blend sex and country music. The old British ballads themselves were plump with the stuff, and long before WWVA, there were protestors. In 1583 Puritan Philip Stubbes damned balladeers in his *Anatomie of Abuses:* "Their heads are fraught with all kinds of lascivious songs, filthy ballads, scurvy rhimes."

"Tam Lin," "Mary Hamilton," and other ancient ballads refer to abortion. "Gil Brenton" tells of supernatural sheets that broadcast a woman's lack of virginity. The popular seventeenth-century ballad "Fair Margaret and Sweet William" contains the moory couplet:

> *I dreamed my bower was full of red swine,*
> *And my bride-bed full of blood.*

The eighteenth-century antiquary Bishop Thomas Percy collected many ballads deemed too vulgar for printed publication. These songs, dating to Elizabethan times, remained unissued until 1868, when Frederick W. Furnivall issued them, in London, as *The Percy Reliques: Loose and Humorous Songs,* making available for the first time golden-oldie lyrics such as "Up start the Crabfish, & catch her by the Cunt" (from "The Sea Crabb," c. 1620) and "Which made him have a mighty mind To clipp, kisse, & to ffuck her" (from "A Friende of Mine," c. 1650).

First published in Britain in 1776, "Our Goodman" is the whimsical ballad of a drunken cuckold. Transported across the sea, it became one of the most widespread songs in America. Various versions of it have been recorded commercially by country singers: "Three Nights' Experience" by Gid Tanner and Fate Norris in 1926 for Columbia (but not released); "Three Nights Experience" by John Evans in 1927 for Brunswick; "Three Nights Experience" by Earl Johnson in 1927 for Okeh; "Four Nights Experience" by Clarence Ashley in 1928 for Gennett; "Six Nights Drunk" by Emmett Bankston and Red Henderson in 1928 for Okeh; "Drunkard's Special" by Coley Jones in 1929 for Columbia; "John the Drunkard" by the Carson Robison Trio in 1929 for Perfect; "Johnny the Drunkard" by Asa Martin in 1930 for Gennett; "Three Nights Drunk" by Gid Tanner and Riley Puckett in 1934 for Bluebird; "Old Man Crisp" by the Jolly Boys of Lafayette in 1937 for Decca; "Five Nights Experience" by Mustard and Gravy (Frank Rice and Ernest Stokes) in 1938 for Bluebird; "Three Nights Experience" by Homer and Jethro in 1947 for King. A piece of "Our Goodman" even appears in a Hollywood Western-swing record of 1948, Tex Williams's "Suspicion" on Capitol. It is doubtful that WWVA's standards of decency would allow for the broadcast of any of these disks.

Another British ballad that became very popular in America is "The Foggy Dew," a plain, flowing celebration of skin-thrill that would flush the face of WWVA's program director. In 1930, in Cade's Cove, Blount County, Tennessee, a Mrs. Samuel Harmon sang a version that she called "The Bugaboo" for a man from the *Journal of American Folklore.*

> *All in the first part of that night,*
> *Me and my love did play;*
> *All in the latter part of that night,*
> *She rolled in my arms till day.*

The first erotic ballad written and published in America is "The Consultation; a new BALLAD, to the tunes of OVER THE WAVES, & JEENY DANG THE WEAVER, and others of equal dignity with the metre," printed in the September 2, 1774, issue of the *Virginia Gazette*. Signed simply "D.C.," the song is about farting, and shitting too. It ends thus:

> *That dulness, gorged with black ey'd peas,*
> > *And feeling foul air rack her,*
> *To give her suffering bowels ease,*
> > *Did volley forth a cracker.*
> *As echo, without bone or skin,*
> > *Exists in verse Nasonian,*
> *So does that fundamental din,*
> > *Baptis'd the Muskitonian.*
> *His great descent still in his mind,*
> > *He deals in matters squalid,*
> *And sedulous, at each behind,*
> > *Announces births more solid.*

Is this the stuff of American music's goldener, purer days? Is this essential of Doc Williams's "character of a music form that draws on the best and noblest of the American experience"?

Augustus Summerfield Merrimon (1830–1892) was a United States Senator and Chief Justice of the Supreme Court of North Carolina. As an ambitious young Asheville attorney, Merrimon kept an energetic, often pretentious journal of his activities. In 1931 the *North Carolina Historical Review* published "The A. S. Merrimon Journal, 1853–1854," and in it are some valuable observations of the haveless Southern whites who were creators and lovers of early country music. In the entry for October 17, 1853, Merrimon described the scene at a court session in Jewell Hill, North Carolina.

The crowd in attendance were "getting in a weaving way" about night. Some twenty or thirty women were present and most of them were drunk.—I do not know any rival for this place in regard to drunkeness, ignorance, superstition and the most brutal debauchery. I regret that it is so, yet it is true. Scores of women attend the court for the sole purpose of drinking and pandering to the lustful passions of dirty men, and I regret so excee[d]ingly to say, that some men, I will not say gentlemen, are guilty of intercourse with these dirty, filthy strumpets, that ought to be, and one would think they are, far above doing such things. . . .

Merrimon's January 24, 1854, entry gives a similar scene at Yancy County Court.

I saw two women drunk and one cursed and swore desperately and proposed to whip some of her male friends that did not please her. Oh, what a shocking sight to see a *woman* drunk. A woman! Ah, a woman drunk! Shame on the unfortunate wretch! Infamy and disgrace are indellibly stamped upon the poor creature while she lives, and when she dies the world will be glad to be rid of a hateful pest and mankind soon forget that so mean a being lived. The men too, scores of them, have been drunk. At different times I noticed groups about over the Court Yard and in the center stood a large gauky looking fellow with a fiddle and he would saw off some silly ditty and two or three drunken fools would dance to the same. . . .

Some of the old ballads dealt with the crueler side of sex. The eighteenth-century Scots ballad "Fair Mary Wallington" culminates in death during a cesarean operation.

> *She took out a razor*
> *That was both sharp and fine,*
> *And out of her left side has taken*
> *The heir of Wallington.*

> *There is a race in Wallington,*
> *And that I rue full sare;*
> *Tho the cradle it be full spread up,*
> *The bride-bed is left bare.*

Early in the eighteenth century, "The Berkshire Tragedy" came to America. It is still alive in the lingering oral tradition in a variety of forms: "Knoxville Girl," "The Waco Girl," and others. It is a song of stark, irrational lust murder.

> *We walked along, we talked along,*
> *Till we came to the levellest ground;*
> *I picked me up a stick of wood*
> *And knocked the poor girl down.*
>
> *She fell upon her bending knees,*
> *Crying, "Lord have mercy on me!*
> *Oh, Willie, oh, Willie, don't murder me now,*
> *For I'm not prepared to die."*
>
> *Little attention did I pay,*
> *I beat her more and more;*
> *I beat her till the blood run down,—*
> *Her hair was yellow as gold.*

This song was cut as "The Knoxville Girl" by the Wilburn Brothers and released in their 1966 Decca album *The Wilburn Brothers Show*. In *Songs That Made America Famous*, issued by Adelphi in 1973, Patrick Sky did a version that he smartly titled "Yonkers Girl" for maximum effect.

Lust murder is also the theme of "The Jealous Lover," called at times "Florella," "Fair Florella," and "Pearl Bryan."

> *Down on her knees before him*
> *She pleaded for her life;*
> *Deep, deep into her bosom*
> *He plunged that fearful knife.*

The ballad "Sir Hugh" has a twist. It tells of the slaying of a young boy by an older woman. Nelstone's Hawaiians (Hubert Nelson and James Touche) cut an eerie steel-guitar version in 1929 for Victor, called "Fatal Flower Garden."

Of all the ancient ballads, perhaps the most striking erotic verse is in "The Knight and Shepherd's Daughter," first published in the eighteenth century. Not "Would You Lay with Me (in a Field of Stone)," nor "You've Never Been This Far Before," nor "The Pill" can approach the plain, moralless lyricism of this ancientry.

> *He took her by the milk-white hand,*
> *And laid her on the ground,*
> *And when he got his will o' her,*
> *He lift her up again.*

Doc Williams is not the only Brown Shirt of innocence in country music. Ray Price (born in Perryville, Texas, on January 12, 1926) was once one of the greatest honky-tonk singers. His earliest records, for the Bullet label, and his work for Columbia throughout the fifties are raw, visceral classics. By the early sixties, Price was becoming more of a pop singer, and by 1963 and his hit recording of "Make the World Go Away," there was more Perry Como in Price's music than Hank Williams, Price's original mentor. Today, Ray Price will tell you that sex belongs in the bedroom, not on the airwaves. The guy's got a way with words.

There are several offensively pious men in country

music. Johnny Cash and his God are a particularly tedious act. The strongest drink Cash serves at his parties is non-alcoholic fruit punch. His perspective of country music's history is as surreal as that of WWVA. In the first show of his "Johnny Cash" series, broadcast by CBS in August of 1976, Cash referred to his mother-in-law, Maybelle Carter, as "one of the most influential instrumentalists in country music." Mother Maybelle Carter's influence as a country-music instrumentalist is equal to that of, say, Rudy Vallee. Each year, Johnny Cash's mind seems to grow more monomaniacal. His 1976 hit "Sold Out of Flagpoles" was an absurd mess of godly patriotism, a song berserk with blandness and as dumb as any in the 1975 film *Nashville*.

More ignorable, perhaps, but no less creepy is Roy Acuff. He was born in Maynardsville, Tennessee, on September 15, 1903. This event has been appropriately written of in *King of Country Music: The Life Story of Roy Acuff*, by Acuff's friend A. C. Dunkleberger, published in 1971 by Williams Printing Company in Nashville.

> In the Smoky Mountains—the GREAT Smokies, they are called—the peaks seem to stretch higher and higher on all sides around you, and from the tallest ones on a clear day you can see for miles to where the horizon touches three other states. On a clear night you can see a million times as far . . . all the way to the stars.
>
> Stars of another firmament are not strangers to the Smokies; some have been born there.
>
> This is the story of a boy, a fiddle, and a dream!
>
> The boy was Roy Acuff. With his fiddle he made his dream come true.
>
> It is an American story—as earthy as the hills of Union County, Tennessee, where he first saw the light of day; an American *SUCCESS* story, for such is the harvest of the years we are going to explore.
>
> Almost it didn't happen. . . .

Good writers make it look so easy! Dunkleberger ends it, 130 pages later.

> And so we shall not terminate with a *PERIOD* this narrative—this biography of a remarkable career. That would denote finality to something that isn't finished.
> We began by saying, "This is the story of a boy, a fiddle and a dream."
> It is that—and the dream, while much of it has been fulfilled, still unfolds.
> So we shall do the unusual—if not, indeed, the unprecedented—where any book is concerned.
> In deference to facts, and to chapters which only time, itself, can write . . . we shall terminate it with a comma—thus

The Acuff biography is not unique among country-music books. Several are as bad, or worse. The first of these junk country books was *My Husband Jimmie Rodgers* by Carrie Rodgers and her friend Dorothy Hendricks (though only Mrs. Rodgers's name appears on the book), published in 1935. The sentences are large, offensive teardrops: "No money for toys! No money to buy—a little white casket." *Hubbin' It: The Life of Bob Wills,* a 1938 book by Ruth Sheldon, was country music's second great contribution to the literature of yech. *Chet Atkins,* a 1967 book by Red O'Donnell of the Nashville *Banner,* is a series of bizarrely truncated paragraphs; reading it is like watching Cheez-Whiz slowly coagulate on someone's chin during lunch. Here is one of Red's finer paragraphs: "A vacation incident in 1966 attests to a guitar's attraction for Atkins." And another, less florid: "Mr. Guitar likes all music."

Warren B. Causey, who for several years also wrote for the *Banner,* is author of *The Stringbean Murders,* a sort of country-music *In Cold Blood* that was published in

1975. Stringbean, who was born David Akeman in Anneville, Kentucky, on June 17, 1916, was a regular on "Hee Haw" and the Grand Ole Opry when he and his wife, Estelle, were murdered by thieves on November 10, 1973. The hero of the story is Tommy Jacobs, the Nashville police detective who solved the case. It isn't a bad book, and there is much grim, gray precision in it: "Police also found three empty beer cans in the kitchen. Three were missing from Stringbean's stock of two six-packs in the refrigerator. Raleigh and Marlboro cigarette butts were in the sink." *The Stringbean Murders* also reports what may be the tritest eulogy on record. It is by Maurice O'Neal, minister of Wingate Church of Christ: "String had a string of friends. Now there is a string of sadness." Death stay thy phantoms.

Not long after the murder of Stringbean, Kinky Friedman and I were sitting at breakfast one Sunday in the restaurant of a Holiday Inn in Houston. There was a quiet, after-church clientele, and Kinky rang a knife against a plate, stood, and solemnly declared, "Someone in this room killed Stringbean." Several persons, who were finished and ready to leave, hesitated lest their departure be interpreted as an admission of guilt.

There is also a novel about country-music crime, *The Grand Ole Opry Murders* by Marvin Kaye, published in 1974. (The paperback edition spurts, "Down-home hate and blue-grass vengeance when death plays Nashville.") Other country-music novels are *High Lonesome World* by Babs H. Deal, *Heart of Nashville* by Robert Vaughan, and, best of a bad lot, *Ruby Red* by William Price Fox. There's a fuckbook called *Snuff Queen,* but I don't recall the writer's name.

I think the essential country-music prose is found in fan publications such as *Music City News, Country Song Roundup,* and *Country Music.* A piece of writing I shall never forget is "Ray Griff: A Man with Three Countries" by Betty Hofer, published in the December 1974 issue of *Country Song Roundup*. Hofer seems to have studied under Red O'Donnell, or perhaps the great Dunkleberger himself:

> He's a man with *THREE* countries.
> Canada . . . the U.S. . . . and country music!

Several of the paragraphs include upward of ten words, and one of them begins, "But Bingo!"

The worst country-music writing, however, is found not in the pus-prose of the fan magazines, but in the pale regional publications of New York. In the cover story of the May 17, 1976, issue of *New York*, "Jimmy Carter's Clockwork Campaign Style" by Aaron Latham (who later blessed us with *Urban Cowboy*), the reader is told that to understand Carter, he must understand country music. Quotes from several country songs follow, but all the songs are from the film *Nashville*; not merely bad country songs, but fake country songs, written by Hollywood actors such as Henry Gibson. Readers feel the ingestion of a wisdom, and turn to the advertisements of Lucite brie-servers. Would *New York* publish an article on black politician Julian Bond that declared an understanding of blues necessary to an understanding of Bond's political style? An article that compounded bigotry with stupidity by quoting extensively from *Porgy and Bess*? But it is so much more comfortable, so much more acceptable to dislike rednecks than blacks.

Steve Young, a country singer born and raised in Alabama, played guitar in the early sixties for a folksy duet called Richard and Jim. Steve first visited California with them, where he attended the wedding of Richard and Mimi Fariña at the home of Joan Baez, who is Mimi's older sister. Steve recalls that Baez, butterfly of egalitarianism and wet-dream queen of liberals everywhere, was quite repulsed by the presence of a white Southern man.

The literature of country music has its scholarly side. Magazines such as *John Edwards Memorial Foundation Quarterly* in Los Angeles, *The Journal of Country Music* in Nashville, and *Old Time Music* in London seethe with matrix numbers, abstract obsessiveness, and historical detail. *The Journal of Country Music,* in its summer 1973 issue, audaciously printed something called "Esoteric-Exoteric Expectations of Redneck Behavior and Country Music" by Patricia Averill. One paragraph begins, "The same narrowing of options before overt actions and the influence of the S-X factor in that process can be seen in the other components of redneck behavior, and have been illustrated by other people." And you thought all they did was fuck chickens and pray.

The standard country-music history text is Bill C. Malone's *Country Music U.S.A.,* published in 1968. Malone's book was the first noble lunge out of darkness. *In a Narrow Grave,* Larry McMurtry's 1968 collection of essays on Texas, contained this note: "I had intended to include an essay on hillbilly music, but the impending publication of Mr. Malone's impressive study made such a chapter unnecessary. If anyone knows more about the subject than he does, God help them."

The most beautiful prose written of country music is probably "Some Real American Music" by Emma Bell Miles, a poet, teacher, and mountain woman of Tennessee, who was born in 1879 and died in 1919. "Some Real American Music" was printed in the June 1904 issue of *Harper's Monthly Magazine* and included in her 1905 book, *The Spirit of the Mountains.* Her treatment of country music is perceptive and bare of misknowing romance, and it has lost none of its power in the many years since its publication. In 1975 the University of Tennessee Press in Knoxville produced a facsimile edition of *The Spirit of the Mountains.* It's a captivating, eerie thing.

But Bingo!

Roy Acuff made his first records in Chicago in October 1936 for the American Record Corporation. Acuff was brought to ARC by William R. Calaway, an artist-and-repertoire man for the company. A native of Boone, North Carolina, Calaway had worked as a talent scout since the 1920s, and had been associated with the Gennett Record Company of Richmond, Indiana, before joining ARC. At ARC Calaway worked not only with country artists, but also with blues performers such as Charley Patton. Calaway had a bad reputation for stealing the copyrights of his singers. During an eight-year period, he deposited approximately 180 songs with the Copyright Office in Washington, D.C. The last copyright he attempted to register was "The Wabash Cannonball" in 1938. Acuff had cut the song for ARC in 1936, but the Carter Family had recorded the same song for Victor in November 1929 and submitted it for copyright through Southern Music in 1933, the year of its release. Calaway died in Orlando, Florida, about 1955. Several New York publishers have tried to contact his spirit, but have got no further than a rapping upon a table. The question remains: Is there P.D. after death?

Calaway had been impressed by Acuff's performances, and especially by a song he had heard Acuff sing during his noon radio program at WROL in Knoxville. The song was "The Great Speckled Bird," and Acuff had got it from Charlie Swain, leader of the Black Shirts, a group who also played at WROL. Acuff holds that he had heard bits of the song throughout his youth, and when he heard the Black Shirts perform a complete version, he had Swain write down a copy of the lyrics for him, for which service Swain charged fifty cents.

The melody of "The Great Speckled Bird" is ancient and British. The Carter Family had used it in their 1929 Victor recording "I'm Thinking Tonight of My Blue Eyes." The same melody was used later in the honky-tonk classic

"The Wild Side of Life," the mournful and bitter song that Texas songwriter William Warren wrote about his wife. (The song was first cut by Jimmy Heap and the Melody Masters for Imperial. Hank Thompson covered it for Capitol. It was released as a B side and became the biggest country hit of 1952.)

Folklorist Vance Randolph collected a version of "The Great Speckled Bird" in Pawhuska, Oklahoma, where it was sung as an Assembly of God Hymn; and Wilbur J. Cash in his 1941 book, *The Mind of the South*, wrote of "a curious song, entitled 'The Great Speckled Bird of God' and sung quaintly to the tune of 'Blue Eyes,'" that was used as the official hymn of the Church of God.

W. J. Cash was right when he described the song as curious. "The Great Speckled Bird" escapes complete comprehension. The title is from the Bible (Jer. 12:9): "Mine heritage is unto me as a speckled bird, the birds round about are against her; come ye, assemble all beasts of the field, come to devour." This line is one of the great mysteries of biblical scholarship. One interpretation is that the speckled bird is a vulture. Others see it as a hen attacked by hawks, a bloodied bird, a fine exotic creature attacked for its plumage, or simply a dull fowl. Some scholars have translated the words into English as, "Mine heritage is unto me as a bird with talons." How could a song rooted in such an abstruse metaphor be anything but curious?

"The Great Speckled Bird" (1937) was Roy Acuff's first hit. It was a great performance and one of the few truly mystical country records ever cut.

Many of the recordings Acuff made before 1940 were fine country sides, but as time passed Acuff's music became stale and tedious. When he first performed at the Grand Ole Opry in February 1938, the Opry was not too concerned with singers. Since its earliest broadcasts in November 1925 (at first the program was described as

only a "barn dance"; late in 1927 it acquired the name
Grand Ole Opry), fiddlers and string bands had been the
featured performers. There were exceptions. The first
and best-known was Uncle Dave Macon (born David
Harrison Macon on October 7, 1870, in Smart Station, near
McCinnville, Tennessee; he died on March 22, 1952, in
Murfreesboro, Tennessee), the singing and banjo-playing
vaudeville star who joined the Opry on December 26,
1925. Later there were the Vagabonds (Herald Goodman,
Curt Poulton, and Dean Upson), the smooth-crooning
trio who joined the Opry in 1931. In 1933 Asher Sizemore
and Little Jimmy, his son, came to the Opry; their specialty
was Mom-death-sin. The Delmore Brothers (Alton, born
on December 25, 1908, in Elkmont, Alabama, and Rabon,
born on December 3, 1916, also in Elkmont; Rabon died
in 1952, Alton in 1964) joined the Opry in the spring of
1933. The Delmores, pioneers of country boogie, made a
music characterized by sharp harmonies, hot guitar licks,
and wry lyrics. In 1936 Pee Wee King (born on February
18, 1914), a polka-playing Polack from Milwaukee, who
led a group called the Golden West Cowboys, came to the
Opry. An agent named J. L. Frank was responsible for
getting Pee Wee King on the Opry, and it was to Frank
that Acuff came after several unsuccessful attempts to
perform on the Opry. Frank spoke with David Stone,
head of WSM's Artists' Service Bureau, and it was done.
Previously Acuff had dealt directly with George Hay,
who didn't feel Acuff belonged with the Opry.

Acuff soon became one of the most popular performers on the Opry. More than any other single person,
he was responsible for bringing about a reversal of the
Opry's original paradigm; never again would the old string
bands be as important as the new vocalists and their new
and synthetic country songs. From now on, the Opry
would reflect the ways of mainstream, commercial country
music. (At times the Opry has pretended a vainglory

purity, as in its ban on the use of full drum kits during Opry broadcasts.)

Roy Acuff was the avatar of the new Opry, and he loved it. During World War II, Dizzy Dean, a friend of Acuff's, started calling him the King of the Hillbillies. This was later changed to the King of Country Music. Acuff reached the apex of his popularity during the forties. Each performance on the Opry of "The Great Speckled Bird," "The Wabash Cannonball," and "Wreck on the Highway" waxed more pompous, as if he were tossing lotus petals of country-music history or baring a pontifical foot for the kissing. In 1948 Acuff ran for governor of Tennessee as the Republican candidate. He and senatorial candidate Carroll Reece toured the state with a twelve-man band, a portable stage, and two truckloads of props. Reece's speech damned the civil-rights movement and the Commies, praised the TVA. Acuff said, "I'm not a politician. I'm just a country boy, trying to run things as honest and square as possible." Tennessee did not bite.

The truth of the matter is that the King of Country Music has not had a Top Ten record in thirty years, and the last time he hit the Top Forty was in 1959. One would tax credibility less by calling Aldo Ray the King of the Cinema. But Acuff has little to worry about financially. In 1942 he put up $25,000 to form Acuff–Rose Publications with Fred Rose, and the company has become the most successful publisher of country music in Nashville.

Roy Acuff enjoys upholding the morals of the United States. John McEuen of the Nitty Gritty Dirt Band, who worked with Acuff and others in the 1971 United Artists album *Will the Circle Be Unbroken*, described the synergy: "Acuff didn't need the money. Wesley Rose talked him into it. He's a little touchy, Acuff. Been in the business like seventy years. He invented the record player. Later he said about us, 'I like those boys, but I can't see 'em with all that hair they got all up around their faces and all.'" Jeff Hanna, also a member of the Nitty Gritty Dirt Band, said, "Acuff made a couple of nasty remarks about Earl Scruggs in front of him. We were sittin' around this big table and Acuff says something about people changin', and then he turns and looks at Earl in a real snide sort of way." McEuen again, "Yeah, right. And then we're driving down the street later with Earl, who's one of those very gentle, soft-spoken, old-time country guys, and he turns to me and he says, 'You know, John, that Acuff really burns my ass. He thinks he invented country music.'"

But, once upon a time, Roy Acuff recorded smut.

At that first recording session in 1936, Acuff and his band cut "When Lulu's Gone" and "Doin' It the Old Fashioned Way," which were issued under the name of the Bang Boys on the Vocalion label late that year. (When the New Lost City Ramblers recorded a seven-inch LP of dirty songs, *Earth Is Earth*, for Folkways in the early 1960s, they took the name of the Bang Boys in commemoration.)

"When Lulu's Gone," rooted in traditional smutsong, is a fast record with a strong bass line and much heady fiddling.

> *I wish I was a diamond ring upon my Lulu's hand,*
> *Every time she'd take her bath, I'd be a lucky man—*
> *Oh, lordy, bang away my Lulu, bang away good and*
>   *strong:*
> *What're ya gonna do for bangin' when Lulu's gone?*

How much more interesting than the dullnesses of senescence and yo-yo!

Clarence Tom Ashley (born on September 29, 1895, in Bristol, Tennessee) was, with Dock Walsh, a founder of the Carolina Tar Heels in 1925. About 1932 Ashley performed with Roy Acuff in a medicine-show act (Acuff wore blackface), and it is interesting that Ashley too recorded a Lulu song, "Shout Little Lulu." It was cut in

1966, when Ashley was seventy-one years old (he died the following year), and released in the Folkways album *Clarence Ashley and Tex Isley*.

> *How many nickels does it take*
> *To see little Lulu's body shake?*
> *It takes a nickel and it takes a dime*
> *To see little Lulu cut her shine.*

The song was also recorded by George Banman Grayson and Henry Whitter in 1928 for Gennett, under the title "Shout Lula." Ashley carried another fine smutsong down through the years. It's called "Farm Girl."

> *I plow her land, and then I sow my seed;*
> *She loves her daddy because I'm long and hard.*

There are more than a few other country songs from the 1920s and '30s that WWVA would hurl. Could Darby and Tarlton's "Ooze Up to Me" even be considered for airplay? What of Fiddlin' Bob Larkin's 1929 Okeh record "Women Wear No Clothes At All"? Or the 1931 Columbia recording of "It Won't Hurt No More" by Buster Carter and Preston Young?

> *Just lay down and open it wide*
> *Because I want to rub it a while.*

The early repertoire of Gene Autry was not unlike that of Jimmie Davis. Before he stopped recording smut in the early 1930s, Autry had cut titles such as "Wild Cat Mama," "She's a Low-Down Mama," "She's a Hum Dum Dinger" (the Jimmie Davis song), and "Do Right Daddy Blues," which includes the memorable stanza:

> *Now you can feel my legs*
> *And you can feel my thighs,*
> *But if you feel my legs*
> *You gotta ride me high.*

This was recorded for Victor on February 18, 1931. Later these lines emerged in "Don't You Make Me High," cut by Merline Johnson (the Yas-Yas Girl) for Vocalion on October 4, 1938.

Cliff Carlisle, born Clifford Raymond Carlisle on May 6, 1904, in Mount Eden, Kentucky, is one of the finest steel-guitarists in country music and one of the most exciting old-timey singers. "My music is a cross between hillbilly and blues," he said. "Even Hawaiian music has sort of a blues to it." Of the three great post-Rodgers yodelers (Autry, Carlisle, and Davis), he yodeled the longest and the best. In July 1933, in New York City, Carlisle recorded two songs about defloration for the American Record Corporation, "Sal's Got a Meat Skin" and "Mouse's Ear Blues."

> *My little mama, she's got a mouse's ear,*
> *My little mama, she's got a mouse's ear,*
> *But she's gonna lose it when I shift my gear.*

> *Gonna take my mouse's ear for a midnight ride,*
> *Gonna take my mouse's ear for a midnight ride,*
> *Gonna use my old straight eight cuz it's long and wide.**

Carlisle cut many such songs: "My Rockin' Mama" for Bluebird in 1936, "High-Steppin' Mama" for Decca in 1937, and, perhaps his best, "That Nasty Swing," recorded for Bluebird in 1934.

* "Mouse's Ear Blues" by Cliff Carlisle. Copyright © 1974 by Acuff–Rose Publications, Inc. Used by permission of the publisher. All rights reserved.

Cliff Bruner's Boys, 1939. Left to right: Moon Mullican, Acee Peveto (steel guitar), Logan Conger, Cliff Bruner, Buddy Dukon, Cotton Plant, KPAC radio announcer.

> *Wind my motor, honey,*
> *I've got a double spring;*
> *Place the needle in that hole*
> *And do that nasty swing.*
> *Yodelayeeyodelayeeyodelayee.*

The master of smutsong in the 1930s was a man named Buddy Jones. He was a close friend of Jimmie Davis's and worked in the Shreveport police force while Davis was involved in city government. He recorded for Decca from 1936 to 1942. (His first recordings were duets with Davis.) The band used in most of Jones's sessions was Cliff Bruner's, which went under different names: Cliff Bruner's Texas Wanderers, Cliff Bruner's Boys, and so on. (Born Clifton L. Bruner on April 25, 1915, in Texas, Cliff started out as a fiddler with Milton Brown and His Musical Brownies in 1936. He formed his own group—

Cliff Bruner's Texas Wanderers in the 1940s. Left to right: Albert Gonzales, Harris Dodd, Lee Bell, John Wallace, Cliff Bruner, Pete Bumgartner, Buddy Dukon.

Bruner, fiddle; Bob Dunn, electric steel guitar; Moon Mullican, piano; Dickie McBride, guitar; Hezzie Brock, bass; and Will Raley, electric mandolin—and recorded extensively for Decca, under his own name and with Jimmie Davis, Buddy Jones, the Shelton Brothers, and others.)

Buddy Jones was born in 1906, and he died on October 20, 1956, following a lunch of catfish and chili. At the time of his death, he was a lieutenant with twenty years behind him on the Shreveport police force. (He had performed his last show in January of 1955, at a local March of Dimes benefit featuring Elvis Presley and Johnny Horton.) Bruner first met Jones in 1935, when Jimmie Davis came to Houston to record at the Rice Hotel. Davis brought Buddy and Buddy's kid brother, Buster, who later wrote many of the songs Buddy recorded and played steel guitar at several of his sessions.

Some of the songs Buddy Jones recorded for Decca are "Butcher Man Blues" (1937), "Evil Stingaree" (1938), "She's Sellin' What She Used to Give Away" (1938), "Small Town Mama" (1938), "Rockin' Rollin' Mama" (1939), "Hold It a Little Longer" (1939), "Roughest Gal in Town" (1939), "Easy Rollin' Sue" (1939), and "She's a Hum-Dum-Dinger" (1941). In his best records, Jones is crude and happy. In "Easy Rollin' Mama," he describes his beloved.

> *She rolls her head,*
> *She rolls her eyes,*
> *But she knocks 'em dead*
> *When she rolls her thighs.*

Bruner recalls that Buddy Jones was a quiet man and "very clean-cut." He didn't smoke, or drink, or have any bad habits as far as Bruner remembers.

Milton Brown and His Musical Brownies recorded a couple of sexy records in the late 1930s for Decca. One was "Somebody's Been Using That Thing," recorded in 1936. The other, more interesting record was "Cheesy Breeze," cut in 1935. "Cheesy Breeze" is basically an instrumental, featuring a severely raunchy break by steel-guitarist Bob Dunn, that ends with a very surreal and essentially lewd couplet.

The Tune Wranglers' 1936 Bluebird recording of "Red's Tight Like That" was based on the 1928 blues hit "It's Tight Like That," recorded by Tampa Red for Vocalion. (Louis Armstrong and Clara Smith both covered the song for Okeh shortly after the original hit. McKinney's Cotton Pickers covered it for Victor.) In the Tune Wranglers' record is one of the strongest lyrics in country music.

> *She couldn't come at all,*
> *She pulled up her stockin' and leaned against the wall.*
> *Oh, it's tight like that.*

"Pussy, Pussy, Pussy" was a minor Western-swing classic, recorded for Vocalion in 1939 by the Light Crust Doughboys, and for Bluebird in 1940 by Bill Boyd and His Cowboy Ramblers. It was a novelty record, a double entendre, not as daring, or as good, as the stuff Davis, Jones, and others had already recorded.

"Truckin'," written by Ted Koehler (author of "Stormy Monday") and Rube Bloom (author of "Fools Rush In"), was one of the most successful songs of 1935. A dance song full of whimsical sexual implications, it was introduced by Cora LaRedd in the twenty-sixth edition of the Cotton Club Parade at the Cotton Club in New York City, and was immediately recorded by many artists. In July and August alone, "Truckin'" was cut by the Mills Blue Rhythm Band, the Little Ramblers, Joe Haymes, Henry Allen, and Duke Ellington. In the months and years that followed "Truckin'," many derivative songs appeared, some of which turned up on country records, such as "Keep On Truckin'" by Smoky Wood and His Wood Chips (Bluebird, 1937), "Can't Nobody Truck Like Me" (written by Moon Mullican) by Cliff Bruner's Texas Wanderers (Decca, 1937), "Everybody's Truckin'" by the Modern Mountaineers (Bluebird, 1937), and "Keep Truckin'" by the Hi Neighbor Boys (Vocalion, 1939). The Modern Mountaineers' record included *that* word.

In his 1947 King record "Let Me Play with Your Poodle" (written by Tampa Red), Hank Penny compared his girlfriend's crotch to "the face of a teddy bear." The record was withdrawn from the market, and a new record (Penny's version of "Open the Door Richard") was issued bearing its catalogue number.

One of my favorite country smut records is "Operation Blues" by Homer Clemons and His Texas Swingbillies. Based somewhat on Georgia Tom's 1930 "Terrible Operation Blues," it was recorded for Blue Bonnet of Dallas in 1947, then leased to Modern of Los Angeles, which issued it in September of that year.

Now, won't you climb up on this table,
Jerk up that gown.
Raise up that left leg,
Let that right leg down;
Pull off them stockin's,
That silk underwear,
Cuz the doctor's got to cut you, mama,
Don't know where.

In the early fifties dirty country songs were rare. (Ted West's "She Bent My Pole" on Republic was one of the last glimmers of a fading genre.) But sleazy country songs were common: grim honky-tonk tales of adultery and shame and tears. Welcome to the Age of Guilt!

Rockabilly brought a lot of visceral fun back into country music, but since the early 1960s the sacred sin-guilt-pain schema has dominated the soul of country music: *Lacrimo ergo sum,* and bring the strings up a few decibels.

Freddy Weller recorded country music's only lesbian song, "Betty Ann and Shirley Cole," released in his 1973 album *Too Much Monkey Business.* There is not a surface plenty of faggotry in country music, either. But if you ever have the opportunity, hear Cowboy Jack Derrick's "Truck Drivin' Man," released by King in 1946. In his raspy baritone, Cowboy Jack anticipates the return of his main squeeze:

When my truck drivin' man comes back to town,
I'll dress up in my silken gown.

Shit, you don't hear Johnny Cash singing stuff like *that!* San Francisco journalist Howie Klein, who in the 1970s specialized in covering country music for queer magazines such as *Vector,* reviewed Willie Nelson's 1975 *Red Headed Stranger* album under the title "Saddle Up": "I'll put Willie's lyrics up against Barry White's as an exponent of the 'gay' experience any day of the week," wrote Howie.

A song very close in spirit to the smutsongs of Jimmie Davis and Buddy Jones is Mack Vickery's "Meat Man," recorded by Jerry Lee Lewis in 1973. The words "Maytag tongue" will live on.

We close our lecture on rustic smut with two thoughts. First: "I'm not a prude; I've been around some in my day. But there are things that are sacred in American life. What are we supposed to do, just go . . . FUCK?" (Roy Rogers, *Esquire*, December 1975). Second: The Country Music Foundation in Nashville possesses two interviews with promoter Oscar Davis (also known as the Baron). In his long and colorful career, Davis had worked intimately with Ernest Tubb, Hank Snow, Roy Acuff, Eddy Arnold, Hank Williams, Elvis Presley (whom Davis introduced to Colonel Tom Parker), and hundreds more. The Country Music Foundation interviews were recorded in July through November of 1974 and comprise thirteen tapes. Davis was in his seventies, partially paralyzed, and he felt the end to be near. He had nothing to lose, and he told it all: a great, glorious, scandalous *Who Fucked Who* of country music, full of homosexuality, pedophilia, and motel drunk-fucks. The CMF allows absolutely no access to these tapes.

And what about dope? Dick Justice recorded a hillbilly version of "Cocaine" for Brunswick in 1929. There is a reference to opium in "Keep on Truckin'" by Smoky Wood and His Wood Chips. "I can sell you morphine, coke, or snow," sings Tommy Duncan in the 1937 recording of "I'm a Ding Dong Daddy from Dumas." (There are other country recordings of "Ding Dong Daddy," such as that of Zeb and Zeke, but none contain this drug line.) The song was written and first performed by Phil Baxter in the summer of 1928. Louis Armstrong cut a hit version of it in 1930, and the Benny Goodman Quartet performed it in the 1937 film *Hollywood Hotel*. Even Arthur Godfrey cut in.

David Allan Coe's "Cocaine Carolina" refers to both

cocaine and heroin, and it was cut in 1975 by none other than Johnny Cash.

I think that country music's only timeless contribution to drug music is "Benzedrine Blues," recorded by the Texas Rhythm Boys for Royalty Records at an indeterminable time in the 1940s.

Five years after amphetamine was first synthesized in 1927, Benzedrine was introduced to the pharmaceutical marketplace and the age of speed began. It soon became a fairly common drug, and magazines enjoyed yelling of its threat to youthful morality. From "Benzedrine Thrill Party," *Whisper* magazine: "The kids become hopped up, not only from the drug but also because they feel they're living dangerously—like those Big Time Broadway–Hollywood heroes do." There is a photo: A girl lies dead in nylon stockings and undies. There is a headline: "Idaho Outlaws Benzedrine As Kids Misuse It."

The melody of "Benzedrine Blues" is a familiar one, very similar to that used by Bill Cox and Cliff Hobbs in their 1937 "Franklin Roosevelt's Back Again," and by Harvey and Earl Shirky in their 1930 "We Have Moonshine in the West Virginia Hills."

> *Throw away your Ovaltine,*
> *Buy yourself some Benzedrine,*
> *And roll, roll, roll on down the line.*
> *On down the line,*
> > *On down the line,*
> *On down the line,*
> > *On down the line:*
> *Just take a pill and roll on down the line.*
> *You can go on a coffee diet,*
> *It makes you laugh and dance all night,*
> *It gives you atomic energy.*

At a 1947 Hank Penny session at Castle Studio in Nashville, someone slipped Benzedrine into Red Foley's Coke. Foley was a boozer, but unlike many of his Nash-

From Hello, I'm Johnny Cash, *a Spire Christian Comic by Johnny Cash with Billy Zeoli and Al Hartley. Copyright © 1976 by House of Cash. Published by Fleming H. Revell Company. Used by permission.*

ville drinking buddies, he was innocent of drugs. His rhythm-guitar work at the session, which produced "Hillbilly Jump," "Got the Louisiana Blues," "Sweet Talkin' Mama," and others, was especially intense. He complained that he couldn't sleep for several days afterward.

Johnny Cash was arrested in El Paso in 1964 for "smuggling and concealing" 688 Dexedrine capsules and 475 Equanil tablets. "I'd talk to the demons," Cash said in 1975, "and they'd talk back to me—and I could *hear* them. I mean, they'd say, 'Go on, John, take twenty more milligrams of Dexedrine, you'll be all right.'"

Lulu of "Hee Haw" (best leg show on TV) was busted in Dallas in the winter of 1970 for possession of five and a half pounds of reefer. On her wall was a Day-Glo poster of Roy Clark which bore the legend TAKE MY SEED, DAUGHTER OF THE FEN.

I asked Cliff Bruner if drugs were popular among Western-swing musicians in Texas. He wrote: "This is a hard question to answer. I must say that a very few musicians fooled around with drugs—and when they did, it was controlled more than today. Only marijuana or a 'Bennie' or so—none of the *hard* drugs (heroin, etc.) like today. We had a few 'boozers' but usually under control while playing."

BENZEDRENE BLUES
(Edwards)
Alvin Edwards and His Band

West Virginia Hills Are in the Bronx, Says Barn Barnum

New York, Feb. 27.—Real hillbillies rarely have good night club acts, says Meyer Horowitz, who ought to know. Jewish and Italian hillbillies usually outshine all others on showmanship, he says.

Meyer is the owner of the Village Barn, New York's most successful night club using the homespun motif. Ever since he opened the Barn eight years ago he has been having a tough time finding sock hillbilly acts.

Native-born hillbillies from the sticks usually provide entertaining music, but in most cases they're short on comedy and showmanship. As a result, synthetic hillbillies are as a rule more desirable in a night club than the real ones.

One of his most successful acts was a trio—Annie, Judy and Zeke—all three of Spanish-American descent.

Crockett's Mountaineers followed for a six-month run. They were part Indian. Then came Louis Pope and Nellie Thompson (Italian and Irish), who stayed for six months.

—*Billboard*,
March 4, 1939

You're Going To
Watch Me Kill Her

Spade Cooley was born in 1910 in Grand, Oklahoma. His full name was Donnell Clyde Cooley. During the late 1940s Spade Cooley and His Orchestra were one of the most popular of the California-based Western-swing bands. These California bands were a new sort of Western swing: slicker, closer to the popular swing music of the era, and wholly devoted to large orchestrations. (In 1949 Tex Williams had a harpist, Spike Featherstone, in his band. In the summer of 1948 it was reported that Ted Daffan was leaving Texas for the Coast, where he would organize a twenty-seven-piece band, but nothing came of it.) Bob Wills and His Texas Playboys moved to the Coast in 1943, and soon Western-swing dances at Venice Pier and Redondo Beach presented not only Wills, but also the new breed of Western-swing bands, led by men such as Spade Cooley, Tex Williams (who had been the

singer on many of Cooley's early records), and Hank
Penny. Hank Thompson, who represents an even later,
more pop-influenced style of Western swing, recalls seeing
Wills and Cooley and others perform at Redondo Beach
while he was stationed by the navy in San Pedro during
the war. Hank says it was not uncommon to see "ten thousand people out at that pier."

Spade Cooley first recorded for Columbia on November 4, 1944, in Hollywood. (He had recorded previously,
but only as part of Cal Shrum's band, about 1941.) At his
first Columbia session, Cooley cut the biggest hit of his
career, "Shame on You," released on January 15, 1945.
Cooley stayed with Columbia until 1946. He recorded for
RCA-Victor from 1947 to 1950, and then he went to Decca,
where he stayed until 1955. Cooley was featured in two
musical films: *Spade Cooley, King of Western Swing*, a
ten-minute short produced in 1945 by Warner Brothers,
and *Spade Cooley and His Orchestra*, a thirty-five-minute
film produced in 1949 by Universal.

In December 1945, Cooley married his second wife,
Ella Mae, who was twenty-one years old. When Cooley
had a television program in the 1950s, Ella Mae played
fiddle in his band. Cooley had three children: a daughter,
Melody, born in 1947, and two sons, John, born in 1933
(with his first wife, Ann), and Donnell, Jr., born in 1948.

In 1945, the year of his second marriage, Spade
Cooley was arrested for rape in California. He was
acquitted.

He retired from television in 1958 and became involved with businessmen in a plan to build a recreational
park in the Mojave Desert, called Water Wonderland.
The digging of artificial lakes began.

Ella Mae bragged to many of her acquaintances that
she fucked Roy Rogers. Spade apparently believed that
for a time, but before he died, says Roy, tried to apologize
to Roy for having accepted Ella Mae's story. (Spade and

Roy were old friends. On several occasions Cooley worked
as a stand-in for Rogers in the younger singer's films.)

On the evening of April 3, 1961, he arrived at his
home in Willow Springs, about eighty-five miles north of
L.A. He had been drinking and eating pills. There was an
argument. Spade began beating Ella Mae. He forced
his daughter to sit.

"You're going to watch me kill her," he said.

Bobbie Bennett, Cooley's female manager, came to
the house. Cooley's wife was naked, bruised and red and
dying. Her breasts had been burned with a cigarette.
Spade stood there, in shock. There was blood on his fancy
cowboy boots. The sheriff was called at eleven o'clock.

On April 25 in Bakersfield, a murder indictment was
returned against Cooley. He was convicted of first-degree
murder, largely on the testimony of his fourteen-year-old
daughter. On August 22 Superior Judge William L. Brad-
shaw sentenced the King of Western Swing to life im-
prisonment. As the verdict was read, Cooley slumped.
In a cracked voice he said there was nothing he wished
to say.

Cooley had written a letter to his friend Hank Penny
on April 10, a week after the murder.

Cooley sat in Vacaville, a prison forty miles northeast of Oakland, for years. In August 1969, it was announced that he had been granted a parole and that he would be released on February 2, 1970. On November 23, he was granted an evening leave to perform in an Oakland show sponsored by the Alameda County Deputy Sheriffs Association. He was received well and given standing applause. During intermission he collapsed and died of a heart attack.

One of Cooley's last Decca recordings in the 1950s featured a woman, Betsy Gay, singing a song Cooley had written: "You Clobbered Me."

Cowboys
and Niggers

Minstrelsy was a Northern love. Its first star was Thomas Dartmouth Rice (1808–1860), a touring actor who parodied the song and steps of an old black stable-worker in Louisville. Rice began performing the "Jim Crow" in 1828. He wrote most of the lyrics around the found refrain:

> Wheel about and turn about and do jis so,
> Eb'ry time I wheel about I jump Jim Crow.

Rice brought the song back to New York City, and it was a success. He traveled abroad, making "Jim Crow" the first international hit of America when he premiered it in London in 1836. The year before, Alexis de Tocqueville had observed in his *Democracy in America* that "the prejudice of race appears to be stronger in the states which have abolished slavery than in those where it still exists; and nowhere is it so important as in those states where servitude never has been known."

The first minstrel troupe was formed in New York City. The Virginia Minstrels (Dan Emmett, Frank Brower, Dick Pelham, and Billy Whitlock) gave their first performance on February 6, 1843, at the Bowery Amphitheatre. Three months later, the Virginia Minstrels had a six-week engagement in London. Other troupes were organized: the Kentucky Minstrels, the Ring and Parker Minstrels, the Congo Melodists (who became Buckley's New Orleans Serenaders), and the Christy Minstrels.

Southern minstrels were rare. Lew Dockstader was from Hartford, Connecticut. Dick José and Honey Boy Evans were from Great Britain. Al Jolson was from New York City. Even Bert Williams, the famous black minstrel, was not of the South.

Minstrelsy lingered into the twentieth century. Issues of *Billboard* in the 1930s still published advertisements for minstrelsy catalogues ("Fast, Furious Fun for Your Minstrel Show"). *Billboard* published a "Minstrelsy" column regularly until June 10, 1939. Then, twenty-three years later, the Rolling Stones gave us a new sort of minstrelsy. It was minstrelsy without blackface, but minstrelsy just the same.

In the early years of the recording industry, minstrel records were common. Some of Edison's most popular cylinders were minstrelsy: Banjoist Vess Ossman's "Darkey Tickle" (1896), "Nigger in a Fit" (1896), and "Little Pickaninnies" (1899); Arthur Collins's "Nigger, Nigger Neber Die" (1899), "Every Race Has a Flag but the Coons" (1900), and "Coonville Cullid Band" (1904); Ada Jones's "Songs My Mammy Sang for Me" (1905), "Bull-Frog and the Coon" (1906), and "If the Man in the Moon Were a Coon" (1906). A 1901 Columbia catalogue lists minstrelsy records such as "De Sweetest 'Backer Is Nigger

COLLINS, ARTHUR, Comedian

Co

COPY'T CHANNELL

COLLINS

Mr. Collins is one of the most successful singers of "coon songs" now before the public. His success in this particular type of song is quite unique and is due in a large measure to the sympathetic, human way in which his own delightful personality reveals itself through his records. In addition he has a splendid voice and a wonderful faculty for making the words sound clear and understandable, which is no easy task in dialect songs. Mr. Collins is quite able to please his hearers in this respect, and he is always entertaining both in solos and in the clever duets made with Mr. Harlan. The charm of this special kind of art seems to have a never-failing appeal for the American public, and we are fortunate to have a past master of the art to represent us.

COLLINS RECORDS

Any Rags (Allen) and *Every Little Bit Added* (Dillon) *Arthur Collins*	16215	10	.85
Every Little Bit Added to What You've Got and *Any Rags—Arthur Collins*	16215	10	.85
Ghost of the Banjo Coon (O'Dea) and *Aunt Mandy—Golden and Hughes*	17011	10	.85
Hot Tamale Man (Ingraham) and *Uncle Josh and the Billiken—Cal Stewart*	16293	10	.85
I Got To See the Minstrel Show and *Medley of Reels—Accordion—Kimmel*	16171	10	.85
I'm Going Way Back Home and *Stormy Sea of Love—O'Connell*	18072	10	.85
I Think I See My Brother Coming and *Flanagan on Broadway Car—Porter*	16015	10	.85
Moving Day (Sterling-Von Tilzer) and *Original Cohens—Jones and Spencer*	16110	10	.85
Preacher and the Bear and *Bake dat Chicken Pie—Collins-Harlan*	17221	10	.85
Steamboat Bill and *Mississippi Dippy Dip—Arthur Collins and Byron G. Harlan*	16937	10	.85
When Uncle Joe Plays a Rag and *Down at Mammy Jinny's—"That Girl"* Q	17118	10	.85

COLLINS and HARLAN—Comic Duets and Specialties

Alexander's Ragtime Band (Berlin) and *Oceana Roll—Eddie Morton*	16908	10	.85
At the Levee on Revival Day and *Darktown Editors—Golden and Heins*	17300	10	.85
Auntie Skinner's Chicken Dinner and *Little Ford Rambled—Murray*	17755	10	.85
Bake Dat Chicken Pie and *Preacher and Bear—Collins*	17221	10	.85
Buzzin' the Bee and *They're Wearing Them Higher—Collins-Harlan*	18210	10	.85
Casey Jones Went Down and *When Midnight Choo-Choo—Collins-Harlan*	17246	10	.85
Cat and the Fly Paper and *Who Do You Love—Collins and Harlan*	16170	10	.85
Closing Time in Country Grocery and *Krausmeyer—Spencer and Holt*	17255	10	.85
Come Along to Caroline and *Don't Leave Me, Daddy—Marion Harris*	18185	10	.85
Come On to Nashville and *Oh! How She Could Yacki Hacki Woo*	18110	10	.85
Down in Bom-Bombay and *Just Try to Picture Me—Collins-Harlan*	17841	10	.85
Down in Georgia on Campmeeting Day and *Oh, You Coon—Jones-Murray*	16018	10	.85
Down in Jungle Town and *Uncle Josh and Lightning Rod Agent—Stewart*	16805	10	.85
Everybody's Jazzin' It and *When He's All Dolled Up—Harlan*	18303	10	.85
Ghost of the Saxophone and *Mammy Blossom's Possum Party—Collins-Harlan*	18354	10	.85
Hello, Summer! and *The Honolulu Blues—Peerless* Qt	18068	10	.85
Honest Injun and *The Two-Key Rag—Collins and Harlan*	18128	10	.85
If You Saw All That I Saw in Arkansaw and *Old Grey Mare—Collins-Harlan*	18387	10	.85
I'm Saving Up Means Get to New Orleans and *My Lovin' Lou—Collins-Harlan*	18089	10	.85
International Rag and *On the Honeymoon Express—Collins-Harlan*	17431	10	.85
I Want to be in Dixie (Berlin) and *Snap Your Fingers (Von Tilzer)* Jolson	17075	10	.85
Just Try to Picture Me and *Down in Bom-Bombay—Collins-Harlan*	17841	10	.85
Kid is Clever and *Yaaka Hula Hickey Dula—Collins-Harlan*	18014	10	.85
Lily of the Valley and *When I Hear That Jazz Band Play—Harris*	18398	10	.85
Mammy Blossom's 'Possum Party and *Ghost of the Saxophone—Collins-Harlan*	18354	10	.85
Mississippi Barbecue (Dave Reed) and *Memphis Blues—Harvey*	17657	10	.85
Mississippi Dippy Dip (Walker) and *Steamboat Bill—Arthur Collins*	16937	10	.85
Moonlight in Jungle Land and *Casey Jones—Murray and American Quartet*	16483	10	.85
My Gal Irene and *Down on Uncle Jasper's Farm—Porter and Harlan*	17307	10	.85
My Lovin' Lou and *I'm Saving Up the Means to Get to N. O.—Collins and Harlan*	18089	10	.85
Nigger Loves His Possum and *Turkey in Straw—Golden*	17256	10	.85
Night Time in Little Italy and *Oh, Lady—Collins-Harlan*	18262	10	.85
Oh! How She Could Yacki Hacki and *Come On to Nashville—Collins-Harlan*	18110	10	.85
Oh, Lady and *Night Time in Little Italy—Collins-Harlan*	18262	10	.85
Old Grey Mare and *If You Saw All That I Saw in Arkansaw—Collins-Harlan*	18387	10	.85
On the Honeymoon Express and *International Rag—Collins-Harlan*	17431	10	.85
Pickin' Cotton and *Mobile Minstrels—Victor Minstrel Co*	17293	10	.85
Put Your Arms Around Me, Honey and *U. S. A. Patrol—Xylophone—Reitz*	16708	10	.85
Sugar Moon and *Down in Turkey Hollow—Billy Golden and Wm. Hughes*	16540	10	.85
That Funny Jazz Band from Dixieland and *Honolulu Hicki Boola Boo—Am.* Qt	18235	10	.85
They're Wearing Them Higher and *Buzzin' the Bee—Collins-Harlan*	18210	10	.85
Two-Key Rag and *Honest Injun—Collins-Harlan*	18128	10	.85
Way Down in Borneo-o-o-o and *On Old Dominion Line—Qt*	18067	10	.85
When the Midnight Choo-Choo and *Casey Jones Went Down—Collins-Harlan*	17246	10	.85
When Uncle Joe Steps Into France and *Good-Bye Alexander—Harris*	18492	10	.85

Twist," "Jolly Darkeys," and "No Coon Can Come Too Black for Me." In its 1917 catalogue, Columbia still advertised coon songs, but a bit more demurely. Under the heading Coon Songs, the reader is advised to "See: Negro Songs and Plantation Airs," where he finds airs such as "Nigger Love a Watermelon, Ha! Ha! Ha!" and "I'se Gwine Back to Dixie." The minstrel Bert Williams was an exclusive Columbia artist.

In its 1920 catalogue, under Coon Songs and Specialties, Victor printed the following:

> NOTE—By "coon songs" are meant up-to-date comic songs in negro dialect. The humor of many of these songs cannot be called refined, and for that reason we have distinguished them from old-fashioned darky humor, these songs being listed under "Fisk Jubilee Quartet," "Negro Songs," and "Tuskegee."

Coon songs were usually published by the important New York companies. "All Coons Look Alike to Me," written by a coon, was copyrighted in 1896 by M. Witmark & Sons, the company that published many of Bob Dylan's songs in the 1960s.

Many minstrel songs are found in the repertoires of early country singers. (Some country singers, such as Jimmie Rodgers, Bob Wills, and Roy Acuff, worked as blackface performers early in their careers.) Records such as Fisher Hendley's "Nigger, Will You Work" (Okeh, 1925), Charlie Parker and Mack Woolbright's "Give That Nigger Ham" (Columbia, 1927), Uncle Tom Collins's "Every Race Has a Flag but the Coons" (Okeh, 1927), Herschell Brown's "Talking Nigger Blues" (Okeh, 1927), Dr. Smith's Champion Hoss Hair Pullers' "Nigger Baby" (Victor, 1928), Uncle Dave Macon's "The Coon That Had the Razor" (Brunswick, 1928), Earl Johnson's Dixie Entertainers' "Nigger in the Cotton Patch" (Okeh, 1929),

JAMUP and HONEY
STARS OF
W S M GRAND OLE OPRY

Hatch Show Print, Nashville, 3, Tenn.

Jamup and Honey (Bunny Biggs and Lee Davis "Honey" Wilds), blackface Opry regulars of the 1930s and '40s.

and Bill Cox's "Nigger Loves a Watermelon" (Supertone, 1929) were drawn from minstrelsy. After 1930 extremely little minstrel material turned up in country records. Some strikingly atavistic performances are "You're Bound To Look like a Monkey" by Milton Brown and His Musical Brownies (Decca, 1935), Jimmie Revard and His Oklahoma Playboys (Bluebird, 1938), and Hank Penny (RCA-

Victor, 1952); "Darktown Poker Club" (written and first recorded by Bert Williams) by Tex Williams (Imperial, 1963); and "Alabama Jubilee" by Jerry Reed (RCA, 1976) and Jerry Lee Lewis (Elektra, 1979).

"Run, Nigger, Run" was cut by several early country artists, including Fiddlin' John Carson, who recorded it for Okeh in 1924, and Uncle Dave Macon, who recorded it for Brunswick in 1925. Before either of these records was made, folklorist Dorothy Scarborough found "Run, Nigger, Run" to be common among black Southerners, and in her 1925 book, *On the Trail of Negro Folk-Songs*, she claimed the song went back to the days of slavery. "Run, Nigger, Run" represented a true kind of musical interaction between black and white, an interaction that had been tamping and defining Southern music since the seventeenth century.

The first important reference to country music in America is the announcement of a fiddling contest in the November 26, 1736, issue of the *Virginia Gazette*.

> We hear, from Hanover County, that on Tuesday next, (being St. Andrew's Day,) some merry-dispos'd Gentlemen of the said County, design to celebrate that Festival, by setting up divers Prizes to be contended for in the following Manner, (to wit,) A neat Hunting-Saddle, with a fine Broad-cloth Housing, fring'd and flower'd &c. to be run for (the Quarter) by any Number of Horses and Mares: A fine Cremona Fiddle to be plaid for, by any Number of Country Fiddlers, (Mr. Langford's Scholars excepted:) With divers other considerable Prizes for Dancing, Singing, Foot-ball-play, Jumping, Wrestling &c. particularly a fine pair of Silk Stockings to be given to the handsomest Maid upon the Green, to be judg'd of by the Company. . . .

In the *Virginia Gazette* of October 7, 1737, is this announcement of a fiddling contest, again part of the St. Andrew's Day festivities.

> That a Violin be played for by 20 Fiddlers, and to
> be given to him that shall be adjudged to play the best.
> No person to have the Liberty of playing unless he brings
> a Fiddle with him. After the Prize is won, they are all to
> play together, and each a different Tune; and to be
> treated by the Company.

Another event of interest was scheduled for that year's
festival.

> That a Cuire of Ballads be sung for, by a Number of
> Songsters; the best Songster to have the Prize, and all of
> them to have Liquor sufficient to clear their Wind-Pipes.

In 1737 appear the earliest references to slave
fiddlers. From the *South Carolina Gazette* of September
17, 1737:

> Any white person that can play on the violin, or a Negro
> may be employ'd by the said Logan living in Union
> Street.

Most of the references to fiddling slaves are found in the
advertisement section of the *Virginia Gazette*. From April
23, 1738:

> Ran away from the Subscriber in Lancaster County
> the 17th instant, a dark Mulatto Fellow, named Will: He
> is a lusty, well-set Fellow, aged about 42 Years; he is
> pretty much Lock-fretten, and has a Lump on the hind
> Part of One of his Legs, near his Heel. He wore a Man's
> Cloth Jacket, a Pair of brown Cotton Breeches, and an
> Ozenbrig Shirt; he carried with him a white Fustian
> Jacket, a lopping Ax, and a Fiddle.

From March 27, 1746:

> Ran away from the Subscriber, living near James-
> Town, last Sunday was Fortnight, a Negroe Man, named

Henry, who formerly belonged to Col. Charles Grymes, of Richmond County: He is about 5 Feet 6 Inches high, thin visag'd, has small Eyes, and a very large Beard; is about 35 Years old; and plays upon the Fiddle. He had a dark-colour'd cloth-coat, double breasted, flourish'd at the knees, and a blue Great Coat. It is suppos'd he is gone to Richmond County, where he has a Wife. Whoever apprehends him, so that he be brought to me near James-Town, shall have a Pistole Reward, besides what the Law allows. Wilham Newgent.

N.B. As he ran away without any Cause, I desire he may be punish'd by Whipping, as the Law directs.

From April 26, 1776:

Run away from the subscriber in Prince George, the 2nd instant (April) three negro fellows, viz. *WILL, DAVIE,* and *WILL.* One of the fellows named Will is near 6 feet high, of a very black complexion, much troubled with fore eyes, and fond of playing the fiddle. Davie is 18 or 19 years old, 5 feet 8 or 9 inches high, of a yellowish complexion, and has what is commonly called a sealled head. Will is about 20 years old, 5 feet 6 or 8 inches high, has a remarkable black smooth skin, a scar on his forehead, and shews his teeth very much when he laughs.

From May 23, 1777:

Run away from the subscriber in Charlotte, the 17th of April last, a negro man named *NED,* who is a well set fellow, about 29 years old, 5 feet 6 or 7 inches high, has remarkable small legs for his size, walks with his toes much turned out, plays on the violin, pretends sometimes to make fiddles, and is very forward in speaking.

From February 26, 1779:

Run away from the subscriber, on the 26th of May, 1777, a likely Virginia born negro fellow, named *HARRY,* about 5 feet 10 or 11 inches high, has been frost bitten and lost some of his toes, two of his fore teeth wide apart, and of a yellowish complexion. I am informed he is lurking about Mr. Joseph Sowell's in Gloucester county, or in that neighborhood; he is very fond of playing the fiddle, and is an artful cunning fellow, and may endeavour to pass for a free man.

From the *Virginia Herald* of January 21, 1800:

RAN AWAY

On the 25th ultimo, from the subscriber, living near Culpepper Courthouse, A Negro Man named Jack, about 30 years old, 5 feet 10 or 11 inches high, very muscular, full faced, wide nostrils, large eyes, a down look, speaks slowly and wore his hair cued; had on when he eloped, a white shirt, grey broadcloth coat, mixed cassimere waistcoat and breeches, a brown hat, faced underneath with green, and a pair of boots. He formerly belonged to Mr. Augustin Baughan, of Fredericksburg, now of Baltimore, and I am told was seen making for Alexandria, with the intention of taking the stage thither: he is artful and can both read and write and is a good fiddler.

This was not too long ago, a mere life span before the birth of men such as Uncle Dave Macon (1870) and W. C. Handy (1873), a mere life span before the phonograph. In the July 25, 1774, entry of *The Journal of Nicholas Cresswell, 1774–1777*, the twenty-three-year-old Englishman described a Southern party. The picture is one that did not fade until the twentieth century.

About noon a Pilot Boat came along side to invite the Captn. to a Barbecue. I went with him and have been highly diverted. These Barbecues are Hogs, roasted whole. This was under a large Tree. A great number of young people met together with a Fiddle and Banjo played by two Negroes, with Plenty of Toddy, which both

Men and Women seem to be very fond of. I believe they
have danced and drunk till there are few sober people
amongst them. I am sorry I was not able to join them. Got
on board late.

The fiddle was the most common musical tool among
both whites and blacks throughout the nineteenth century.
One of the first New Orleans balls, described in 1802,
featured a band of six black musicians, most of whom
played fiddles. A directory of 217 jazz musicians who
worked in the Storyville district of New Orleans between
January 1, 1898, and November 17, 1917, reveals that
there were more fiddlers in these early jazz bands than
trumpeters, banjoists, or saxophonists. In *Blues: An
Anthology*, W. C. Handy tells that his original band,
organized in the first decade of this century, consisted of
a cornetist (Handy), a saxophonist, a clarinetist, a trom-
bonist, a guitarist, a bass player, and three fiddlers (Ed
and Paul Wyer and Jim Turner). The song version of
"Memphis Blues" (the original, copyrighted in 1912, was
purely instrumental), published in 1913, refers to a jazz
fiddler.

In her 1942 book, *Slave Songs of the Georgia Sea
Islands,* Lydia Parrish wrote of her encounter in 1932 with
Green Harris, a black fiddler who was born in 1856. Harris
told her that the fiddle, although sinful, was the favored
instrument of Southern blacks.

Leroy Parker, who played at Mamie Smith's second
session, on February 14, 1920, in New York City, was the
first blues fiddler to record. In 1922 George Bell replaced
Parker as fiddler on Mamie's records. Fiddler Armand J.
Piron and his New Orleans Orchestra first recorded in
1923. Bessie Smith recorded with fiddler Robert Robbins
in 1924. In 1925 blues singer Clara Smith cut a song with
fiddler Leon Abbey; that same year, blues fiddler Lonnie
Johnson made his first records. Jelly Roll Morton recorded

with a pair of fiddlers in 1926. Peg Leg Howell used Eddie Anthony on fiddle in some 1927 recordings. In 1929 Charley Patton recorded with fiddler Henry Sims, who cut two records under his own name that year, using Patton on guitar. In 1930 the Mississippi Sheiks, a black group that featured much fiddling, made their first records. In 1942 Muddy Waters sang on several recordings by the Son Simms Four, the leader of whom, Son Simms, was a Mississippi fiddler and, some think, the same man who had accompanied Charley Patton twelve years before. The black fiddling tradition lingers. In 1972 fiddler Claude Williams, who was born in 1908 in Oklahoma, cut a beautiful and not at all archaic album with pianist Jay McShann for Sackville Records, a small Canadian company. Williams was the fiddler with Andy Kirk and His Twelve Clouds of Joy in the 1920s and '30s.

Black fiddle music was not too different from its white source. Henry Sims's style of fiddling with Charley Patton, who had a wholly black vocal style, is like the work of many white country fiddlers of the day. It is rawer and empty of the speed and tremolo of Mississippi fiddle bands such as the Leake County Revelers, Ming's Pep Steppers, the Mississippi Possum Hunters, Narmour & Smith, and the Ray Brothers, but its tones are plain proof of a century of cultural seepage in Mississippi, a century of windings and flowings that spilled onto the lap of the 1920s both Henry Sims and the Mississippi Possum Hunters.

Sam Chatman, guitarist with the Mississippi Sheiks, recalled that "my father, he played the fiddle—old songs like 'Turkey in the Straw' and such." Honeyboy Edwards, born in 1915 in Itta Bena, Mississippi, is another blues singer whose father played fiddle. Skip James, born in 1902 in Bentola, Mississippi, recalls attending country dances where a black man named Green McCloud fiddled. Fred McDowell, born about 1905 in Rossville, Mississippi, also remembers black fiddlers playing at dances. Gatemouth Brown, born in 1914 in Vinton, Louisiana (but raised in Texas), played fiddle before he took to the guitar. Brown includes modern country songs, such as Johnny Horton's "The Battle of New Orleans," in his performances.

Butch Cage (born James Cage on March 16, 1894, near Meadville, Mississippi) was a black fiddler who recorded by himself and with other blues singers. Cage held the fiddle to his chest as he played, a style favored by old-timey country fiddlers such as Eck Robertson. Cage remembered two other black fiddlers he knew in Franklin County, Mississippi: Frank Felters and Old Man Carol Williams. As a young man, Cage heard the older fiddlers perform "Arkansas Traveler," "Hell Broke Loose in Georgia," "Old Wagoner," and other songs associated with white fiddling.

Guitars had been played in America since the eighteenth century, but it was not until the latter part of the next century that they became commoner than fiddles among rural musicians. The rise of the guitar was part economic and part religious. It was easier to build and maintain than the fiddle, and it was less frowned upon by religious groups, especially black, who had used the fiddle as a goat's-ass symbol of sin since early in the 1700s.

The technique of slide-guitar playing, associated with blues musicians, and that of steel guitar, associated with country musicians, have a common source in popular Hawaiian music of the late nineteenth century. The guitar was probably introduced to the Hawaiian Islands by Spanish and Portuguese sailors and Mexican cowboys who were brought in when cattle ranching became an important industry, but it did not become an integral part of Hawaiian music until after 1879, when a group of Portuguese immigrants, three of whom were instrument makers, arrived from Madeira.

The Hawaiian guitar style, forerunner of the American slide and steel styles, centered on the use of a hard, smooth object upon the strings to effect a slithery, airy sound, an exaggerated glissando, instead of the defined notation of finger stops. The Hawaiian style is said to have been invented by Joseph Kekuku, a student at the Kamehameha Boys School in Oahu, about 1894. Kekuku discovered the effect of using a comb or a knife on the strings of his guitar, then used a metal bar for even greater effect. His invention caught on quickly. It is difficult to believe that no one in the history of Western civilization toyed with the effects of odd objects upon a guitar's strings before Kekuku came along, but he must remain the documented, and in his own day uncontested, inventor of the Hawaiian guitar style.

The style came to America in the 1890s and took the attention of the pop masses as yodeling had years before. W. C. Handy recalled seeing a black man play upon his guitar's strings with the blade of a knife in 1903.

By 1920 the record companies were deeply involved in Hawaiian guitar music. The most popular artists were Louise & Ferera (the husband-wife team who recorded for Brunswick, Columbia, and Victor), the Toots Paka Hawaiian Company, Lua & Kaili, and the Hawaiian Quintette. Some of these performers, such as Pale K. Lua and David Kaili, were real Hawaiians, but others, such as Frank Ferera, the most famous of the early Hawaiian guitarists, were not. (Ferera was a Portuguese cowboy. He came to America with the troupe of Keoki E. Awai to entertain at the Panama Pacific Exposition in 1914, and soon he and his wife, Helen Louise, began recording.)

Sol Hoopii, often considered the best and most important Hawaiian guitarist, came to America in 1919. In 1925 he formed a group with Lani McIntire and Glennwood Leslie, and the group began recording for Columbia. Hoopii appeared in several films: *Bird of Paradise, Flirtation Walk, Sing Me a Song of the Islands, Waikiki Wed-*

LOUISE, Helen and Frank FERERA, Hawaiian guitar duets.

Everybody Hula *and* He Lei No Kiulani. (A Wreath for Princess Kiulani) (Edwards)	A2253 10 .75
Hapa Haole Hula Girl *and* On the Beach at Waikiki.	A1935 10 .75
Hawaiian Medley. Introducing (I) "Moanalua Hula," (II) "Maunawili," (III) "Neleana" *and* Pua Mohala. Henry N. Clark *and Hawaiian Octette.*	A1993 10 .75
Hawaiian Medley. Introducing (I) "Waikiki Mermaid," (II) "Uua O Ka Palai" *and* Hawaiian Medley. Introducing (I) "Kamehameha March," (II) "Ainehau," (III) "Adois Ke Aloha."	A2158 10 .75
Hawaiian Two-steps, Medley of. Introducing "Maui" and "Aloha Oe" *and* Wailana Waltz. (Drowsy Waters)	A2016 10 .75
Hawaiian Waltzes, Medley of. *and* My Old Kentucky Home.	A1814 10 .75
He Lei No Kaiulani. (A Wreath for Princess Kaiulani) *and* Everybody Hula.	A2253 10 .75
Manna Kea Medley *and* That Ukulele Band.	A2033 10 .75
My Old Kentucky Home *and* Medley of Hawaiian Waltzes.	A1814 10 .75
On the Beach at Waikike *and* Hapa Haole Hula Girl.	A1935 10 .75
Palakiki Blues *and* Pua Carnation. (Carnation Flower.) Introducing "Wiliwili Wai." (Surging Waters)	A2214 10 .75
Songs From Hawaii. Introducing "Maui Girl" (Waltz Medley) *and Hawaiian-Portuguese Tango. Louise, Ferera and Kainoa.*	A2119 10 .75.
That Ukulele Band *and* Manna Kea Medley.	A2033 10 .75
Wailana Waltz. (Drowsy Waters) *and* Hawaiian Medley Two-step. Introducing "Maui" and "Aloha Oe."	A2016 10 .75

Louise & Ferera

ding, and many Charlie Chan episodes. In 1938 he became an evangelist, and on November 16, 1953, he died.

Hawaiian guitar music was popular until the late 1940s. Decca's 1942 popular catalogue listed more than five hundred Hawaiian titles. Two Decca artists, Bing Crosby and Jimmie Davis, recorded sessions with Lani McIntire and His Hawaiians. (Crosby appeared with Hoopii in *Waikiki Wedding.*)

The first blues guitarist to record in a Hawaiian-derived style was Blind Lemon Jefferson (1897–1930), who played slide guitar in "Jack o' Diamond Blues" in May 1926. Lemon (and this was his given name; he had an older brother named Izakiah) was born blind in Couchman, Texas, a small place near Mexia that is no longer found on maps. He made his living in the red-light district of Dallas. Jefferson was a grotesque creature, a beastly fat man who cared for nothing but sex and whiskey. J. Mayo Williams, the recording manager of Paramount's race division, knew Jefferson's needs, and after each session he paid the blind man his due: a few paper dollars, a bottle of bootleg whiskey, and a whore who didn't sound at Lemon's dull lumberings.

Blues guitarists throughout the South fitted metal tubes or bottlenecks onto their fingers, like Blind Lemon Jefferson. The sound was usually not too different from that produced by the Hawaiian guitarists. It was less tied to melody than to interpolation, and it was raunchier. The blues guitarists never favored the Hawaiian custom of resting the guitar flat upon the lap, but held to the Spanish position. One of the few bluesmen who played lap-style was Bukka White (1909–1977).

In the 1930s the influence of the Hawaiian guitarists had changed the sound of the blues. The slide style became a watermark of both rural and urban bluesmen, a ubiquitous sound that was no less common in the Mississippi Delta than in Chicago. Bluesman Casey Bill Weldon was billed on some of his records as the Hawaiian Guitar Wizard. One of the most effective slide guitarists of those years was Scrapper Blackwell, who recorded with the Nashville pianist and singer Leroy Carr in the late 1920s and early '30s.

In 1954 Elmore James, a master of the electric slide guitar, who was born in Canton, Mississippi, on January 18, 1918, and died in Chicago on May 23, 1963, recorded a tribute to his musical roots for Flair Records in Chicago. It was called "Hawaiian Boogie."

Five months after Blind Lemon Jefferson made his first slide-guitar records in 1926, Frank Hutchison, a white man born in Raleigh County, West Virginia, on March 20, 1897, became the first country performer to record in the same style. This was in New York in October 1926, and the session resulted in Hutchison's first Okeh single, "Worried Blues" c/w "Train That Carried the Girl from Town." Hutchison held his guitar in the Hawaiian fashion, as would many country musicians after him. His style was cleaner, faster, and more concerned with harmonics than that of Blind Lemon. Hutchison recorded until September 1929, then worked as a steamboat entertainer and store owner. He died on November 9, 1945.

Frank Hutchison's "K.C. Blues," cut in New York City on June 9, 1929, is one of the most striking of the old-timey country records, not merely for its splendid guitar work, but also for an occurrence halfway through it. To Hutchison's mind, the song is ended. There is a small silence as the men from Okeh signal that he must continue, that the record must be longer than the minute and fifty seconds he has given them. Hutchison's solution is to speak.

"All right, boys. This is Frank Hutchison, settin' back in the Union Square *Ho*tel, just gettin' right on the good corn liquor."

Then he resumed playing. It was the time of Prohibition, but Okeh released the record anyway.

Black "guitarists called their Hawaiian-derived style "slide" or "bottleneck," but country musicians called it "steel." In the mid-1920s, the Dopera Brothers, Ed and Rudy, manufactured their all-metal National guitar, and in 1929 they produced the first wood-and-metal dobro. Both guitars were constructed with aluminum resonator discs (the National had three, the dobro one) to effect natural amplification. Patents were licensed to several firms to make dobros. Although many black musicians used Dopera guitars, these guitars were most popular among country musicians.

Darby and Tarlton made their first records in 1927. Jimmy Tarlton, born on May 8, 1892, in Chesterfield County, South Carolina, adopted the bottleneck style in 1902 after observing its use by black guitarists. He began using a steel bar in 1923, when he saw Frank Ferera perform in California, and he settled upon the use of an automobile wrist-pin in the late 1920s. Tarlton played a

National guitar on most of his recordings. Like many other country artists of the 1920s and '30s, Darby and Tarlton made a severely black-sounding music. Some of their records, such as "Slow Wicked Blues," would be barely recognizable as the stuff of white boys were it not for Tarlton's yodeling.

Cliff Carlisle, who first recorded in 1933, was also very influenced by blues. Carlisle was a more emphatic, more urbane steel-guitarist than Tarlton, and his tough, swooning steel work was the perfect complement to the raunchy double-entendre songs that were his specialty.

Jimmie Rodgers, who made black music accessible to white audiences, used many steel-guitarists at his sessions: E. T. Cozzens (the first, in February 1928), John Westbrook, Lani McIntire, and others. His August 1929 recording of "Everybody Does It in Hawaii" featured a trio of steel-guitarists, perhaps Sol Hoopii's group. The following December, King Oliver and His Orchestra cut the song. In May 1931, Rodgers cut a new version of "Everybody Does It in Hawaii," again with three steel guitars. This recording was issued on "Jimmie Rodgers' Puzzle Record," a disc that had three different lead-in grooves. Each time you put the needle to the record, you heard one of three recordings (the other two were "Blue Yodel" and "Train Whistle Blues") that had been pressed onto a single disc in parallel grooves. The first such record had been issued by Victor about 1920; it was called "The Conundrum (What Will I Play Next)" and described in the Victor catalogue as "Four short selections, any one of which the needle may decide to play." In 1975 Arista issued an album by Monty Python, *Matching Tie and Handkerchief*, that had two different lead-in grooves on one of its sides. It was wrongly advertised as the world's first three-sided record.

Roy Harvey of Beckley, West Virginia, who recorded with Charlie Poole's North Carolina Ramblers from 1926 to 1929 and with various other artists during the same period, was a steel-guitarist of extreme subtlety. He recorded "Guitar Rag" as a duet with Jesse Jackson, another West Virginia guitarist, in 1930 for Brunswick. ("Guitar Rag" was a steel-guitar version of a song by the same name that Sylvester Weaver, an obscure blues musician, recorded for Okeh in 1923.) The Hokum Boys cut it in 1931 for Romeo. Leon McAuliffe used the title "Steel Guitar Rag" when he cut it with Bob Wills and His Texas Playboys in 1936.

One of the greatest popularizers of the dobro sound was James Clell Summey (1914–1975), who joined Roy Acuff in 1933. Acuff called this group, which included three other men, the Tennessee Crackerjacks. In 1935 he changed the group's name to the Crazy Tennesseeans, a misspelling he used for his early records. Summey's dobro work is responsible for the strong, haunting quality of Acuff's earliest and best records. Two of his finest dobro performances were cut at Acuff's March 1937 session: "Steel Guitar Chimes" and "Steel Guitar Blues." Summey quit Acuff in January 1939 (in this same month Acuff changed the name of his group to the Smoky Mountain Boys; Harry Stone, the manager of WSM, felt the old name was too derogatory) and was replaced by Pete Kirby, or Bashful Brother Oswald. By that time, the steel guitar had replaced the fiddle as the signature instrument of country music.

Some country singers experimented with the steel-guitar sound in their recordings, but returned to the plainer sound of standard guitar accompaniment. Gene Autry was one of these singers. In 1931 he cut several songs with steel-guitarist Frankie Marvin, who had recorded on his own for Edison, Brunswick, and other labels, and with his brother as Frankie and Johnny.

Some older artists still use dobros in their bands, and in the late 1970s a few younger singers, such as David

Allan Coe and Tompall Glaser, got a striking sound in
their records by using dobros instead of more modern
steel guitars. And what is commonly called the steel
guitar today is a drastically different instrument, a
drastically different sound.

The first electric lap steel was manufactured by
Rickenbacker in 1931. By 1935 several country steel-
guitarists were using amplified guitars, usually acoustic
models with electrical pick-ups. Unlike most dobro-
players, the first amplified guitar players held the instrument in the Spanish position. Bob Dunn was probably the
first amplified steel-guitarist. He joined Milton Brown and
His Musical Brownies late in 1934 (he had toured with
vaudeville bands since 1927) and added a stunning new
energy to the group's records when he started recording
with them in January 1935 at the band's second session.
(The Brownies had first recorded on April 4, 1934, at the
Texas Hotel in San Antonio.) Cliff Bruner remembers
Dunn's guitar to have been a mongrel of wood and metal.

"He had an old guitar he picked up down in Mexico,
a Mexican guitar that had a homemade pick-up on it. And
he would have to magnetize his strings. He carried a
magnet with him. He used this magnet to magnetize the
strings, and he had a homemade pick-up built to go on it.
Bad amplifiers, too, at those times."

Bob Dunn was the lord of the steel guitar. In the
1930s, he wrought a music full of electric wonders. Great
yelling dissonances burst from his bastard tool like glass
against a stone wall. Three years before Django Reinhardt
made his first records, Dunn had a style as subtle and
involved as Reinhardt's would be, but Dunn had a daring, febrile energy that neither Reinhardt nor the effete
jazzbos who came in his wake could comprehend. Today
there are people who hear the influence of Django Reinhardt in Bob Dunn's music, as if it were unthinkable that
this Texas gentleman could create such a music on
his own.

Dunn's best work was in Brownies records such as "Cheesy Breeze," "Who's Sorry Now," "You're Tired of Me" (all cut in 1935), and "Somebody's Been Using That Thing" and "Yes Sir!" (both cut in 1936), where he mixed loud, lucid notes with fast, jagged triplets and grabbed at variously toned shreds of melody that complemented the song with bizarre, lizard-eye concision. These solos lunged drunkenly, or rushed, graceful as a hawk, from here to there to here. He even made "Shine on Harvest Moon" sound dirty.

Milton Brown was severely injured in a car wreck on the night of April 13, 1936, as he was driving to Fort Worth from Crystal Springs on the Jacksboro Highway. He was brought to a hospital, but complications arose and he died on April 18, at the age of thirty-two. Such was his local popularity that thirty-five hundred people came to the funeral. Cliff Bruner, who had joined the Brownies in 1936, thinks Brown's death could have been prevented.

"He had a punctured lung, and they had the old family doctor. A new doctor came in and said, 'If you let me, I'll save Milton's life.' See, it wasn't all that serious. He's sittin' up in bed talkin' to me the next morning. And they let pneumonia set in, and this was before penicillin and all that. He'd just had a punctured lung; pneumonia set in and killed him. It was uncalled for, actually.

"At that time, he had the number-one band. After his death, his brother tried to keep the group together, but he just didn't have the leadership. I'd have never left Milton, I'd have never had a band of my own if Milton had lived. I'd have been happy just working in his band, 'cause he was the greatest."

After the Brownies broke up in 1936, Bob Dunn started recording for Decca with his own group, the Vagabonds, and with Cliff Bruner's bands. Some of his Vagabond recordings, such as "Blue Skies" and "Toodle-Doodle-Oo," a derivative of "It's Tight Like That," were as good as any of his work with the Brownies, and his work with Cliff Bruner produced many of Western-swing's raunchiest and best records. In the 1930s Western-swing musicians in Texas interacted so much that the recording histories of many of the most important men, such as Dunn, are hard to unravel. A good example is "Two More Years" by Leon Selph's Blue Ridge Playboys, released by Decca in 1938. In reality, Leon Selph was nowhere in sight when "Two More Years" was cut, for he was in trouble with the musician's union at the time. The vocal was by Floyd Tillman, who was in the Blue Ridge Playboys, but the other musicians included Cliff Bruner on fiddle, Bob Dunn on steel guitar, and Moon Mullican on piano, all of whom were in the Texas Wanderers, Bruner's band.

Bob Dunn stopped recording in the 1940s, after which he taught music and operated a music store in Houston. According to Cliff Bruner, Dunn died about 1970.

"He had retired. He'd taught a lot. Y'know, Bob had a master's degree in music. Possibly his doctor's degree. He was a graduate of the conservatory here in Houston. He was a very finished musician, and he taught a long time. He had a big music store, a big business, and he sold it and was going to retire and enjoy his earnings, and he found out he had cancer. It was a terrible thing. Dickie McBride died one day and Bob died the next day, both in the same hospital. One on the first floor and one on the second. A real tragedy.

"I always considered Bob a genius. He was futuristic, that's the way Bob was. He originated the whole thing. He was a wonderful guy, one of the nicest guys that ever lived. He was, you know, caught takin' a drink once in a while, but he quit that in his older days. He was a nice guy."

There are other tales of Bob Dunn's being caught taking a drink. One Western-swing veteran said it was

Cliff Bruner's Boys, 1940. Left to right: Harris Dodd, Logan Conger, Cliff Bruner, Buddy Dukon, Eddie Caldwell, Curly DeLouche, Link Davis, Johnny Thames.

always wise to bring a backup steel-guitarist with you when you played a date with Dunn, just in case he wilted off his chair in the middle of a set.

After Dunn's first recordings with the Brownies, amplified steel playing flourished in Texas. Ted Daffan (born Theron Eugene Daffan on September 21, 1912, in Beauregarde Parish, Louisiana) recorded with Shelly Lee Alley and His Alley Cats and Leon Selph's Bar-X Cowboys (both Houston bands) before forming his own band in 1939. Daffan wrote and recorded the classic "Born To Lose" for Okeh in 1943.

"I was nineteen years old when I first saw the Hawaiian guitar played. A cousin of mine who played standard had come down from New Orleans to visit us in

Houston. He was working with a local Houston boy named Clayton Wilson, and Clayton played the steel guitar. That was the first time I'd ever seen it played, and I fell in love with it. I immediately bought a five-dollar guitar at a pawnshop and got a fifty-cent instruction book and started in. This was during the Depression; there was no money for lessons or training, anything like that. But I did teach myself to read, write, and arrange.

"In thirty-three I was playing Hawaiian music and I had a group called the Blue Islanders on KTRH. In thirty-four I started playing steel with a little group here in Houston called the Blue Ridge Playboys. About a year later I joined the Bar-X Cowboys.

"The amplifiers with pick-ups had just come on the market, so I immediately purchased one. That was one of the first ones on the market. It was called a Volatone. It was necessary in order to play dance jobs. I first played one late in thirty-four. I first recorded with an electric steel in December of thirty-nine.

"After I had turned country, there was a great steel player working with Milton Brown and His Brownies, called Bob Dunn. I admired his steel playing terrifically, but I could never duplicate it. He had a very individualist style, and I never even tried. I stuck mostly to straight lead. He played a very sophisticated jazz steel. Bob Wills, of course, had a great steel player, Leon McAuliffe."

Al Dexter was born Clarence Albert Poindexter on May 4, 1902, in Jacksonville, Texas; he died of a heart attack on January 28, 1984, at his home on Lake Lewisville, near Dallas. His 1943 recording of "Pistol Packin' Mama" for Okeh was the biggest-selling record of the year and the first country recording to hit the top of the pop charts. Within six months of its release, the record sold a million copies, and sheet music sales hit two hundred thousand. The Duke of Windsor was caught humming it, *Life* called it "a national earache," jukebox operators

The BAR-X COWBOYS

B-8440 { I'm Just
an Out-
cast—
FT—VR
My Dark
Eyed
Sweet-
heart—
FT—VR

B-8487 { Blue
Bonnet
Gover-
nor—
FT—VR
Blue
Steele Blues—FT

B-8546 { Sunset Valley—FT—VR
South—FT

B-8577 { When Mama Goes Out the Maid
Comes In—FT—VR
Houston Shuffle—FT

B-8723 { Let's Go Honky-Tonkin' Tonight
—FT—VR
Hang Over Blues

during the Petrillo Ban (a strike by the American Federation of Musicians that crippled the record business in 1942 and 1943) paid as much as ten dollars for a black-market copy of it, Frank Sinatra sang it for fourteen weeks straight on "Your Hit Parade," and Bing Crosby had one of the biggest hits of the decade when he covered it for Decca. The song also entered folk tradition (in her 1961 Folkways album, Aunt Molly Jackson of Kentucky sang it and claimed she was its source), and was revived in a rockabilly version by Mac Curtis in 1975. Al Dexter never heard of Aunt Molly Jackson. It is not too uncommon for pop hits to be collected in the hills by folklorists. In 1959 D. K. Wilgus, professor of English and Anglo-American Folksong at U.C.L.A., recorded performances of Bill Justis's "Raunchy" and the Everly Brothers' "Bye Bye Love" by the Sammie Walker Family of Summer Shade, Kentucky. In June 1965, Wilgus recorded a hot "Blue Suede Shoes" by Aunt Ollie Gilbert of Mountain View, Arkansas.

In 1975 Dexter told me the story of his million-dollar song. "I used to go sit around these honky-tonks, beer joints. At one time I owned a tavern, the Round-Up Club, in Turnertown, Texas. I had a bunch of girls workin', and there was a little cross-eyed feller who brought a girl in one night by the name of Jo Ann, and he asked me if I'd give her a job, and I said yeah. I had a pretty good-sized business. This was over in the east Texas oil field. I gave her a job. The next day three or four women came up in the same V-8 Ford that little cross-eyed feller drove up in the day before, and they're lookin' for Jo Ann. This woman said she's gonna kill her and wanted me to fire her and all that. So I told all this to Jo Ann. That guy, his name was Webb Jay, and he's cross-eyed as he can be. Jo Ann, she always said, 'I love that little cross-eyed man.' She didn't know he's a married man.

"So, I sold that place. Later on, about two or three years later, I was sittin' in this joint over close to Long-

Ted Daffan, back when lapels were lapels.

view, tryin' to get ideas for a song, and the jukebox is playin' that song of Bob Wills's, 'Take Me Back to Tulsa.' It's an eight-bar verse, eight-bar chorus, eight-bar verse, eight-bar chorus. A repetitious thing. So I said, 'I'm gonna write me a song on that same pattern.' Simple melody. Everyplace you go then, nine times out of ten the jukebox be playin' that song. It's just that old P.D. song 'Take Me Back to Texas.' So I'm sittin' there, watchin' things happen, and in came this gal Jo Ann. She's scratched up and looks like she's been fightin' wildcats. I said, 'Well, godsakes, Jo Ann, what happened?' And she said, 'Jay's old

Al Dexter, c. 1940.

lady's after me with a gun.' I said, 'I told you to leave that married man alone, that woman gonna kill you 'bout that man.' She said, 'Yeah, but Dex'—she always called me Dex—'but Dex, I love that little cross-eyed man.' Woman had chased her about two miles through wire fences, through briars, and everything else. She was a pretty girl, 'bout eighteen, twenty years old. So I got the idea, 'Lay that pistol down, babe, lay that pistol down.' Got a woman after ya with a gun, y'know, you can't outrun the darned thing, so you gotta beg her to lay it down. So I went out to the car and started writin' these lyrics. I sang it over and over so I wouldn't forget it, and then I had my song."

Al Dexter had used an electric steel-guitarist named Bobby Simon in his first Vocalion recordings in 1936.

"Bobby, he was a Spaniard from San Antone. He was a very refined Spaniard, though. He played electric steel guitar and take-off guitar. That was the first one I ever saw. It had a little-bitty body and an electric pick-up on it, and he played it Spanish style. That's the one I recorded 'Honky Tonk Blues' with."

Leon McAuliffe, the best-known steel-guitarist of Western swing, performed with Bob Wills from 1935 (McAuliffe was eighteen then) to 1942. His first experience with an electric guitar was in Fort Worth, when Bob Dunn let the younger musician play a while with his. In the spring of 1935, Wills bought McAuliffe an amplified steel guitar. Leon admits that he was a less able artist than Dunn, who could swim farther from the constraints of melody than McAuliffe. If McAuliffe had been capable of Dunn's free-yelling style, Wills probably would not have allowed it in his music. It is hard to imagine Bob Dunn appearing as a guest soloist in the Lawrence Welk show, "Top Tunes and New Talent," as McAuliffe did in September 1957.

After World War II, Leon McAuliffe began recording with his own band, and he continued to record by himself into the 1970s. He started with the short-lived Majestic Records, then had a Top Ten hit, "Panhandle Rag," with Columbia in 1949. After Columbia he recorded for Russell Sims's Cimarron label, Starday (some of his Starday work was reissued by Mercury), Capitol, and Stoneway. Since 1954 McAuliffe has operated radio station KAMO in Rogers, Arkansas.

Many other good steel-guitarists passed through the Texas Playboys. One of them, Noel Boggs, did the soundtrack for *War of the Worlds* in 1953.

The amplified steel guitar changed in the mid-1940s.

It stood on four legs, like an insect, and had up to four separate eight-string necks. A complex system of cables, pulleys, and rods connected to foot pedals (and later knee pedals) enabled the guitarist to weirdize the pitch of individual strings and to make chords and voicings that none had heard before. The pedal steel was the invention of John Moore, a machinist and amateur musician who lived in Winsted, Connecticut. Moore worked with the Gibson company to produce the Gibson Electraharp, the first pedal steel guitar. The Bigsby company and others began manufacturing pedal steels also.

Pedal steel guitars were harder to master than conventional guitars. Men sat at this strange shining tool, their fingers gleaming with metal—doctoral, they seemed, and mystical, too. The most popular pedal steel players in the late 1940s and early '50s were Joaquin Murphy and Speedy West.

West, who was born Wesley Webb West on January 25, 1924, in Springfield, Missouri, began playing a National steel guitar about 1937. He moved to Los Angeles in June 1946, seeking work in the music business. In 1948 he bought the second pedal steel Bigsby manufactured and, that same year, worked with both Spade Cooley and Hank Penny. In the early 1950s Speedy was one of the most popular session men in L.A., recording over six thousand records with 177 singers in five years. Many of the singers Speedy recorded with were country, but many of them were pop singers who wanted this new, mesmerizing sound in their music. In February 1952, a representative month, Speedy recorded with Rex Allen, the Bell Sisters, Jimmy Boyd, Tommy Duncan, Tennessee Ernie Ford, Johnny Horton, Spike Jones, Frankie Laine, Ella Mae Morse, Tex Ritter, Fabor Robison, Billy Strange, Merle Travis, and others. (By today's standards, West was not paid too well for his session work, about $1,000 a month.)

In two 1952 recordings, Hank Thompson's "Waiting

in the Lobby of Your Heart" (Capitol) and Slim Whitman's "Song of the Old Water Wheel" (Imperial), Speedy West used a bizarre, high-volume wah-wah effect that got the attention of the industry. Soon the pedal steel work heard in records coming from Nashville was louder, more emphatic than it had been.

The man who made the pedal steel the most important part of the Nashville sound was Webb Pierce (born on August 8, 1926, in West Monroe, Louisiana), one of the greatest honky-tonk singers of the 1950s. After a handful of recordings for Pacemaker and Four-Star, Pierce signed with Decca in 1952. His first release, "Wondering," was a Top Ten hit (only one country artist, Eddy Arnold, has had more hits in his career than Pierce). He was best, and most successful, with hard-core, honky-tonk stuff. "Back Street Affair," his first Number One hit, was a song of adultery. "There Stands the Glass," a hit during the winter of 1953–1954, is one of the classic booze songs and one of the strongest records of the fifties. It was released in October and very quickly banned by many stations, beginning with WXGI in Richmond, Virginia. The February 13 issue of *Billboard* reported that the record "is growing by leaps and bounds ever since the ban of the tune by many radio stations." The authors of "There Stands the Glass" wrote a sequel, "Throw Away the Glass."

There was steel in Pierce's music from the beginning, and with each record it pulsed stronger and louder. In "Wondering" the steel is barely noticeable, but for a small flourish at the end; in "That Heart Belongs to Me," Pierce's second hit, there is a full solo; in "Back Street Affair" and "That's Me Without You" the steel flows through the whole of the music; in "There Stands the Glass," the steel is the dominant instrument; in "Slowly," the biggest country hit of 1954, the steel is the force of the song. Bud Isaacs, the man who played a Bigsby steel on "Slowly," birthed the Nashville steel sound that still prevails: those dark swoonings fluid as seaweed in a bay, and often as turgid.

When honky-tonk's popularity waned, so did Webb Pierce's. He fared well, though, and today he is a millionaire with a specially built ramp at his home to accommodate the comings and goings of tourists by the busful. Webb has a guitar-shaped swimming pool and unappreciative neighbors. During the 1976 Muscular Dystrophy Telethon, Webb donated $100. What a sport.

Charley Ryan (born December 19, 1915, in Graceville, Minnesota) recorded a series of rockabilly records in the late fifties that used steel-guitar work to achieve a variety of weird affects. In "Hot Rod Lincoln," which he recorded on his own Souvenir label in Spokane in 1955, steel-guitarist Neal Livingston wrought sounds of speed, sirens, and whiplash behind Ryan's tough boogie beat and amphetamine vocal. Ryan had been playing, in his phrase, "country music with a beat" since about 1947. His first record, "Double Track Woman" c/w "Daddy Can I Night Herd in the Sky," was released by Keyboard in 1951. The original version of "Hot Rod Lincoln" (the flip-side was "Hank Williams Goodbye") went largely unnoticed, but when Ryan recut it for Four-Star in 1960, it became a hit in both the country and pop markets. (The previous year had seen the first steel-guitar pop hit, Santo & Johnny's "Sleep Walk.")

Instead of using pedal steel guitars, blues artists held to the older slide and bottleneck styles, increasing the volume of their amplifiers as years passed. In the late 1940s and early '50s, as the pedal steel became the major tool of country music, the electric slide was the major tool of blues, and its masters were men such as Lowell Fulson and Elmore James. (Fulson was born in 1921 in Tulsa. His grandfather was a fiddler, and the first band Fulson was in, in 1938, was Dan Wright's String Band, which played a mixture of blues, pop, and country. The group consisted of two guitars, three fiddles, two mandolins, and two banjos. Fulson began recording in 1946 and through the years he made records for Big Town, Gilt-Edge, Swing Time, Aladdin, Checker, Kent, and other labels. Fulson's older records are very rare, but, like Elmore James's, they hold some of the classic and most powerful electric slide performances of the era.)

The connection between the pedal steel of country music and the electric slide guitar of blues has become very tenuous to the ear. There is an occasional clarity, as in Chuck Berry's steely "Deep Feeling," the flip-side of his 1957 hit "School Days." In 1961 Doug Quattlebaum, a blues singer born in 1927 in Florence, South Carolina, cut an album for Bluesville, *Softee Man Blues*, with a National steel guitar. But Freddie Roulette is the best example of the common stem of country and blues guitarists.

Roulette was born on May 3, 1939, in Evanston, Illinois, north of Chicago. He has recorded with blues singers such as Johnny Walker, Earl Hooker, and Charlie Musselwhite, who's white. Roulette is the first black performer since Doug Quattlebaum to cut a steel-guitar album. The album, *Sweet Funky Steel*, was released by Janus in 1973. Roulette, who plays a National eight-string, cut the album with the accompaniment of saxophones, guitar, fiddle (Sugarcane Harris), bass, and drums. One of the songs is titled "Joaquin," a tribute to Joaquin Murphey, the steel-guitarist of the 1940s. Asked of his influences, Freddie Roulette said, "Country and Western. I play steel guitar because I couldn't get out of a regular guitar what I could get out of steel."

Though he may be the last, Freddie Roulette is not the first blues performer to admit being influenced by country music. Blues singer John Jackson, born in 1924 in Rapahannock County, Virginia, has a great liking for country artists such as Jimmie Rodgers, the Delmore Brothers, and Uncle Dave Macon. Jackson was surprised when it was revealed to him that Uncle Dave Macon was white. (On October 6, 1924, Thomas Edison listened to Uncle Dave Macon's Vocalion recording of "Bile Them Cabbage Down" to decide if Uncle Dave should record for the Edison company. He made a note: "This also might do—if he is a colored man, if not they will detect it.") Jackson recorded Jimmie Rodgers's "T.B. Blues" in 1965 and the Delmore Brothers' "Gonna Lay Down My Old Guitar" in 1967. Snooks Eaglin, who was born Ford Eaglin in 1936 in New Orleans, is another blues singer who admits a liking of Jimmie Rodgers. In 1958 Eaglin recorded Rodgers's "Waiting for a Train" under the title "A Thousand Miles from Nowhere." Furry Lewis also cut "Waiting for a Train," under the title "The Dying Hobo," and attempted a yodel in it. The first stanza of "Waiting for a Train" was used by Peg Leg Howell in two records, "Broke and Hungry Blues" and "Away from Home," both cut six months after Rodgers's song.

Some of the most ancient British ballads became a part of black musical tradition in America. In the 1920s folklorist Virginia Bates of Fort Worth collected a version of "Barbara Allen" by a black woman near Hearne, Texas. In this variant, the Scotch lady Barbara Allen had become a black boy called Boberick Allen. Another black version of "Barbara Allen" was collected by Dorothy Scarborough in Virginia and included in her book *On the Trail of Negro Folk-Songs*. Scarborough also found black versions of "The Maid Freed from the Gallows," "Lord Lovel," and "Lady Isabel and the Elf-Knight," three more British ballads brought to America in the eighteenth century. "Our Goodman," the ancient song of the drunken cuckold, which surfaced in so many country records, was recorded by several blues singers: Blind Boy Fuller ("Cat Man Blues"), Coley Jones ("Drunkard's Special"), and others.

One of the earliest tellings of the enculturation of

slaves to white society in America is in *The Present State of Virginia* by Hugh Jones, published in London in 1724.

> The Negroes are not only encreased by fresh Supplies from Africa and the West India Islands, but also are very prolifick among themselves; and they that are born there talk good English, and affect our Language, Habits, and Customs.

Writing in his journal on January 30, 1774, Philip Vickers Fithian tells of a party in Virginia. The two boys he mentions, Ben and Harry, are white.

> This Evening the Negroes collected themselves into the School-Room, & began to play the Fiddle, & dance— I was in Mr Randolph's Room;—I went among them, Ben, & Harry were of the company—Harry was dancing with his Coat off—I dispersed them however immediately.

In the early 1950s the Louisiana-born singer and harp player Little Walter performed at a club in Dallas. The way someone described it, the scene seems not too different from that long-ago night in Virginia.

> In those days they strung a rope down the center of the dance floor to keep white and colored apart, but before Walter was through, that rope was down and things were right. Even the law was too hung up on the scene to keep control.

The Mississippi Sheiks, Charlie Patton, Son House, and other Mississippi blues artists derived much of their income by playing for white parties in the first part of this century; Yank Rachell and others did the same in Tennessee. Patton and Son House were received decently in white homes, and both often ate and slept in them.

Some of the most fascinating records made are those

of Henry Thomas, the mysterious black singer who cut twenty-three sides for Vocalion in the years 1927 to 1929. He was a tramp, born in 1874 on a farm in Upshur County, Texas. His parents were freed slaves. Thomas was best known in the towns connected by the tracks of the Texas & Pacific Railroad, but he knew many other railroad routes: the Cottonbelt, the Katy, the Santa Fe, and more. There were people in Texas, old and cayman-skinned and smiling, who remember Henry Thomas— how he bragged in 1893 of his visit to the Chicago Columbian Exposition, how he bragged in 1904 of his visit to the St. Louis World's Fair, how he jumped a train to Chicago in 1927 and made phonograph records, how weeks later those phonograph records were brought to Texas by train, and how you could walk into a record store in Wichita Falls and buy them, black and lustrous and full of Henry Thomas's wild, fiery noise.

More than anyone else, Henry Thomas offers a taste of what Southern street music of the nineteenth century was like. He accompanied himself not only with guitar, but with syrinxes, or panpipes, which he made of bamboo. (In 1883, when Henry Thomas was nine years old, Joel Chandler Harris wrote to *The Critic* to say that, contrary to the cliches of minstrelsy, he had never seen a slave play a banjo. "I have heard them make sweet music with the quills—panpipes; I have heard them play passably on the fiddle; . . . I have heard them blow a trumpet with surprising skill; but I have never seen a banjo.")

Henry Thomas's music is the oldest form of blues captured by a record company's greed. The earliest blues records, those of Mamie Smith, Lucille Hegamin, Ethel Waters, Bessie Smith, Ma Rainey, and others who recorded between 1920 and 1925, were a very modern, sophisticated style blues: urbanely written songs set to jazz orchestrations.

The use of the word *blue* to describe an emotional

state of depression or discomfort is traceable to the early sixteenth century. In the eighteenth century, the colloquialism "blue devils" referred to melancholia (the poet Burns wrote of his "blue devilism" in a 1787 letter). The first published occurrence of "the blues" was in America in 1807, when Washington Irving described "a fit of the blues" in *Salmagundi; or, the Whim-Whams and Opinions of Launcelot Langstaff, Esq., and Others.* The December 1883 issue of *Harper's* included a short story in which was written, "Come to me when you have the blues." How many songs have you heard *that* line in? (In *The Posthumous Papers of the Pickwick Club,* published in 1837, Charles Dickens used the word "funky." It is not true, however, that Philly International tried to trace Dickens's telephone number for the purpose of assigning liner notes.)

The eighteenth century, as well as the nineteenth, lingers in Henry Thomas's blues. The sound of his panpipes, breezy and trilling and half-real, is the sound of an America that was the world's last blue-skied Babylon, an America that the itinerant Anglican Charles Woodmason called "low, lazy, sluttish, heathenish, hellish." He looked at the Carolina backcountry of the late eighteenth century as one would the griseous ass of Satan. He describes Southern women:

> They draw their Shift as tight as possible to the Body, and pin it close, to shew the roundness of their Breasts, and slender Waists (for they are generally finely shaped) and draw their Petticoat close to their Hips to show the fineness of their Limbs—so that they might as well be in Puri Naturalibus.

And their white-trash husbands. It sickened him to see them "swopping wives as cattle." He estimated in his journal that 95 percent of the girls he married were visibly pregnant and that nine-tenths of the settlers had

venereal disease. A century later this culture birthed
Charlie Poole, the grandest drunk in the history of country music. The epic binge that caused Poole's death at
the age of thirty-nine on May 21, 1931, is a part of
Carolina legendry.

Henry Thomas's "Red River Blues" is of a style that
predates the standard verse structure of the blues. It is a
blues that has not yet been tamed.

> *Which-a-way do the Red River run?*
> *Which-a-way do the Red River run?*
> *Which-a-way do the Red River run, poor boy?*
> *Which-a-way do the Red River run?*
> *Yes, she runs north and south,*
> *It runs north and south.*
> *Which-a-way do the Red River run, poor boy?*
> *Well, it runs north and south.*

His "Lovin' Babe" is closer to the blues of the twentieth
century.

> *Look where the evenin' sun is gone,*
> *Look where the evenin' sun's gone,*
> *Look where that evenin' sun done gone.*
>
> *Just make me one pallet on your floor,*
> *Ah, make me a pallet on your floor,*
> *Oh, make it so your husband never know.*

The records of Henry Thomas are more than primitive blues. They are testimony of the mongrelization of
black and white music. Thomas's "John Henry," "Arkansas," "The Fox and the Hounds," "Jonah in the Wilder-
ness," "Shanty Blues," and "When the Train Comes Along"
were all recorded by Uncle Dave Macon, most of them

earlier in the decade. His "Charmin' Betsy" was also recorded by Fiddlin' John Carson and the Georgia banjo player Land Norris; both recordings predate Thomas's. "Fishing Blues" was later cut by Opry star Lew Childre. "Old Country Stomp" seems echoic of the sort of party Philip Vickers Fithian described a century before Thomas's birth.

No one knows what became of Henry Thomas. Mack McCormack, a consultant to the Smithsonian Institution, thinks he encountered Thomas in Houston one afternoon in 1949. He recalls that Thomas stood about six feet three inches and that he wore several layers of clothes (McCormack counted three overcoats). By now Henry Thomas is buried, and with him an ocean of tales. In 1974 Herwin Records of Glen Cove, New York, produced an album of his complete recorded works.

The ballad of "Frankie and Johnny" is common to blacks and whites, but it originated among blacks in 1899. Allen Britt shot Frankie Baker of 212 Targee Street in St. Louis on October 15, 1899. The song was written by Mammy Lou, a singer at Babe Conner's cabaret in St. Louis. In the 1920s, the song was recorded by blues singer Mississippi John Hurt and by country singers such as Jimmie Rodgers, Charlie Poole ("Leaving Home"), and Darby and Tarlton ("Frankie Dean"); it was also recorded by pop bands.

"Casey Jones," a ballad associated with whites, was written by a black man. Casey Jones (born Jonathan Luther Jones on March 14, 1862, in Kentucky) was killed at 3:52 A.M., April 30, 1900, when he ran the Illinois Central Train No. 1, of which he was engineer, into the rear of a freight train near the Vaughan, Mississippi, railroad station. Wallace Saunders, a black engine-wiper at the Canton, Mississippi, roundhouse, wrote the song a few days later. It was recorded in the 1920s by both Fiddlin' John Carson and Furry Lewis.

Furry Lewis's 1928 "Kassie Jones" held an intriguing couplet:

> *Had it written on the back of my shirt:*
> *Natural-born eastman, don't have to work.*

Twenty years before, when there were neither blues records nor country records, folklorist Howard W. Odum collected a song that was later published in the 1925 book he wrote with Guy B. Johnson, *The Negro and His Songs*.

> *I got it writ on de tail o' my shirt:*
> *I'm a natu'el-bohn eastman, don't have to work.*

In Jimmie Rodgers's "Blue Yodel No. 9," recorded in 1930, the same couplet appears, with slight changes (Rodgers is not a natural-born eastman, but a Tennessee hustler). Gene Autry uses the couplet in his 1931 "Do Right Daddy Blues." Autry is neither a natural-born eastman nor a Tennessee hustler, but, as expected, a do-right daddy. Although it did not contain the couplet, Jimmie Davis's 1934 "Shirt Tail Blues" paid hip, oblique homage to it with its title. In 1951 Harmonica Frank Floyd cut "Rockin' Chair Daddy" for Sun. Harmonica Frank derived much of his song from "Blue Yodel No. 9," including:

> *Rockin' chair daddy don't have to work,*
> *I told her my name was on the tail of my shirt.*

The couplet surfaced in Waylon Jennings's 1975 recording of "Waymore's Blues." Waylon is neither a natural-born eastman, a Tennessee hustler, a do-right daddy, nor a rockin'-chair daddy, but, simply, no ordinary dude. Last seen, the couplet drifted by in Mel Tillis's 1976 hit, "Good Woman Blues." *Panta rei*, indeed.

Hear Buck Owens's 1971 hit "Rollin' in My Sweet Baby's Arms." (When the bluegrass group Country

Gazette appeared on "Hee Haw" that year, they intended
to perform this same song. They ran through it before the
taping, and Buck Owens told them the song was too
risqué, that they should perform something else. They
did, and Buck had a hit.) Flatt and Scruggs recorded
"Roll in My Sweet Baby's Arms" in 1950 for Mercury. In
1931 it was recorded as "I'll Roll in My Sweet Baby's
Arms" by Buster Carter and Preston Young for Columbia.
Carter copyrighted the song on October 9, 1931. A similar
song had been collected earlier. In his 1932 book, *Episodes
in Black and White,* Francis Goodwin printed a verse he
had heard sung by a black man in Alabama.

> *I gwine ter lar roun' town twell de sun go down,*
> *Den it doan do me no harm, fer to roll in my honey's arm.*

Robert W. Gordon edited a column, "Old Songs That Men
Have Sung," that was published in *Adventure* from 1923
to 1927. In his column of January 10, 1924, he printed a
stanza sent to him by a reader who had heard it sung by
blacks in railroad construction camps of the South.

> *I ain't goin' to work on the railroad,*
> *I ain't goin' to work on the farm;*
> *I'll lay round town till the pay-train comes,*
> *And roll in my Dony's arms.*

In *The Negro and His Songs,* Odum and Johnson printed
a couplet similar to a verse of "Roll in My Sweet Baby's
Arms."

> *Where were you las' night when I was sick in bed?*
> *Down town wid some other gal, wusn't here to hole my*
>   *head.*

The most powerful white blues of the 1920s is "Country Blues," cut in 1928 for Brunswick by Dock Boggs

(1898–1971). It is a sere, droning thing, moanful and mean, too, pulled from more ancient songs, black and white.

> All around this old jailhouse is hainted, good people,
> Forty dollars won't pay my fine.
> Corn whiskey has surrounded my body, poor boy,
> Pretty women is a-troublin' my mind.*

Boggs later cut two songs that are almost identical to "Country Blues": "Sugar Baby" for Brunswick and "Old Rub Alcohol Blues" for Lonesome Ace. "Wild Bill Jones," recorded by James Luther Dickinson in 1971 and included in his Atlantic album, *Dixie Fried,* is a dark, gale-force reworking of some ancient Southern lyrics; a verse of "Country Blues" is worked in beautifully. *Dixie Fried* is one of the most bizarrely powerful musics of this century: a loud, moralless baptism of rhythm. There are the Night Caps' "Wine," Carl Perkins's "Dixie Fried," warm, visceral graftings of Dock Boggs and a thousand more drunken voices of an older, more tenebrious South, and a prowling, surly version of Bob Dylan's "John Brown" that wields an unfriendly mirror at its author's eyes.

Black blood flows in the music of Jimmie Rodgers and Cliff Carlisle; it was in Gene Autry's and Jimmie Davis's, too, before they went pop in the late 1930s. It has been suggested, strongly, that Davis often bought songs outright from black men, but the former governor said this was not true when he was asked about it by Doug Green, oral historian of the Country Music Foundation in Nashville. There is also black blood in the music of less bluesy country singers.

"Hesitation Blues" was recorded by Reaves White County Ramblers (1927), Milton Brown and His Musical

---

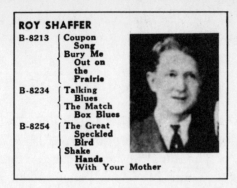

ROY SHAFFER

B-8213	Coupon Song Bury Me Out on the Prairie
B-8234	Talking Blues The Match Box Blues
B-8254	The Great Speckled Bird Shake Hands With Your Mother

Brownies (1936), and Hank Penny and His Radio Cowboys (1939). Lyrics from "Hesitation Blues" surfaced in Charlie Poole's "If the River Was Whiskey" (Poole also recorded Handy's "Beale Street Blues," under the title "Rambling Blues"), and Fiddlin' John Carson's "Whatcha Gonna Do When Your Licker Gives Out," which was derived from "Crawdad Song." (One of Fiddlin' John's songs, "It's a Shame To Whip Your Wife on Sunday," later turned up on a Leadbelly record.) Copyrighted by W. C. Handy in 1915 as "The Hesitating Blues," the song is related to an older black song, "Honey Take a Whiff on Me." Charlie Poole cut a variant of this, "Take a Drink on Me."

Dick Justice, a West Virginia singer who recorded for Brunswick in the late 1920s, cut Luke Jordan's "Cocaine," Bayless Rose's "Black Dog Blues," and "Brownskin Blues," derived from Blind Lemon Jefferson's songs "Dark Horse Blues" and "Stocking Feet Blues."

Blind Lemon Jefferson's "Matchbox Blues," recorded for Okeh in March 1927, was done by Kentucky mandolinist and miner Larry Hensley (1934), Joe Shelton (1935), Roy Shaffer (1939), Roy Newman and His Boys (1939), Carl Perkins (1957), and Jerry Lee Lewis (1958). Lines from the song were used by Jimmie Davis in "High Behind Blues" (1932). The essence of the song's lyrics

did not originate with Blind Lemon Jefferson but with Ma
Rainey's 1924 record "Lost Wandering Blues."

> *Lord, I stand here wondering,*
> *Will a matchbox hold my clothes?*

Some country artists found themselves in the race
section of record company catalogues, and were not
pleased by it. The Allen Brothers (Austin Ambrose Allen,
born February 7, 1901, and Lee William Allen, born June
1, 1906, both in Sewanee, Tennessee) made their first
records for Columbia on April 7, 1927; they recorded for
Victor from October 1928 to May 1931. Their version of
the old Papa Charlie Jackson song "Salty Dog Blues," cut
at their first session, was issued by Columbia in its 14000
Race Series instead of its 15000 Hillbilly Series. The Allen
Brothers filed suit for $250,000, but the suit was dropped
before it came to litigation. (In the 1950s Maudie Bowen,
a white lady, won a libel suit against the Anderson, South
Carolina, *Daily Mail*, which had mistakingly published
an item about Mrs. Bowen in its Negro News section.)
The Allen Brothers recorded more black-derived songs,
such as Alec Johnson's "Maybe Next Week Sometime."
When their recording careers ended in 1934, Austin became a singing waiter in New York and Lee became an
electrician in Tennessee. Austin also became an electrician
in the 1940s. He died on January 5, 1959, in Williamston,
South Carolina. Lee Allen lives in Lebanon, Tennessee.

The Oklahoma Blue Ridge Playboys agreed to have
some of their records, such as "Cross Tie Blues" and "Pour-
ing Down Blues" (both of 1930), released in a race series,
but they used the name Buster and Jack for these releases.

Western-swing bands of the 1930s and '40s used a lot
of black material, but not in such a vivid manner as the
older country artists. The black music Bob Wills chose to
perform was often effete. At the first two Texas Playboys
sessions, on September 23 and 24, 1935, Wills and his

band recorded twenty songs. Twelve of these were Tin Pan Alley songs or standard jazz pieces from the previous decade; four were original compositions; three were old country songs; and one was a fairly contemporary blues (Big Bill Broonzy's "I Can't Be Satisfied"). Overall, it was old stuff: "I Can't Give You Anything But Love" was a hit in 1928 (three years after Wills cut it, Katherine Hepburn sang it in *Bringing Up Baby*). "Four or Five Times" was copyrighted in April 1927 and was a hit for Jimmie Noone's Apex Club Orchestra, McKinney's Cotton Pickers, and other bands in 1928; Milton Brown had cut the song in April 1934. "Mexicali Rose" was a hit in 1923. "Wang Wang Blues" was a hit for Paul Whiteman in 1921 (one of the song's authors, Henry Busse, played trumpet in Whiteman's orchestra). "I Ain't Got Nobody" was copyrighted in February 1916. "St. Louis Blues" was a hit in 1914; Milton Brown had recorded it in January 1935 (even Guy Lombardo and His Royal Canadians had cut it). "Sitting on Top of the World," recorded by the Mississippi Sheiks in February 1930, had already been recorded by three country acts: Joe Evans (1931), Leon's Lone Star Cowboys (1932), and Milton Brown (1934).

It was uncommon for Wills to record anything of modern origin that he and the Playboys did not compose. A 1937 recording of Jimmie Lunceford's 1934 hit "White Heat" is as close as Wills came to recording the music of his contemporaries.

"Brain Cloudy Blues," recorded in 1946, includes a good deal of Kokomo Arnold's first record, "Milk Cow Blues," of 1935, which includes a good deal of Sleepy John Estes's 1930 recording of the same name; and there were three other cuts of "Milk Cow Blues" between those of Estes and Arnold: Big Bill Broonzy's (1934), Tampa Red's (1935), and the Birmingham Serenaders' (1935). Cliff Bruner's Texas Wanderers were the first country band to cut it, in 1936. In 1938 Bob Crosby's Bob Cats recorded an instrumental version, and in 1941 Johnnie Lee

Wills, Bob's brother, recorded it. Johnnie Lee had never heard any of the blues versions and was introduced to the song by Cotton Thompson, a member of the band. Thompson sang on Johnnie Lee's record, and it sold well. In 1974 Johnnie Lee Wills said of "Milk Cow Blues," "I was the first one ever recorded that." Bob Wills finally cut "Milk Cow Blues" in 1969. Henry C. Speir (1895–1972), the Mississippi-born talent scout for Paramount and other record companies, held that he helped Kokomo Arnold write "Milk Cow Blues."

Other Western-swing bands were more imaginative than Wills in their use of black music. Milton Brown and His Musical Brownies covered Tampa Red's 1934 "Somebody's Been Using That Thing," a descendant of his 1928 "Tight Like That." Jimmie Revard and His Oklahoma Playboys cut the ancient "Blues in the Bottle" (another country band, Prince Albert Hunt's Texas Ramblers, recorded the blowsiest, most beautiful version of this song in 1928).

Luis Russell was a jazz pianist, writer, and bandleader, born in Careening Clay, Panama, on August 6, 1902. He began working in 1917 as a piano player in a silent-film theater. In 1919 he won $3,000 in a lottery and moved with his mother and sister to New Orleans, where he joined the Arnold DuPas Orchestra at the Cadillac Club. In 1926 Russell's Hot Six made their first records. He changed the name of his group, and its size, regularly: Luis Russell's Heebie Jeebie Stompers, Luis Russell and His Burning Eight, Luis and His Ginger Snaps, Luis and His Orchestra. In 1934 Russell made his last recordings. He worked as a chauffeur in New York City in the early 1960s and died there on December 11, 1963.

Luis Russell was crazy, and great. On January 15, 1929, he recorded a song for Okeh titled "The Call of the Freaks," a macabre, funereal thing without words, composed by Russell's drummer, Paul Barbarin. On September

6, 1929, Russell recorded "The New Call of the Freaks." It was essentially the same song, except for a ghostly, drunken chanting that rose at its end.

> *Stick out your can, here comes the garbage man.*
> *In the mornin'.*
> *Stick out your can, here comes the garbage man.*
> *In the evenin'.*
> *Stick out your can, here comes the garbage man.**

The record ended with a fade-out effect, the world's first. It all seemed satanic, but very funny.

From somewhere Milton Brown and His Musical Brownies got "The New Call of the Freaks" and cut it under the title "Garbage Man Blues" at their first session, on April 4, 1934. It was faster, and those jittery, eldritch words were babbled-sung throughout. To hear "Garbage Man Blues" is to feel the space between Bob Wills and Milton Brown. Roy Newman and His Boys covered "Garbage Man Blues" for Vocalion in 1935.

Country music's last transfusion of black blood came in the days of rock-and-roll. Ernest Tubb cut "Kansas City Blues" for Decca in 1954; that same year, Leon McAuliffe covered the Chords' "Sh'Boom" for Columbia. Bull Moose Jackson's 1947 "I Want a Bowlegged Woman" was cut by Jimmy Ballard on King. The Dominoes' 1951 hymn to duji-dick, "Sixty Minute Man," was cut by Hardrock Gunter & Roberta Lee (Decca), the York Brothers (King), and, of course, Jerry Lee Lewis (Sun). (These were the sort of songs that caused headlines such as "Urge Cleanup on Smut Songs," which *Variety* yelled on November 3, 1954.) Bill Haley turned Guitar Slim's

* "The Call of the Freaks" by Luis Russell and Paul Barbarin. Copyright © 1929 by Edwin H. Morris & Company, Inc. Copyright renewed. Used by permission.

"Later for You Baby" into his 1955 "See You Later Alligator." Mac Wiseman cut the Clovers' "One Mint Julep" in 1956.

R&B singer Wilbert Harrison covered Terry Fell's 1954 country hit, "Don't Drop It." Later, in the spring of 1959, Harrison had a double-barreled Number One R&B and pop hit with "Kansas City," a song swiped from Little Willie Littlefield's 1952 "K.C. Loving." It has been argued that Littlefield's original was inspired by Denver Darling's "Juke Joint Mama." Illinois-born Denver Darling (his real name!), the swishiest country singer of his day, specialized in World War II hate songs. "Cowards Over Pearl Harbor," "We're Gonna Have to Slap the Dirty Little Jap," "Mussolini's Letter to Hitler," "The Devil and Mr. Hitler," "I'm a Pris'ner of War," and "When Mussolini Laid His Pistol Down' are some of the titles he recorded for Decca. Bob Wills cut a handful of World War II songs, including three Darling wrote: "Stars and Stripes on Iwo Jima," "Empty Chair at the Christmas Table," and "White Cross on Okinawa." Cliff Bruner made only one statement on the subject: "Draft Board Blues."

Other R&B performers looked toward country music. Hank Williams's hit "Lovesick Blues" was covered for Decca by Eddie Crosby in the spring of 1949. Stick McGhee cut an instrumental version of "Tennessee Waltz" for Atlantic in November 1950. The song was also cut by Bobby Comstock (Blaze, 1959) and Daddy Stovepipe (Heritage, 1960). Darrell Glenn cut "Crying in the Chapel," which was written by his father, for Valley in the summer of 1953. Rex Allen covered it for Decca and got a Top Ten country hit, but an even better-known cover is that of the Orioles for Jubilee, the biggest R&B hit of the year. Wynonie Harris's 1951 hit "Bloodshot Eyes" was a cover of Hank Penny's Western-swing recording of the year before. Harris cut two other country songs: Moon Mullican's "Triflin' Woman Blues" and Louie Innis's "Good Morning, Judge."

Harris's version was better than the original, and one of the consummate records of his career. The song fit his persona well. It is a cruel and funny song; very sexy, very unromantic, and very liquorish. Harris was the greatest of the jump blues singers, a lord of excess from Omaha, Nebraska. ("Wynonie was a mess, man," said musician Melvin Moore. "All he wanted to do was rock 'em and roll 'em.") He recorded from 1944, when he sang with Lucky Millinder and His Orchestra, to 1964, for many labels: Philo, Aladdin, Bullet, King, Apollo, Atco, Roulette, and more. His biggest hit was the 1949 "All She Wants To Do Is Rock" (King). When Wynonie realized he was dying, he called all his friends together for a wild, drunken bash. He died in June 1969, in Los Angeles. He was fifty-three years old, and he rocked until the end.

Several of Jimmie Rodgers's songs have been cut by black artists. The Memphis Sheiks did "He's in the Jailhouse Now" for Victor in 1930; Fats Domino cut "Waiting for a Train" under the title "Helping Hand" for Imperial in 1955; Memphis Slim did a version of "T for Texas" for Folkways in 1960.

Bull Moose Jackson covered Wayne Raney's 1949 "Why Don't You Haul Off and Love Me" and Moon Mullican's 1951 "Cherokee Boogie." Ivory Joe Hunter covered "Jealous Heart," Al Morgan's 1949 country hit. Louis Jordan covered Tex Williams's 1950 "Tamburitza Boogie." Ray Charles cut Bob Wills's "Roly Poly" in 1952. Earl Hooker cut "Steel Guitar Rag" and "Red River Valley" in 1953, and Ernest Tubb's "Walkin' the Floor over You" in the late sixties. Eddy Arnold's 1947 hit "It's a Sin" was cut by Tarheel Slim and Little Ann in 1961. Hank Williams's songs were cut by many R&B acts, such as the Pearls ("Your Cheatin' Heart"), Bobby Comstock ("Jambalaya"), and Fats Domino ("Jambalaya"). Big Bill Broonzy cut "Sixteen Tons" in 1956. Junior Parker cut Willie Nelson's "Funny How Time Slips Away" in 1972. Ray Charles's best-selling album was *Modern Sounds in*

Country & Western Music, which included Jimmie Davis's "You Are My Sunshine" (how many R&B versions of *that* are there?) and Ted Daffan's "Born To Lose." Charles's 1959 version of Hank Snow's "I'm Movin' On" was the source of the Rolling Stones's song. He recorded two more country albums, in 1962 and 1965. Esther Phillips cut a country album for Lenox in 1963 (reissued by Atlantic in 1966); the Supremes, for Motown in 1965; Joe Tex, for Atlantic in 1968; and Bobby Blue Bland, for ABC in 1975 (the much awaited and discussed Bobby Bland and George Jones duet album has still not occurred, however).

Most R&B companies were involved in country music as well. Early on, Apollo Records had its green-label Hillbilly Novelty releases by the likes of Smilin' Eddie Hill and the Tennessee Mountain Boys. In January 1949 both Specialty and Mercury inaugurated country lines. In Specialty's 700 Series were Earl Nunn, Johnny Crockett, and others; Mercury's 6100 Series featured Bill Nettles, Louie Innis, and others. Gotham, the Philadelphia company that issued Jimmy Preston's "Rock the Joint" in the summer of 1949, released records by Faron Young and others in its 1951–53 Folk Series. Aladdin's subsidiary label, Intro, formed in March 1950, was devoted exclusively to country. One of the country releases in the Chess 4800 Series, "If You Don't Someone Else Will" by Jimmy & Johnny, reached Number Six on the C&W charts in the fall of 1954. Rockin' Records was a small company that began in Los Angeles late in 1952. Rockin' 516, released in the summer of 1953, was "Heaven Only Knows" by the R&B group the Charms. Less congruous with the label's name was Rockin' 514, a new version of "Orange Blossom Special" by the Rouse Brothers.

The first country artist to record with a black musician was Jimmie Rodgers, who used Louis Armstrong on cornet in his July 16, 1930, recording of "Blue Yodel No. 9." This was Armstrong's first session after moving to California earlier in the summer, and when asked about it later in his life, he could not recall the circumstances that led to it. The unidentified pianist in the record is surely not Earl Hines or Lil Armstrong, contrary to what has been said and written. In 1970 Louis Armstrong, by then a pop act, cut a fake country album. Someone asked him if it were a change of direction and he said, "I was doing that same kind of work forty years ago."

Jimmie Davis was the second country singer to record with black accompaniment. On February 8, 1932, he cut four songs in Dallas with blues singer and steel-guitarist Oscar Woods. (Davis had first used a steel-guitarist, Snoozer Quinn, at his May 26, 1931, session in Charlotte.) Woods, like Davis, lived in Shreveport, and it seems the two men were very close. Davis arranged for Woods and his friend Ed Schaffer to cut a record the same day as his own session; this record, "Nok-'Em-All Blues" c/w "Flying Crow Blues," was released under the name Eddie and Oscar. Woods and Schaffer had recorded once before for Victor, as the Shreveport Home Wreckers. This session, on May 5, 1930, seems also to have been arranged by Davis, for he recorded the day before in the same city. In 1936, two years after Davis joined Decca, Woods recorded for that company under the name of the Lone Wolf. In 1937 Davis arranged for the black group Kitty Gray and Her Wampus Cats to record for ARC-BRC. The group featured Oscar Woods. In October 1940, John Lomax found Oscar Woods playing in the streets of Shreveport. That was the last he was seen.

Davis was not the first country artist to help a blues singer's career. Willie F. Narmour, the fiddler who recorded with guitarist Shell W. Smith as Narmour & Smith, got Okeh to sign Mississippi John Hurt in 1928. Narmour, Smith, and Hurt were neighbors in Carroll County, Mississippi.

In the early 1930s, the Texas singer Al Dexter worked with an all-black band.

"Yeah, that was what I started out with. I had a

saxophone, a piano, and drums, a bass. You see, when I
started out it was hard times. The early thirties. A quarter
was a quarter then. The big ones eat the little ones. I was
barnstormin' around and playin' these joints and passin'
the hat. I went up to the radio station, got me a little
thirty-minute program. One day this little black woman
came up to me and said, 'How'd you like to play at my
place?' I said, 'Where is your place?' She said, 'I have
the Avalon Club over here in Longview. Get yourself a
little band. I'll give you two dollars a man, plus your tips,
your kitty.' That sounded all right to me. I was happy to
get any salary at all, y'see.

"So I went around, tried to get some white musicians
to work with me; they wouldn't work with me. They
wanted to play Benny Goodman stuff, that kind of music.
I just wanted to sing songs, play music. So I met a nigro
down there at Longview. He'd been playin' with white
musicians. His name was Claude Crawford. I said, 'Claude,
would you work with me?' He said, 'Yes, Mr. Al, whataya
got?' So I told him and he said, 'That sounds pretty good
to me, Mr. Al.' He was a great big guy, weighed two
hundred and thirty pounds, and he could sure play a
piano. He said, 'You don't mind playin' with colored
people, do you?' And I said, 'Not a bit.' So we got a guy
who used to play saxophone with Louis Jordan. Lee
Siegler was his name; he come from Arkansas. Got a boy
by the name of Hicks. He played guitar, and he played
drums. I just kept hirin' 'em. Al Dexter and His Colored
Band, all-nigro band. [Laughs.] We had 'em dancin' to
death."

Dexter never recorded with black musicians, but he
planned to on one occasion.

"There was a colored guitar player I had one time. I
sold him a guitar. Boy, he could play it, I'm tellin' you
the truth. He wanted me to take him in and record him
sometime, and I intended to, but he got killed. I can't
think of his name now."

Dexter acknowledges taking "New Jelly Roll Blues," his first record, from a black source. Peg Leg Howell and His Gang cut "New Jelly Roll Blues" for Okeh in the spring of 1927. By then versions of "Jelly Roll Blues" were common.

One night in the late 1930s, Bob Wills got drunk and hired a black trumpet player in Tulsa. The next morning he fired him.

It is a very intriguing fact that Charlie Parker often made late-night music with Ray Price's band in the early 1950s. If any tapes of these sessions were made, they did not survive. Ray Price went middle-of-the-road in the sixties, but Charlie Parker had beat him to it: Hear his 1950 Mercury album *Charlie Parker with Strings*.

White musicians have been common in R&B. All the black artists who have recorded in Memphis, Muscle Shoals, and several other Southern cities since the 1950s have mostly used white musicians. Every time you hear an Otis Redding record, you're hearing a bunch of white boys.

Deford Bailey was born in 1899 in Carthage, Tennessee, and died on July 2, 1982, in Nashville. The first black Opry star, Bailey made twice as many Opry appearances in 1928 as any other performer. He recorded for Columbia in April 1927, but the records were not released. That same month, he recorded for Brunswick at two New York sessions. (Brunswick did not issue Bailey's records in its race series.) He made his last records for Victor, on October 2, 1928. Bailey ended his career in 1941. He refused an offer to play a role in *W. W. and the Dixie Dance Kings*, a 1975 movie starring Burt Reynolds; the part went to Memphis blues singer Furry Lewis. He had lived in Nashville since he moved there from Carthage in 1922.

Charley Pride, country music's only black star since Deford Bailey, was born in Sledge, Mississippi, on March 8, 1938. He signed with RCA in 1966 and had his first hit, "Just Between You and Me," in December of that year.

He made his Opry debut on January 14, 1967, and was brought back for three encores.

The first black girl singer to play the Opry was Linda Martell. She appeared there in August 1969. Plantation released an album by her, *Color Me Country.*

In 1971 Otis Williams, the former lead singer of the Charms, a black group that recorded for Rockin' and DeLuxe in the 1950s, cut a country album for Pete Drake's Stop label, *Otis Williams and the Midnight Cowboys.* "I Wanna Go Country," a single from the album, was a minor hit that spring.

> *Well, I can see what happened to Jerry Lee,*
> *And I want the same thing for me.*

Blacks are not a common subject in country music, but they do occasionally appear. Hank Williams recorded "The Funeral" in 1949. Though credited to Fred Rose, it was derived, as were most of the Luke the Drifter records, from an earlier stage recitation. "The Funeral" speaks of a black preacher with "countenance grotesque." "Ethiopian face" is rhymed with "crushed, undyin' race." Twenty years later the Flying Burrito Brothers parodied "The Funeral," substituting a dumb hippy boy for the dead tar baby.

"Black Diamond," recorded by both Stuart Hamblen and Hank Snow, tells of a World War II soldier injured in battle on a tropical island. He lay there, his hip shattered, till "an angel of mercy with a bone through his nose" carried him off to his cave in the hills. His face is described as one "that would've given death a scare." Hank Snow continued to perform "Black Diamond" into the seventies, not only in concert, but on TV shows as well.

The song Merle Haggard wrote after his 1969 "Okie from Muskogee" was "Irma Jackson," a soft tale of inter-racial sex. Capitol did not permit him to record the song then, but he did cut it in 1972. Billy Joe Shaver's "Black Rose," cut for Monument in 1973, was about the same thing. "I'm a White Boy" is a song Merle Haggard wrote but did not record. "I'm proud and white," wrote Merle. "Daddy's name wasn't Willie Woodrow; I wasn't born in no ghetto." Jim Mundy cut it for ABC-Dot in 1975.

In the mid-1920s the KKK label of Indianapolis, Indiana, released a series of records with titles such as "Why I Am a Klansman," "Cross in the Wildwood," "The Bright Fiery Cross," and "Wake Up America and Kluck, Kluck, Kluck." Thomas Edison listened to the records on July 24, 1924, to see if they were suitable for release on his label. He noted that "Why I Am a Klansman" had a "fair tune," but his final advice was, "Don't bother with this trash."

In the 1960s the Reb Rebel label was formed in Crowley, Louisiana. Crowley had been a recording center

---

FOLK SONGS OF AMERICA

M-G-M 10630 - LUKE the Drifter with Musical Accompaniment

BEYOND THE SUNSET	Comp: Brock-Rowswell
Time: 2:58	Pub: Robbins Music Corp. (ASCAP)
THE FUNERAL	Comp: Anonymous
Time: 3:03	Pub: Public Domain

M-G-M RECORDS take pride in introducing a great new Folk artist with this release: someone you might call a country bard. He goes under the name of Luke the Drifter, a name you'll find is an appropriate one. It's appropriate because Luke seems just that: a drifter - a drifter, however, with a love of people and a kindly observant eye, and one who can put his impressions into a touching poetic form. We called Luke a bard, and that's just what he seems to be; what else was a bard but a man who wandered and noted the sadness and the joys of people along the way, and put that joy and sadness into poems and songs to touch the hearts of his very inspirers? In BEYOND THE SUNSET, Luke touches in words and hymn-like song the subject of the death of a loved one. In simple, sturdy lines, he traces the saddened reactions of the bereaved, tracing the while his hopes that he soon will be reunited with the lost one BEYOND THE SUNSET. In THE FUNERAL, Luke takes us to a little colored church where we share the tragedy that has befallen a mother and father through the death of their child. Luke helps us see with compassion the universal mystery of the "going-before" of a loved one and outlines the bit of bittersweet joy that faith in God leaves one at such a time. This is an unusual record and a great one! Rarely have such moving experiences been imprisoned in the grooves of a lowly phonograph record. Here is a memorable disk that will be treasured long by many!

MGM press release introducing Luke the Drifter, February 1950.

SATURDAY'S PROGRAM.

WSM (282.8 Meters).

6:45—Dinner concert by Andrew Jackson hotel orchestra, directed by Beasley Smith (one hour).
7:15—Bedtime story interlude (¼ hour).
8:00—Uncle Jimmie Thompson, fiddler, accompanied by his niece, Mrs. Eva Thompson Jones (¼ hour).
8:30—Crook Brothers barn dance orchestra (½ hour).
9:00—Miss Glenna Strickland, popular pianist (¼ hour).
9:15—Fields and Martin, Hawaiian guitarists (¼ hour).
9:30—Obed Pickard, one-man orchestra (¼ hour).
9:45—Binkley Brothers, fiddle and guitar (½ hour).
10:15—Sid Hardreader, fiddler (½ hour).
10:45—DeFord Bailey, harmonica wizard (¼ hour).

WDAD (226 Meters).

Silent pending installations.

SUNDAY'S PROGRAM.

WSM (282.8 Meters).

7:30—Service from the Firsst Presbyterian church; sermon by Dr. James I. Vance, pastor (1½ hours).

Nashville Banner, *November 20, 1926.*

since the fifties, when Jay D. Miller cut sessions on Lightnin' Slim, Lazy Lester, Slim Harpo, and others, for his own Feature label and for Excello in Nashville. Miller sold Reb Rebel records in his North Parkeson Street music store. The most popular Red Rebel artist is Johnny Rebel, whose records include "Move Them Niggers North," "Stay away from Dixie," "Nigger, Nigger," "Some Niggers Never Die (They Just Smell That Way)," and "Nigger Hatin' Me." Another Red Rebel artist, James Crow, has a more bluesy style than Mr. Rebel. In "Cowboys and Niggers," he sings of his travail in a deep, blowsy baritone.

The house next door to me
Has been sold to niggers.

About 1973 a well-known country singer whose work is often marked by an excessive poignancy recorded a song called "I Was Born in a One-Nigger Town," one of the best performances of his career. The record was not released.

Well, I used to think that he was black becuz the man was
  sick.
Us honkies hate them niggers cuz they got them big long
  dicks.
What a fuckin' disappointment when they trot you into
  class
And ya gotta hate your classmate for the color of his ass.

Oh, I was born in a one-nigger town;
The only black man that we had for miles and miles
  around.
Well, I was seventeen before I realized my fate:
What a fuckin' disadvantage when ya never learn to hate.

The singer was Tom T. Hall, and the song dates from the period of his Number One hit "I Love" (". . . little baby ducks . . .").

I asked Warren Smith if he had gotten any bad reactions to "Ubangi Stomp" in 1956.

"No. Strange enough, a lot of people, they all liked it. We played a lot of dances, y'know, where there was a lot of colored people there, and they danced the devil out of it."

In the 1980s country music and R&B still hold strong similarities. Look at the soul charts; look at the country charts. Both are dominated by records with dumb lyrics and fat, sticky orchestrations. As it is writ: Everybody does it in Hawaii.

Yeah, But They Break If You Sit On Them

In the seventeenth century, Savinien Cyrano de Bergerac closed his eyes and imagined a talking machine, a box of springs that spoke. Two hundred years later, in 1857, E. L. Scott de Martinville constructed and patented a mechanism that traced the ripplings of sound waves onto a hand-powered, lampblacked cylinder. He called it a phonautograph. Scott's machine could record sound waves, but it couldn't re-create them. On a laboratory work sheet of July 18, 1877, Thomas Edison noted that he had discovered the basic principle of mechanical sound re-creation. On February 19, 1878, he was granted a patent for his device, which he called a phonograph.

In April 1878, Edison took his curious machine to Washington, D.C., where he demonstrated it before the National Academy of Sciences and for Rutherford B. Hayes at the White House. Later that same month, the Edison

Speaking Phonograph Company was incorporated in Norwalk, Connecticut.

On October 8, 1887, a new company, the Edison Phonograph Company, was founded in West Orange, New Jersey. That same year, the American Graphophone Company was founded in Bridgeport, Connecticut. On March 26, 1888, Jesse H. Lippincott, a young investor who desired to control the new industry, purchased the sales rights of the American Graphophone Company, and on June 28 he purchased the Edison Phonograph Company from Edison for $500,000. With his purchases, Lippincott formed the North American Phonograph Company on July 14, 1888.

The North American Phonograph Company leased phonographs through various member companies, each of which had a territory to operate within. One of the most important of these member companies was the Columbia Phonograph Company, which covered Delaware, Maryland, and the District of Columbia. It joined the North American Phonograph Company in January 1889. This territory had been covered by the American Graphophone Company, and when this older company began to fall, Columbia bought up its stock over a period of two years, 1893–95.

When the North American Phonograph Company went into liquidation in 1896, Thomas Edison formed a new company of his own, the National Phonograph Company. Edison remained in the record business until 1929, two years before his death. He held to the end that the phonograph was his dearest invention.

In 1897 Emile Berliner formed the National Gramophone Company in Philadelphia. In 1887 Berliner had applied for a patent for flat disc records, and in late 1894 he began selling the first American discs. (Berliner had marketed several "toy" discs in Germany, in 1889–90.) In 1900 Berliner ceased making records in America because of a patent-infringement suit brought against him by Edison. Eventually it was ruled that Berliner's discs did not infringe on Edison's patent, but by then, Berliner was financially ruined. During the trial, Berliner licensed Eldridge R. Johnson, owner of the Johnson Machine Works in Camden, New Jersey, to manufacture his discs. Johnson called his company the Consolidated Talking Machine Company. In 1901, when Berliner was acquitted in court, Johnson renamed his company the Victor Talking Machine Company. Victor was incorporated in Camden on October 3, 1901.

Victor fast became the most successful company in the industry. On December 7, 1926, Eldridge Johnson sold out to a group of New York bankers, who, on January 4, 1929, merged Victor with the Radio Corporation of America (RCA), owner of the National Broadcasting Company (NBC). RCA had been formed by Westinghouse and General Electric on September 9, 1926, to absorb the assets of Marconi, which had been declared "alien-controlled" during World War I; NBC had been formed on September 9, 1926, by RCA.

In 1902 Columbia began producing discs under its own name (the company had sold "toy" discs as early as 1899 and some grown-up discs in late 1901, but under the cover of the Climax label), while continuing to make cylinders until 1908. (The last cylinders were made by Edison in 1929.) Paper labels were first used, by Eldridge Johnson, in 1900 (Edison, however, had experimented with little ringlike paper labels for his cylinders in the early 1890s—they kept falling off); before that, titles had been carved into records like a potter's signature. It was also in 1900 that the first two-sided discs appeared, produced most likely as test pressings by Eldridge Johnson. Commercial introduction of two-sided discs was in 1904, when they were sold in Europe by the Odeon label of the General Phonograph Corporation. In 1908 Columbia and

Victor started selling two-sided discs in America. (From 1904 to 1906 Columbia had marketed them experimentally on a very small scale.)

In 1918 the General Phonograph Corporation, which was financed by the Lindstrom Company of Germany, formed the Okeh label in New York City. That same year, the Aeolian Company, which had been making gramophones for three years, started its own label, Aeolian-Vocalion, also in New York City. (This label became simply Vocalion in 1921.)

The Pathé-Frères Phonograph Company of Paris started its American Pathé label in 1914, two years after first importing discs to the U.S. In 1922 Pathé formed the Perfect label in Brooklyn (the office moved to Manhattan in 1928, but the factory stayed in Brooklyn). The company was reorganized as the Pathé Phonograph and Radio Corporation in 1922.

The Cameo Record Corporation was started in 1922 in New York City. Cameo formed the Lincoln label in 1922 and the Romeo and Variety labels in 1926. In 1927 J. McPherson bought both Cameo and Pathé and formed Cameo-Pathé.

The Plaza Music Company was formed in the early teens in New York City; it founded the Banner label in 1921 and took over the Regal label from the Emerson Phonograph Company (founded in 1916 in New York City) in 1922. Regal was the first of the budget labels: A Regal disc cost fifty cents while most other records in 1922 cost upward of eighty-five cents. This brought about a price war that raged for twenty years. In the fall of 1936, Sears Roebuck was selling records on its Conqueror label at the price of six for fifty-five cents.

In August of 1929, Cameo-Pathé and the Regal Record Company (formerly the Plaza Music Company) merged with the Scranton Button Company, operator of an independent record-pressing plant. This was the birth of the American Record Corporation (ARC). At the time of the merger, Cameo-Pathé had the Cameo, Lincoln, Pathé, Perfect, Romeo, and Variety labels, and Regal had the Banner, Domino, Jewel, Oriole, and Regal labels. Some of these labels had strict retail markets, such as Oriole, which sold only at McCrory's stores, and Romeo, which sold only at S. H. Kress stores. (Dime-store labels were common in the late 1920s and 1930s. Most of them were discontinued in 1938, but Conqueror, which started in 1929 as the Sears Roebuck label for ARC recordings, lasted till 1942.)

ARC withdrew the Lincoln label in 1929, and Cameo followed in 1930. ARC also added labels, such as Broadway, acquired from Paramount in 1930 (Paramount, founded in 1917 by the Wisconsin Chair Company, had formed Broadway as a budget label in 1926; an older Broadway label had existed since 1924), and the Sears Roebuck label, Conqueror.

With its many small labels, ARC created a whirl of pop, jazz, blues, country, and sacred noise. A single recording was often released on several labels. For example, on January 13, 1930, in New York City, the Dorsey Brothers' Orchestra recorded "Have a Little Faith in Me"

COLUMBIA RECORDS	Number	Size	Price

JASS BAND RECORDS.

	Number	Size	Price
Darktown Strutters' Ball. (Brooks) Fox-trot *and* Indiana (Hanley) One-step. Original Dixieland Jass Band.	A2297	10	.75
Indiana (Hanley) One-step *and* Darktown Strutters' Ball (Brooks) Original Dixieland Jass Band.	A2297	10	.75
It's a Long, Long Time. (Vail) Fox-trot *and* Just the Kind of a Girl (You'd Love to Make Your Wife.) (H. Von Tilzer) One-step. Borbee's "Jass" Orchestra.	A2233	10	.75

"Jass Band Records," Columbia catalogue, September 1917.

for ARC, and it was released on Banner, Broadway, Cameo, Conqueror, Domino, Jewel, Oriole, Perfect, Regal, and Romeo; plus two Australian labels, Clifford and Australian Vocalion; and a British label, Imperial.

In October 1930, Consolidated Film Industries, Inc., bought ARC. In December 1931, this same company bought the Brunswick Record Corporation (BRC) from Warner Brothers Pictures, who had bought it in April 1930 from the Brunswick-Balke-Collender Company of Chicago. (This is the same Brunswick, founded as a billiards manufacturer in 1845 in Cincinnati, and merged in 1879, that is familiar to devotees of "Bowling for Dollars.") BRC's Brunswick label, formed in 1920, was an important producer of race and hillbilly records. The Brunswick 100 Series, Songs from Dixie, was started in April 1927 and at the time of BRC's sale to Consolidated Film Industries, had released sides by Deford Bailey, Dr. Humphrey Bates and His Possum Hunters, Dock Boggs, Dick Justice, Buell Kazee, the Kessinger Brothers, Bradley Kincaid, Bascom Lamar Lunsford, Uncle Dave Macon, and others. (The series continued to January 1934.) BRC had also taken over the Vocalion label in December 1924. The BRC budget label, Melotone, was formed in 1930.

In 1925 English Columbia, which Columbia had operated since 1922, bought a controlling interest in the parent company. In December 1931 or January 1932, English Columbia sold the American company to Grigsby-Grunow, which had grown rich from its manufacture of Majestic radios. But three years later Grigsby-Grunow went into liquidation, and, late in 1934, the BRC division of Consolidated Film Industries' ARC-BRC conglomerate purchased the Columbia Phonograph Company. The Columbia purchase included the Okeh label, which Columbia had taken over from the General Phonograph Corporation in October 1926.

On December 17, 1938, the Columbia Broadcasting

System (CBS) purchased from Consolidated Film Industries, Inc., the capital stock of ARC-BRC. This was the start of CBS's involvement in the recording industry. CBS's first move was to rename the ARC-BRC complex the Columbia Record Corporation.

The budget labels, except for Conqueror, which lingered, were discontinued by CBS. The ARC-BRC prestige label was Brunswick, but in 1940 CBS killed Brunswick and made Columbia its most expensive label. Vocalion, the cheaper label, was also killed, and Okeh was substituted for it.

In August 1934 Decca was formed here by English Decca. Capitol Records began in Los Angeles as Liberty in April 1942. (The label's name was changed to Capitol two months later, on June 1.) In January 1947 MGM Records was formed in New York by its parent film company in Los Angeles.

There had always been small, independent record companies (as early as June 1922, Johnny and Reb Spikes, black music-store owners in Los Angeles, formed their own "all-colored" label, Sunshine; the company only lasted for three records, the fate of many indies to come). But beginning in the 1940s, independent record companies bloomed thick across the country.

In November 1942 Herman Lubinsky founded Savoy Records in downtown Newark. That same November, in Los Angeles, Otis René started Excelsior. In 1943 Ike and Bess Berman founded Apollo Records in New York. (Though Apollo originated on 125th Street in Harlem, by 1945 it was operating downtown.) In 1944 Jules Braun started DeLuxe in Linden, New Jersey; Al Greene began National in New York; Robert Scherman opened Premier in Los Angeles (this was in the early part of 1944; by October Premier had become Atlas); Richard Nelson founded Gilt-Edge, also in Los Angeles; Otis René inaugurated Exclusive as a sister label of his Excelsior;

Irving Berman formed Regis in Newark; and, in the autumn, Syd Nathan founded King Records in Cincinnati. In January 1945, Manor was started as a branch of Irving Berman's Regis in Newark, and Bill Quinn began Gulf in Houston.

During that spring of 1945, as the end of World War II approached, the real flood commenced. In New York there came Majestic Records, headed by former New York City mayor Jimmy Walker, and Irving Field and Viola Marsham's Super Disc. In Los Angeles came Leroy Hurte's Bronze, Daniel O'Brien's Melodisc; then, in May, the Modern label of Joe, Jules, and Saul Bihari, and, also in May, Ed and Leo Mesner's Philo Records (which became Aladdin ten months later). That summer, Richard Nelson started Four-Star in Los Angeles. In Chicago, in February, men in nice suits opened Mercury. In January 1946 Al Middleman's Juke Box Records started in New York. Jim Bulleit founded Bullet Records in Nashville that March. Swing Time and Down Beat were started by Jack Lauderdale in Los Angeles; Fortune was begun by Trianon Publications in Detroit; and Harlem was formed by J. Mayo Williams in New York. At the end of 1946, Bill Quinn started Gold Star to take the place of Gulf; Al Middleman began Sterling as a subsidiary of Juke Box; and Specialty Records was formed in Los Angeles.

In the fall of 1947 Herb Abramson and Ahmet Ertegun began Atlantic Records in New York. In December Leonard and Phil Chess started Aristocrat Records in Chicago. (Three years later, in the summer of 1950, Aristocrat became Chess Records.) In 1948 came Saul Kahl's Freedom label in Houston. In the late summer of that year, Jerry Blaine's Jubilee Records came into being in New York, and in November, Coral was formed by Decca. In 1949 Lew Chudd started Imperial in Los Angeles; Dave and Jules Braun began Regal in Linden, New Jersey; Don Robey opened Peacock in Houston; and

Randy Wood began Dot in Gallatin, Tennessee. At the end of the year, in Houston, Macy Lela Henry started Macy's Records.

In 1950 came Tennessee Records in Nashville and Lillian McMurry's Trumpet in Jackson, Mississippi. Aladdin inaugurated its Intro subsidiary in March of that year. The RPM label was started by Modern in the fall. The Gilt-Edge label was revived by Four-Star as a Pasadena hillbilly imprint in September. In December King began its Federal line. In the spring of 1951 the Okeh label was revived by Columbia. That summer United Records started in Chicago. In the fall came Ernie Young's Nashboro label in Nashville. Al Silver founded the Herald and Ember labels in New York. At the end of the year, Ewart Abner started Chance Records in Chicago. (Late in 1953 the fading Chance label served as the basis for Vivian Carter and Jimmy Bracken's successful Vee-Jay Records.)

In September 1952 Ernie Young formed Excello Records as a part of his Nashboro company in Nashville. Also in 1952 came three Memphis companies: James Mattis's Duke (soon acquired by Don Robey's Peacock in Houston), Lester Bihari's Meteor, and Sam Phillips's Sun.

In January 1953 Coral reactivated the Brunswick label. That same month, Republic Records started in Nashville. The Starday label was begun in Beaumont, Texas, by Pappy Daily and Jack Starnes. (It moved to Nashville in 1957.) In September came Epic Records, "with Radial Sound"; then George Goldner's Rama Records in New York (a subsidiary of his Latin label, Tico); and, also in New York, Archie Bleyer's Cadence label. Hickory Records started in Nashville in January 1954. Leiber and Stoller formed their Spark label in Los Angeles in April, the same month that Atlantic launched its Cat label. And so on. These and many other independent companies

Hank Williams and his sister, Irene, c. 1924. (Photo courtesy of the Bruce Gidoll Collection.)

had come (and, some of them, gone) by the summer of Elvis's emergence.

The independents, or mongrel companies, as they were called by the major labels, often worked with products that the majors would have no part of. Theirs was, and is still, an avant-garde of economic necessity. It was not a major company that released Hank Williams's first records in January 1947, but Sterling, a New York indie so ill-anchored that it changed its telephone number at least five times in three years. (Similarly, it wasn't a major label that issued the Beatles' first records in America, but Vee-Jay, a Chicago mongrel that released mostly R&B.)

Hank Williams was twenty-three when he made those first records, for Sterling, on December 11, 1946. Born

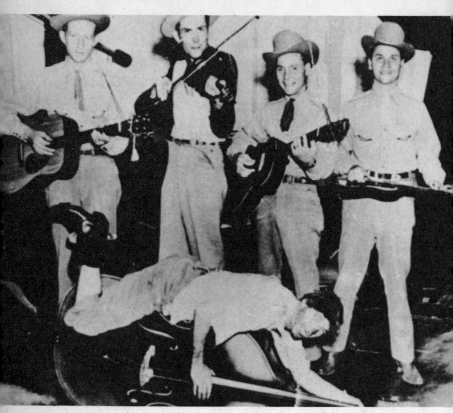

Hank on fiddle, in the WSFA studio, Montgomery, c. 1938. (Photo courtesy of the Bruce Gidoll Collection.)

near Georgiana, Alabama, on September 17, 1923, Williams grew up several miles north of there, in the town of Greenville. It was in Greenville that young Hank met and was influenced by Tee-Tot, the black musician who has figured prominently, though vaguely, in numerous romantic biographies of Williams. Tee-Tot's real name was Rufe Payne, and he was a resident of Greenville till his death about 1950. Farther north, in Montgomery,

Hank began performing at radio station WSFA in 1936; he was still working there when he journeyed to Nashville and met Fred Rose in the autumn of 1946. It was Rose, a Tin Pan Alley veteran, who connected Williams with Sterling, the new subsidiary of Al Middleman's year-old Juke Box Record Company, which was located at 7 West 46th Street in New York. (Roy Milton was Middleman's only hit act. "R.M. Blues," "Milton's Boogie," and others had been successful Juke Box releases in 1946. But as the year ended, Milton and His Solid Senders were about to sign with Specialty.) As it turned out, Hank Williams was Sterling's first country artist.

"For singing real country songs Hank Williams is a favorite wherever he is heard," proclaimed the advertise-

Miss Audrey, Hank, Hank's Mom, Unknown Soldier, Montgomery, 1945. (Photo courtesy of the Bruce Gidoll Collection.)

ment for Sterling 201, "Calling You" and "Never Again
(Will I Knock on Your Door)," in the January 18, 1947,
issue of *Billboard*. (Sterling 202 and 203, also advertised,
were by the Oklahoma Wranglers.) This record did not
receive much notice, nor did Hank's second release,
"Wealth Won't Save Your Soul" and "When God Comes
and Gathers His Jewels," advertised three weeks later.
There were two more Sterling releases by Williams in
the month that followed.

By then, another new, but much larger, label had
been started: MGM. Fred Rose got the Sterling masters
and negotiated Williams's signing to MGM. "Move It
On Over" was released in May 1947, and by midsummer
it was high on the hillbilly charts, right behind Tex
Williams's immense crossover hit, "Smoke! Smoke! Smoke!
(That Cigarette)."

"Rootie Tootie," Hank's proto-rockabilly record, was
released in December; "Honky Tonkin'" came out in
March 1948. At this time, Williams was still broadcasting
regularly as a WSFA staff artist. By August, however, he
moved on to the big, new KWKH "Louisiana Hayride,"
which began in Shreveport in April as the Saturday-night
competition of the WSM "Grand Ole Opry." It was late in
the year when Williams performed "Lovesick Blues" on the
Hayride, and his recording of it was released in January
1949. (In its February 26 issue, *Billboard* praised "Hank's
razz-mah-tazz approach.") "Lovesick Blues" hit the hillbilly charts in early March. A month later, when it was
at Number Three, Rex Griffin's 1939 Decca version of the
song was reissued by Coral. On June 4, 1949, Williams's
record hit Number One on the hillbilly charts (or, as in
two weeks *Billboard* would begin to call them, country and
western charts). A few nights later, on June 11, he performed the song at his "Grand Ole Opry" debut. After a
two-week tour of U.S. Air Force bases in England and
Europe in November, he ended the year ranking second

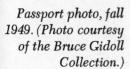

Passport photo, fall 1949. (Photo courtesy of the Bruce Gidoll Collection.)

only to Eddy Arnold as *Billboard*'s Top Folk Artist, and the hits kept coming.

In the spring and summer of 1950, "Long Gone Lonesome Blues" and "Why Don't You Love Me" were back-to-back Number One c/w hits for him. That autumn, he became a television star as well, performing on WSM–TV. In the summer of 1951, Tony Bennett covered his "Cold, Cold Heart" and had a Number One pop hit. A year later Rosemary Clooney's cover of "Half as Much" went to Number Two on the pop charts. (Mitch Miller, who produced both these covers, for Columbia, was eager to sign Williams. If he had, the ensuing collaboration likely would have telescoped the next decade of country-

music history, and the odious "countrypolitan" Nashville
sound of the mid-sixties very well might have bloomed in
1952. As the man says: Whatever.) By August Hank himself was on the pop charts: "Jambalaya" crossed over to
become a minor pop sensation.

But within a month, Hank Williams, stubbornly
adhering to the belief that guilt and weakness conquer
all, had been thrown off the Opry for being a drunken
bum, and was living in a wretched condition at his
mother's boardinghouse at 315 North McDonough in
Montgomery. During this time he pined for his faithless
wife, Miss Audrey; drank; shot chloral hydrate (the
favored drug of Dante Gabriel Rossetti, who could have
had his own slot at WSFA); drank; fell down and cracked
his skull; and wrote "I'll Never Get Out of This World
Alive." Thus, having finally wised up, he fled for once and
all, toward that darker maternal sanctuary.

In October, it was reported that Hank had been wel-
comed back to the KWKH Louisiana Hayride and that he
"has gained thirty pounds and . . . is in the best of health."
On the twentieth of the month, without fully divorcing
Miss Audrey, he married Miss Billie Jones of Bossier City,
Louisiana, on the stage of the New Orleans Municipal
Auditorium. Ticket prices ranged from $1 to $2.80, and
more than fourteen thousand attended. Several weeks
later, in the first hours of the new year, 1953—"I'll Never
Get Out of This World Alive" was on the charts—Hank
Williams died in the backseat of a chauffeured car en
route to an engagement in Canton, Ohio. He was twenty-
nine years old; and it had been a wonderful six years.

"They came from everywhere," declared the Montgomery *Advertiser* on January 5, the day after the funeral;
"dressed in their Sunday best, babies in their arms, hob-
bling on crutches and canes, Negroes, Jews, Catholics,
Protestants, small children, and wrinkled faced old men
and women. Some brought their lunch. . . ."

A legal battle erupted, the contestants for Hank's estate being Audrey Williams, Billie Jones Williams (who went on to marry singer Johnny Horton, another lucky guy), and Hank's mom, Mrs. W.W. Stone. Those with no claim wept, as "tribute records" (ah, euphemy) flooded forth: "The Death of Hank Williams" by Jack Cardell (King) came first, followed by "Hank Williams Will Live Forever" by Johnnie and Jack (RCA-Victor), "Tribute to Hank Williams" by Joe Rumore with J.T. Adams and the Men of Texas (Republic), "In Memory of Hank Williams" by Arthur Smith (MGM), "The Life of Hank Williams" by Hawkshaw Hawkins (King), "The Death of Hank Williams" by Jimmie Logsdon (Decca), "That Heaven Bound Train" by Johnny Ryon (Coral), and "The Last Letter," Mississippi disc jockey Jimmy Swan's reading of a letter to Hank by MGM boss Frank Walker (MGM).

But one cannot weep and mourn forever, and commerce often healeth a sorrowed heart. Thus, in the May 2 *Billboard*: "THE ONE AND ONLY! AUDREY (Mrs. Hank) WILLIAMS❋THE GIRL FOR WHOM THE LATE, GREAT HANK WILLIAMS WROTE HIS FAMOUS SONGS!" was "now available as a single or with her own all-star show for auditoriums, parks, fairs, theaters, T.V." Available indeed.

A year after Hank died, the January 1954 issue of *Country Song Roundup* published the lyrics to a song he had supposedly left behind: "My Cold, Cold Heart Is Melted Now." In death as in life, a sharpie with the metaphors.

In an interview with Fred Rose published in the *Alabama Journal* on September 21, 1954, a reporter asked him who the next country-boy superstar would be. Rose named Al Terry from Lafayette, Louisiana, and Jack Turner, from Montgomery.

But, ah yes, the mongrel labels. Many of them mostly employed black artists (Chess, Vee-Jay, and so on), and some mostly employed white artists (Dot, Cadence, and so on), but, as we've seen, the indies discovered early in the game that musical miscegenation often led to profits. Aladdin, with its great jump blues and black rock artists, also had a hillbilly series that was released on its Intro label. Savoy released not only jazz and R&B, but also country; they cut both Charlie Parker and the Texas Top Hands. King issued some of the finest R&B records of the 1940s and also some of the finest country records. Bullet recorded everyone from Owen Bradley to Milton Berle to Wynonie Harris to Bob Crosby to Sheb Wooley (Bullet's first artist) to Minnie Pearl to Cecil Gant to Jimmy Work. Jubilee cut both doo-wop records (the rarest R&B record, "Stormy Weather" by the Five Sharps, was on Jubilee; a copy of it was sold at auction in 1977 for $3,866) and Jew comedy routines.

Things were never easy for the mongrel labels. Sometimes a hit record brought ruin to a label. It happened like this: Mongrels had no distribution systems of their own (this is what made them independent, really), and the distributors they used usually, or often, took advantage of the situation. When a record is distributed, payment for that record is not made directly to the record company, but through the distributor, which is actually the wholesale arm of the company. When an independent label had a hit, that meant many more copies of the record had to be manufactured than usual. If the hit sold a million units, the company owed whatever pressing plant it used a whole lot of money for manufacturing those million records. The income from the hit would easily have covered manufacturing costs and left a juicy profit. But often when the company went to its distributor to collect the money its million-seller had made, the response was, "What hit? It sold twenty thousand units." Most independents had neither the money nor the courage (for some distributors long, long ago were tied in with The Boys) to initiate legal action. Lacking the money or the credit to cover its pressing-plant bills, the mongrel went into liquidation.

But where in this century-old pail of convolutions do the first country recordings occur? It is commonly said that the first country record made was the June 30, 1922, Victor recording "Sallie Goodin" c/w "Arkansaw Traveler" by fiddlers Eck Robertson (born Alexander Campbell Robertson on November 20, 1887, in Delaney, Arkansas) and Henry C. Gilliland (from Altus, Oklahoma, Gilliland was born about 1848). This may be the first country record by authentic country artists, but there were many earlier recordings of country songs by artists who probably had their roots in pop. Should these records be excluded from consideration because of their pop context? If yes, what of most of the records currently on the *Billboard* country charts?

Len Spencer had recorded "Arkansas Traveler" for Climax (Columbia) in late 1901 (this recording was also issued by Victor several years later). The Victor Military Band cut "Soldier's Joy," a traditional rural fiddling tune before 1920. There were other records like these: stylized adulterations of a music that the record companies felt was not commercial in its real state. This is not too different from the way record companies treated black music before 1920. A 1917 Columbia catalogue includes several recordings of blues, but they are all performed by Prince's Band (Charles A. Prince was the musical director of Columbia), or by minstrel acts such as Collins and Harlan. A 1920 Victor catalogue has a special category: "Blue" Records. Titles include "Hesitation Blues," "Alcoholic Blues," "Kansas City Blues," "Mournin' Blues," "Dallas Blues," and others. Most of these are performed by the Victor Military Band, the rest by small pop groups such as the All Star Trio, who do a saxophone-xylophone-piano version of "Alcoholic Blues," described in the catalogue as a fox trot.

Advertisements published in the spring of 1892 by the Louisiana Phonograph Company, Ltd., of 128 Cravier Street, New Orleans, list two groups of recordings by a man named Louis Vasnier. One is a series of black-dialect recitations called Brudder Rasmus Sermons. There are seven of these, including "End ob de Worl," "Charity ob de Heart," and "Why You Are Black." The catalogue states, "These sermons, while very humorous, are characteristic Negro delineations and are faithful reproductions of a dusky style of pulpit oratory that is rapidly passing away. The sermons are very popular amongst both whites and blacks and have proved to be among the most profitable of all exhibition records." The other group is of coon songs. There are eight titles, including "Black Pickininny," "Coon with a Razor," and "Turkey in de Straw." All these songs are accompanied by banjo, the typical instrument of minstrelsy.

No one has come forward with a Louisiana Phonograph Company record, but it is not impossible that the company, located in the deep South, recorded not only coon songs, but some real country, blues, and jazz records.

Northeast
Mississippi, 1953

The gun, a Ruger .22, is on the table, and it is three o'clock in the afternoon. In an hour Willis and Tommy and John will arrive, and the country singer will shoot them after they close the door behind them. Then he will put on his hat and leave. He will return to Oregon, slowly, not using the new highways. In Oregon he will call the Nashvill office and ask the details of the awful, awful accident. I've been hunting, out on the Cape, he will say. I just got back this morning.

He will call Robert in L.A., then, and tell him how he shot Willis and Tommy and John. And he will demand what is rightfully his.

Everything will have been so easy. It isn't even a sin. It can't be, not when you hate them so much. And Tommy, especially him, patting my back with the smell of Louise still on his hand.

After he meets with Robert, he will take his wife to Spain, and they'll just set in the sand drinking and smoking and sleeping. And when they get back he'll go get them a television at Uneeda, like he's been promising. All of it, just a Viceroy away.

There is a knock. The country star holds the gun with both hands.

"It's open."

They came in, the three of them, or maybe just the one or two. He was shot in the face. When he was found next morning by the colored cleaning woman, there was a paper sack over his head, stuck fast and black with dried blood.

Index